An Autobiography

Peter Alliss
An Autobiography

FONTANA/COLLINS

First published in Great Britain
by William Collins 1981
First issued in Fontana Paperbacks 1982

Copyright © Peter Alliss 1981

Set in 10 on 11 point Plantin
Made and printed in Great Britain by
William Collins Sons & Co. Ltd, Glasgow
Produced by Lennard Books
The words of 'And yet, and yet'
are reproduced on page 241
by kind permission of Big Ben Music Ltd.

For BJ, AJ,
and all the Allisses everywhere

Also, of course, Bob Ferrier

Contents

Introduction

Throughout my youth, and even into my National Service years, I didn't really understand golf. I suppose I didn't give the game much thought. It was there, like my parents and my brother, a part of life that was so absolutely normal that it did not require any thought. Later in life, when I did begin to think of it more objectively, I gradually came to see what an enormous treasure trove it is – of incident, experience, places, situations, and above all of people. Professional tournament golf is not a physically tough game in the sense that there is no physical contact involved. It is not explosive, and in a way not glamorous, but rather gradual, languid, long-drawn-out. Yet in the past twenty years – and in particular for me in the last ten years – it has become a monster attraction. Not with quite the same appeal as football, nor with the massive concentration on individuals like Muhammad Ali or Bjorn Borg, yet in its way golf is very similar in its overall impact.

The rewards in the game now are enormous, as great as in any other sport, so much so that I believe they are becoming almost obscene. If these rewards were cut by half, the top fellows would still be very well paid. So many people have written about the art of the game, the craft of the game, the pleasures of the game – in short, what golf means. That road has been well trodden, but one of its particular attractions to me is that it is an old game, a game that has evolved over centuries, in which now, generally speaking, there is no referee, no umpire to blame, no goalkeeper to blame. You are on your own, with the Rules of Golf and a powerful moral code bearing down on you to obey these rules. I think this is one of the most critical factors in the game. The rules are lengthy and complicated. Some people seem to think they are a criminal code, and are constantly seeking ways of getting round them. I prefer to think that the rules are a Bill of Rights, for the protection of the player, the protection of all the players. And yet situations can arise which permit you to follow the rules, but not play golf in the spirit of the game or in the spirit that the rules intended.

A classic example is that if your ball is unplayable, and by widening your stance a little you can just about get your heel on the edge of some grass cuttings, then you are perfectly entitled to relief under the rules. This I find difficult to accept. But if you want to reform the game, where do you start? There are some forty-one rules in a ninety-page booklet with I don't know how many appendices and definitions, and it is much easier to say they should be simplified than to do it. Henry Longhurst for years preached that the rules should be written on the back of an envelope. The old Scottish adage, 'Play the ball as it lies, and do not touch the ball between tee and green', is the ultimate in simplicity, and might work. Peter Thomson used to say, 'Tee it up, keep hitting it until you hole out, and if you want to touch the ball for any reason, pick it up, drop it within one club's length, and count one penalty stroke.' That might work, too.

The game has its sensuous pleasures, when you make the perfect swing and execute the shot precisely as you had planned it. There is perhaps not the ecstatic thrill of Bobby Charlton blasting the roof of the net from thirty yards; Denis Compton hooking one off his chest at the last possible moment, or Gary Sobers hitting six sixes in a row with sheer animalistic, massive blows. But it does get close. There may be even more delight in bringing off a deft little shot, like the downhill lie in thick grass just behind a bunker, when you have to get it out, up, over and hold it on the green, the kind of thing that Ballesteros, with his marvellous finger-tip control, can do so well and which other players, say Faldo or Norman, may not be able to do quite so well. They are broadsword men, Ballesteros is a rapier man, an artist. I have an enormous regard for him. Yet the greatest pleasure comes, I think, from the big shot perfectly done. Strangely enough I don't remember too many shots from my career, although I played my share of good ones, but one that I do remember, clear as a bell over the years, is the fairway wood I hit to the last hole at Royal Birkdale, when O'Connor and I beat Palmer and Marr in the 1965 Ryder Cup match. The shot was hit with all my power, all my control, all my calculation, and it came off perfectly, the ball doing exactly as it was told, and finishing twelve feet from the hole.

And the moments of high drama in the game are surely the equal of anything in any sport. I get very emotional, nervous even, watching one of the great men of the game coming to the 36th hole of the World Match Play, for instance, at Wentworth, stepping up to the second shot and you know that a long shot with a straight-faced club is easy for him, but he must hit the green to win the match. Will he do it? The final hole of the Open Championship, wherever it might be, with the great man marching up into that vast arena, the huge stands and 12,000 or 15,000 people crowding around the final green. Great moments – and great opportunities they are to look at character, to look at the differences between a Nicklaus and a Player, the sombre Faldo, the exuberant Trevino, the casual Barnes, the niggly ones, the ones who try to pretend they are not niggly. Terribly exposed, championship golfers – no place to hide out there. Championship golf is mentally a very hard game. I think I have only known four players who have said in a manner which I could believe that they actually enjoyed the competitiveness of it all. Palmer, Nicklaus, Nagle and Thomson.

When I look back on my own life in golf, it is clear that it has given me travel, conversation, and has taught me about humanity, and I hope humility. Those early Canada Cup and World Cup and Ryder Cup matches let me travel the world to 'faraway places with strange-sounding names', and at someone else's expense, and happily it is that way still. I am still childish enough to be thrilled by travelling first-class, whether it be in planes or trains, or whatever, simply because I think I have earned it. If I hadn't earned it, but inherited it, it wouldn't quite be the same. Even more important, those early exhibition matches let me see my own country, which ought to be the beginning of travel for everyone – and taught me how to find my way around it, locate and get myself to such as Churleston Golf Club, Chorlton-cum-Hardy and Royal Norwich, to be on time, and to talk to people.

Conversations with all sorts of people have been just as important as travel. I have been able to meet so many different people and have conversations about so many things, that it has been massively rewarding. Bing Crosby, Bobby Jones, Dwight D. Eisenhower, Harold Wilson, Douglas Bader, countless others – this strange game has made it all possible. And the opportunity of visiting clubs like Muirfield (The Honourable Company of Edinburgh Golfers – what a gorgeous title) and Royal St George's, or for that matter Altrincham 'Muni' in the halcyon days of Hugh Lewis. Wondering a long time ago if I would ever be allowed to enter the Ferndown clubhouse, and later the Royal and Ancient, and now that I can do these things, doing them with a touch of pride, and awe.

What an institution it is, the clubhouse, and the bar. I often think that the golf club bar is built before the course, and is really the key factor in the club. How marvellous if one could sit quietly in a corner, unseen, and listen to all the stories, the lies, the fantasizing about the round, about those silly buggers on the committee, and how 'we' could run it better than they, and how all secretaries are idiots, all professionals are boorish louts who never have what you want in the shop – all the instant likes and dislikes and totally irrational opinions.

The game lends itself to fantasies about our abilities. I learned about that early in life, at Ferndown. My father's shop window had the best view in the place. I often thought he could see everything with a pair of old binoculars which had belonged to my grandfather. One day I played a round, on my own, and when I came in, he said, 'How did you do today?'

I said, 'Oh, 67 today, dad.'

He said, 'Oh that's very good – what did you do on the 10th?'

'Four,' I said. 'On in two and putted it up close.'

'But you missed that short one,' says he.

'Well,' I said, 'I just . . .'

He then said to me, 'I saw it. Now it doesn't matter to me, I don't care; but you're only kidding yourself.'

I have never forgotten that, but I guess we all still do it.

People often ask me about the golf swing, and the secret of the game. And I tell them that I don't believe there is any one secret to this perplexing, complicated game. I try to suggest that it is a matter of synchronizing two separate planes of movement, and I liken it to the action of a windmill. If you consider the body of the windmill turning in a horizontal plane, like the screw top of a jar, and the sails turning in a not-quite-vertical plane, then that is more or less what happens. But one simple fact eludes most of us, and in particular the better players – it is damned difficult to do it, to synchronize these movements. And when you think of the speed of the clubhead at impact, and a small, flat surface meeting a very small round surface, the margin for error is meagre indeed.

I often wonder just what the club golfer gets out of the game. Oh, I know there is the cameraderie of the club, the social elements involved, the friendships, the fresh air, the fact that even in city or suburban clubs we can see the sky, which some of us don't often do, but what I do not know is why so many people are content to play so badly. Some people play only three or four times a year, and you don't expect much from them, but others play every week and they can be quite dreadful. They have no idea of grip, stance, anything. They have all the equipment, too. Yet they don't seem to make any particular effort to get better. Perhaps it is a British trait, the old Corinthian philosophy that one learns by playing, and not by practising. If you spent an entire day practising chipping, or bunker shots, you might be dubbed 'bloody pothunter'. Yet I suppose all club golfers are sustained by hope and fantasy, the hope that the one perfect shot will bring them back next time, the fantasy that the one particular shot they played today was in fact perfect, when perhaps it fell rather short of that. And always, of course, the 'one good shot' is the big hit, the smashing drive that went out maybe 230 yards and stayed on the fairway. It is never a delicate little chip which finished one foot from the hole, or the twenty-foot putt that broke two ways, and was holed.

So much – for the time being – about playing the game. Let me also add that, from my viewpoint of fifty years, I have the greatest admiration for the golf tournament spectator. Since I have been involved in television commentary, I have made some effort to walk where the spectators walk, and I conclude that they are abused. They pay a lot of money to see very little. They must not move, they must not run, they must cross here, they must not cross there, they cannot take a picture, and they are now paying five or six pounds a day for these privileges. They are out in the pouring rain, scrambling over sandhills, they'll pay three quid for a steak sandwich which is all gristle, then trek to some distant car park to find their car stuck fast in mud.

God bless them all, for they are an integral part of this wonderful, puzzling, infuriating and rewarding game. I count myself fortunate to have spent my life in it.

CHAPTER ONE

Ferndown

For me, the grass started to grow, the sun first shone, the world began, on 28 February 1931. I was born in a handsome bungalow on the edge of the Wannsee golf club. A momentous day, I would have to say, and my mother may well have agreed but for different reasons, since she was delivered of a monster of better than fourteen pounds. And no doubt well pleased to be rid of me. My father, Percy Alliss, had gone to Germany in 1926 to be senior professional at the Golf-und-Land Club, Wannsee, an appointment at the time as lucrative as any in Europe. In hindsight, it seems a remarkable thing for him to have done. He had served in the Argyll and Sutherland Highlanders in the Great War, had been wounded twice fighting the Germans, and here he was in the thick of them, only eight years after it had ended. Very brave of him, I'd say, at the age of twenty-nine. He was the first celebrated golfer from abroad, the first foreigner, to be a club professional in Germany, and at Wannsee found a tremendous teaching programme waiting for him.

Only a small slice of the population played golf, but it was the top slice, the people of influence, wealth, power, an aristocracy for whom the will to win, the will to be best, the will to dominate, was all. This attitude is characteristically German, and my mother seemed particularly aware of it. She didn't much like the Germans; she saw them as arrogant bullies. However, they were willing and able to pay for the best things, and for my parents the early years in Berlin were good years. This was the Germany famously portrayed in fiction by Christopher Isherwood, but I do not believe the decadence touched the Allisses at Wannsee.

The surroundings were superb, even idyllic – the lovely course set through dense pine forests, the beautiful lake of Wannsee, a handsome, spacious clubhouse with all the facilities, which famous people of the day made use of – Marlene Dietrich, Marion Davies, Richard Tauber, Fritz Kreisler. Father refused unconditionally to teach Kreisler, or to encourage him to play golf, on the grounds that the famous violinist could not possibly risk his hands playing the game, and father would not be responsible for that. Yet Kreisler at the time was so interested he would come out to the club and just watch father teaching someone else, or hitting balls, for an hour or more. Von Ribbentrop was another keen supporter of the club at the time, and I am sure it was a busy and profitable life for my parents.

Yet there comes a time in life when we realize that nothing lasts for ever. Berlin for the Allisses lost its charm. The late twenties and the turn of the thirties was a time of slump and depression around the world, and by 1931 the Nazi party in Germany was growing stronger and more in evidence. There were early rumblings of trouble and sweeping change, though I imagine few people could have foreseen the staggering disasters of the two decades that lay ahead for Germany, and for much of the rest of the world. Father decided that home was the place for us. Even then, before Hitler came to power, getting out of the country was difficult; transferring capital out was very difficult. Towards the end of 1931, when I was all of eight months old and my brother Alec was seven years old, the move was made. The family anecdote, often told, is that on the train to the border there was a snap police check and search for currency. Mother spotted this, said to father quickly, 'Give me the money,' and promptly tucked the boodle into her bloomers. She then played the part of the English milady, summoning up her plummiest accent and raising her voice in the traditional English manner with foreigners, and talked her way, as it were, across the border.

My guess is that father did fairly well financially from his five years 'sur le continong'. Another family anecdote, told as often but less gleefully, is of the £3000 he left in Germany because he could not get it out. That was a hefty sum of money, particularly in those days, but after twelve years of the Hitler regime, World War II and the Allied bombings, the presence of your friendly Red Army and the continuing occupation of the city for over thirty-five years by four powers – after all that, I fear the Alliss £3000 is one treasure trove that will never be uncovered.

The year 1931, 'my' year, the year of Ramsay MacDonald and his National Government, was, if not a crisis then at least a turning point in the history of that generation of the Alliss clan, and this might be a sensible point to take a look at my parents. What does anyone owe to parents? We all consider it, or wonder about it, from time to time. One can say easily, they give us everything. They do give us life, for better or worse, the most stupendous gift of all. In my case they sustained me one way or the other through almost half of my life to date, and they certainly put their mark on me. What is it that Muriel Spark's redoubtable schoolteacher Miss Jean Brodie says? 'Give me a girl at an impressionable age, and she's mine for ever.' But the irony of the business of being a parent, as I was to discover, is that no one can teach you how to do it; you can't take a university degree in the subject, Dr Spock or no Dr Spock. You have to do it, you have to become a parent, and learn the game by being one. And being a parent, I have concluded as the years roll past, is very, very difficult.

My father, born in 1897, was a Yorkshire lad, one of a big family engaged in a small-holding, market-gardening business in which he worked briefly. The Hallamshire Golf Club in Sheffield, where he did some caddying in his early teens, introduced him to the delights of the ancient game. He served in the Argylls during the Great War – all his brothers, big guys, were Coldstream Guardsmen. He and his brother George were very good cricketers, father a pretty good slow right-arm bowler and a handy bat, and they were both on standby for a trial for Yorkshire. George was very much under the wing of Sir Stuart Goodwin, the Sheffield steel magnate who was to promote the Ryder Cup match of 1957 at Lindrick – I played in it! – and endowed the Professional Golfers' Association with a fund to finance future matches.

By the time the Great War broke out, father had achieved some kind of status at Hallamshire. The call to cricket never did come from Yorkshire, and he became an assistant at Stanmore. After the war, he became an assistant at the famous Royal Porthcawl club in South Wales, and presently got his first full professional's job at the Clyne Golf Club, near Swansea. Here, mother enters the story. She too was from Yorkshire, from Hull, where her father, 'Cap'n' Joseph Rust, a fisherman, had become one of the founders of the Icelandic fishing grounds, owning his own trawler. He fished all the coasts, and eventually moved round to Swansea, where the Rust family became quite prominent. Uncle Stanley Rust, for example, was largely responsible for extending the railway system into Swansea Docks, and for building up the docks themselves. Cap'n Joseph, I suspect, made a good deal of money but rather inconsiderately died in his forties. His widow had a house, money, possessions, and lived for fifty more years. When she died, she left everyone £5000 in her will – myself, my brother, all the cousins. The only problem was that, with the passage of time, there was only some £1900 in the kitty.

Mother was an artistic, theatrical type, a church organist with an excellent mezzosoprano voice. She had many diplomas for piano and voice, and really wanted to make a career of music. But in those days, around 1920, show business of any kind, and particularly in South Wales, was considered about the same as going on the streets. Instead, she ran into Percy Alliss, they fell in love and married, and life took off at another tangent.

My father, I must say, was never into the politics of envy, to use the current phrase. For example, just before we left Berlin in 1931, he, the young Henry Cotton and Aubrey Boomer found they were not eligible for the Ryder Cup match of that year because they were based in Europe! Boomer was in France, Cotton in Belgium. So they decided to go off to the US on their own, have a whirl at the American tournaments, and pool their winnings. Boomer was hopelessly out of touch with his game and soon dropped out and went home. Cotton was plagued by a massive attack of boils and for a long spell was stretched out in bed supported by pillows in considerable pain. Alliss soldiered on. He went up to Canada and tied with Walter Hagen for the Canadian Open, only to lose the play-off. He won a tidy sum of money although, split three ways, it did not amount to much. But he never complained over that kind of thing, and was never resentful. If he had been a little more ruthless at times, perhaps he would have been an even greater success in tournament and championship play.

Another problem was the business of serving 'the toffs'. My father was never much of a believer in class, the idea of one person being superior or inferior to another. He took a rather pragmatic, even at times sardonic, view of serving the wealthy and the snobbish. He reckoned that they were there to be catered for and looked after just like anyone else. If others wanted to poke slight fun at them, so be it, but the thing was to smile, to be polite, no matter what. If you smiled, you might get a tip. If you smiled fifty times a day, you might get ten tips. But if you frowned and snarled and said 'Whaddya want?' then you would get positively no tip at all. So it was all part of business, quite calculated, nothing inferior or demeaning about it – it was just a game that you played.

All this rubbed off on me, and stayed with me for a long

time. Father was a kind man with a gentle sense of humour. He was a great newspaper reader, another trait which I inherited. He read the *Mirror* for Cassandra, the *Daily Mail* and the *News Chronicle*. He was a Liberal for a long time, switching to Conservative after World War II, and although the Tories disappointed him often enough, he thought their ideas were, in the main, for the best. He was a meticulous man, without being over-fussy. He couldn't do with dirty, unkempt finger nails, dirty clothes, rumpled shirts. He was a neat, tidy, tweedy man, clean shoes, always well-turned out. I can't imagine what he would think of the decline in manners and standards in the eighties.

Mother was much more outgoing, enthusiastic, impulsive. She'd say she didn't smoke – yet have two or three cigarettes a day. She'd say she didn't believe in drink – she was from a rather Chapel family – but she'd have her whisky and lemonade, and perhaps another, two or three times a week. She could be tempestuous and moody. I see lots of her in me. People think of me as being quiet and calm, but I can be very moody, and there is a mean streak there, oh, a mean streak.

Looking back from the age of fifty, one of the fascinating things is how little I remember of my life before the age of eight or nine, in the period before the war. The analysts tell us that by the age of twelve any child's personality is fully formed. There are certainly personality traits and behaviour patterns in me that I remember clearly in my parents. No doubt I was moulded in those years, but I have very little recall of people and places and happenings. One thing that may have been planted in my subconscious was that people in golf seldom stuck in the same place. My father moved from Berlin to Beaconsfield Golf Club – and a pleasant place it was for a year or two – before he moved north to Templenewsam, in Leeds. This looked like a plum job – thirty-six holes of busy public golf, lots of traffic, lots of turnover, and something of a real homecoming since my parents were both Yorkshire folk, but somehow it didn't work out. Things simply did not gel for that generation of the Allisses in Leeds, and early in 1939 father moved south, to Ferndown in Dorset. For me, Ferndown was where life really began.

I lived at Ferndown and its surrounds for the best part of thirty years: lovely Ferndown, seven miles north of Bournemouth, in the heather and pine country which I adore, in what must be one of the most mellow corners of England. So much of what I am today was given firm shape at Ferndown, in the 1940s. My father, although he was forty-two when the war broke out, immediately rushed off and joined the Dorsetshire Regiment. It seemed no more than a 'Beau Geste' when they threw him out very quickly, in 1940, because of 'lumbago'. His condition deteriorated and he spent much of the next two years in a wheelchair, having manipulative treatment without much effect. Eventually Major Mason, a club member who had a house by the 18th fairway, and incidentally was managing director of Mason's A1 Sauce, insisted that my father should go to London and let Sir John Weir, one of the King's physicians, have a look at him.

Sir John discovered that there was a displacement at the base of the spine, and they were able to trace it back to Wannsee in Berlin. My father had been jogging back to the house from the club one night, through the woods, when his foot went into a rabbit hole and he stumbled. He had thought nothing of it at the time. Under Sir John Weir's supervision, he had eight months of treatment, tedious and expensive, before he could walk again, but thereafter he was soon as busy as ever at the club – Ferndown was not quite as dead as many golf clubs during the war.

Ferndown in those days was a small village, and I'm happy to say it still is, by and large. Life ended at ten-thirty at night when the last bus left Bournemouth, in my terms the big city seven miles away, for a twenty-five-minute journey. There was no question of staying out after that time. At home there was no television to watch, and for information only the newspapers and the radio, which probably made me the avid reader and listener – some people might say talker – that I am. I do like to listen to people with a good command of English. I am sure standards have fallen in this respect. I'm not talking about accents – nothing wrong with them. I adore on the radio people like Benny Green and Terry Wogan. Green, a former jazz musician, played tenor sax and is a London boy with an unmistakeable accent he does nothing to disguise, but marvellously fluent, weaving words to tell good stories. I do like story-tellers, which is why I so enjoyed being with Henry Longhurst in his last few years. Wogan, in an Irish idiom, is another of the breed. Like Keith Waterhouse in the *Daily Mirror* and elsewhere. Bright, funny, in love with words, words, words.

I don't recall ever being afraid during the war. No doubt I took a romantic view of it, as a child would, and I remember patrolling the garden with an air rifle when I was ten or eleven, ready for German paratroops. One odd thing about the English, and the times, was that I don't remember anyone ever saying, 'If we win the war . . .' It was always '*When* we win the war . . .', although God knows there were many times when we should have lost the thing. I also remember seeing dog-fights and vapour trails in the sky. We were just too far west to see the real air battles. Poole Harbour seemed a prime place for an invasion, just as it became the same for launching one, but Portsmouth and Southampton probably had priority over Bournemouth as Luftwaffe targets. So the great happenings of the war – Dunkirk and the Fall of France, Hitler's invasion of Russia, Pearl Harbor, Stalingrad, El Alamein, Hiroshima – washed over the young Alliss and it all finished as I got into my teens.

School days were pretty enjoyable, as I recall. At one

period I was at Queen Elizabeth Grammar School at Wimborne, and very nice it was. However, I was removed from there and installed in modest Crosby House, a private school in Bournemouth, directed by one Mrs Violet Weymouth, a chain-smoking dragon lady. It seemed that at Queen Elizabeth I had been caught copying the book of a boy next to me, and we were both hopelessly wrong, or rather he was hopelessly wrong. I got a good hiding. It was a rather severe one, in fact, and mother did not like it, did not like it at all. I was removed. I was also no scholar, and even then was always around the golf course, playing golf after my fashion. The whole ambience then, as now, was golf. As I grew up, the names I heard across the table and around the house were Whitcombe, Compston, Hagen, Sarazen, Padgham, Duncan, Craid Wood, Diegel, Cotton, Snead, Nelson. When I was a mere infant, I had a set of clubs, two feet long, and knocked up and down the garden with a ping-pong ball. And there was the presence of the great man Percy Alliss, who had known them all and was Match Play Champion, a Ryder Cup player and German Open Champion over and over again. For my brother Alec and myself, life had to mean golf.

At the golf club I was pottering and interfering from my earliest days. After school in the afternoon, I'd head for the golf course, to Jim Dean, the head greenkeeper and his assistant Jimmy Bracher. During holidays, I'd spend hours on Bracher's tractor, up and down the fairways, or poking around in the rough looking for golf balls, putting when I had a chance, raking bunkers or whatever, and, whenever I could, playing. Wartime, and quite a few of the post-war years, meant austerity. The times and the people I knew made their marks on me. I became very conscious of, and appreciative of, food and new clothes, of not wasting anything, of making do.

And when my father was ill, or very busy at the club, there were other people who took his place – Joe Close,

Steve Prentice, Ted Chubb, and Daddy Longmore who would give me sixpence for every hole I won from him. Ralph Close, nicknamed 'Joe', I had watched for some time with great awe. He was a former Army major, a retired dental surgeon, who had a house on the golf course, and I respectfully watched him come and go. One day he asked if I would like to play nine holes. I jumped at the chance and it was the first of hundreds of rounds we played together. He'd give me first half a crown, then later five bob, for nine holes. I thought he must be a millionaire. Then there was Harold Wakefield, from the oil family; Ralph Langton, whose family owned a brewery on the Isle of Wight, and Major Ruttle, with wide business interests through the Gresham Trust, in printing, hotels, the shoe business and much else. There were others and they were all kind and encouraging to me. Close was a fiery character, a stickler for etiquette and politeness and doing the right thing and never taking the Lord's name in vain. These men taught me hard lessons about gamesmanship, about life, in which they were widely experienced, and about complete respect for the Laws of the Game. I learned from these men about morals, ethics, the fact that there must be rules which we must obey if we are to live in peace in a civilized community.

Ted Chubb rather surprised me when he told me he considered himself very fortunate to be a member of Ferndown, which in the main had a membership of 'professional' men – doctors, lawyers, chemists, dentists – whereas he was just a small shopkeeper from Bournemouth, with a tobacconist-newsagent's business. So from these early days I had an awareness of 'one's place' and how one relates to it and to others. I don't believe I am talking about class here, that odd English system that identifies and categorizes a man as soon as he speaks, although there may be a suggestion of that in it, but rather the business of knowing that no one can barge in where he pleases, or do anything he pleases, that we all know and accept that there are some lines drawn in life over which we should not cross without invitation.

This rather small group of men, plus the family of Tricketts from Tricketts Corner, and during the war a few Americans from St Leonard's Hospital were the people who played golf with me. The vast mass of Ferndown members seemingly ignored me. Perhaps I was just a fixture around the place. Perhaps I was just the pro's son. Perhaps they thought my father was wealthy (he was not). Perhaps they thought I was privileged and that my father was surely bent on making me a world champion. Not so. Of course I don't really know what they thought, since they didn't confide in me, but the truth was I don't remember playing golf with my father very much, and he certainly never gave me many formal lessons. We'd mainly just talk about the game from time to time, and usually only when I started the conversation. By the time I was fifteen, I could play well, scratch in fact. The game never seemed particularly difficult. I could always hit the ball. I left school at fifteen and turned to golf for my living.

In 1946, when the world was breathing more evenly, the war veterans were returning, and some form of professional tournament circuit was stammering back into shape, my father took me up to the Boys' Championship at Bruntsfield, Edinburgh. I found a place in the England team to play the Scottish boys – we beat them handily – our team including such names as Arthur Perowne, Michael Pearson and Guy Wolstenholme. I got through to the semi-final of the championship, where I was beaten by a little fellow called Donald Dunston, who promptly lost to a Scot, A. F. D. Macgregor, in the final. That done, I became a professional golfer, assistant, unpaid, at Ferndown GC. Well pleased with myself I no doubt was. I picked up all the small repair work done in a professional's shop, but by then club-making by hand was long gone, save for a few specialists. I got by with the pennies I earned playing with my retired chums. In 1947 I was presumptuous enough to tackle the Open Championship at Hoylake, aged sixteen and a half. I scored 79 at Arrowe Park, 86 at Hoylake and failed to qualify. The title was taken by one Fred Daly, and I stole back to Dorset, obscurity and the five-bob matches.

When I reached seventeen, however, I made my first sortie into the hard world of major tournament golf. My father gave me £50. I was to go to the Spalding Tournament at St Andrews, the *Yorkshire Evening News* Tournament at Leeds, and the Brand-Lochryn event at Mere, near Manchester. The £50 was all I had to cover the trip – which was due to last three weeks! My father declared that if the money ran out, I'd have to get myself home as best I could, walking if necessary. There would be no more money. If I won any, so much the better. Brother Alec would go along as chaperone, sharing in the £50 expenses. Contrary to the general belief, this was the first direct cash donation my father made me.

Off we went to St Andrews and my first sight of the venerable home of golf and its dreaded Old Course. I hacked my way round the confounded place twice for a total of 153 strokes. I was convinced that this total would not be enough to qualify. Then, as now, all the players entering the competition played the first and second rounds, then approximately fifty per cent of the best scorers up to that point went on to play the third and fourth rounds of the 72-hole competition. Alec and I stood at the railing behind the last green feeling rather sulky at the thought of being out of the tournament by perhaps only one stroke when along came Charlie Ward, a senior hand and a bright spark. Charlie was a great statistician – he always knew the state of play. I said, 'Well, we're just going to pack up and get home – we won't qualify here.' Said Charlie, 'Well, son, I'll just bet you half a crown that you do qualify.' I, big spender, said, 'You're on.' Charlie knew that an older professional, John Higham, was on the course at that moment and had taken 48 strokes for the first nine holes and therefore would have a very high score which would push the qualifying mark up, and that everyone on the 153 mark would qualify after all. He took my half crown, and confessed later, 'I knew about Higham, but there's a little lesson for you.' I never did get the half crown back but I was happy to lose it and play all four rounds in my first professional tournament.

Moortown, Leeds, the next stop, gave me another little lesson, or experience – I failed to qualify there. But Mere, the last stop on our pilgrimage, became one of my very favourite golf courses. I was the youngest competitor, and I finished fifth, tied with such august names as Fred Daly, the Open Champion, Dai Rees, Max Faulkner and Aldo Casera of Italy. I also won a prize for assistant professional, and my total cheque was for £57 10s. I went home with money in my pocket, feeling as though I had won the Open Championship. Father was delighted. I thought this tournament golf game was a doddle, easy as shooting fish in a barrel. Moortown was instantly forgotten. Father of course, laid the cold hand of reason on my fevered brow by saying that was how it was to be from now on, that I must finance myself from my winnings, cover my expenses from tournament to tournament, and if I didn't then I should just come home. But that didn't faze me. I was off and running into a grand career. I was a tournament golf professional, What could be better? It was to last for a quarter of a century, and it was to bring me days of wine and roses, the best of times, the worst of times, reaping and sowing, anguish, joy, ecstasy, foreign places, foreign people, good guys, bad guys and, more than anything else, many a hard, hard lesson in the perplexities of living.

CHAPTER TWO

Wentworth

I played about half a dozen tournaments in 1949, including the Spalding event at Worthing where, after an opening 74, three 67s put me into eighth place. There were some early rumblings in the newspapers about a 'boy wonder', Leonard Crawley of the *Daily Telegraph* wrote of a future 'Open Champion', and there was some speculation about a place for the young Alliss in the Ryder Cup match – the professionals of Great Britain and Ireland against those of the United States of America – scheduled for Ganton in Yorkshire towards the end of the season. But something more irresistible, and in the long run no doubt much better for me, called. National Service. I joined up in June 1949, and served my time in the RAF Regiment at such famed watering places as Warrington, Catterick Camp and Watchet, near Minehead in Somerset. Watchet was only eighty-five miles from Ferndown, but it took more than six hours by train. There were no motorways and damned few cars in those days, still in the aftermath, as we were, of the war and still to be freed from the austerities of Chancellor Sir Stafford Cripps. National Service was extended from eighteen months to two years just five weeks before I was due to come out.

When I was released in 1951, and went back to Ferndown, I saw the place through very different eyes. I don't remember ever as a child having family holidays in the ordinary sense. Occasionally I'd be taken to South Wales and the Rust family but the Allisses themselves never packed up bag and baggage and pail and spade and set off for the seaside as an ordinary family would. Ferndown had been my life. Now in 1951 it suddenly seemed

30

diminished. After all, I had been in the Services, been to Catterick! I was just pottering around the place, living at home with my parents, free and rent-free, but without an income from either my father or the club and living on the pennies I could get from playing the odd round with my few friends. So I developed an ambivalent attitude to the old place, a love-hate relationship which bothers me to this day, although I still enjoy going back. It did not seem to hold much future for an ambitious young fellow. And as I picked up the threads of my game, after playing not more than fifty rounds in two years, and began competing in tournaments again, the impression grew in me distinctly that many of the members seemed happier to talk to me when I came back to the club having done badly in a tournament rather than when I had done well. They really did nothing to help my career. Time after time I would see three of them go out to play and never consider asking me to make up the four. Then they'd come back into the clubhouse and cheerfully lose £20 or £30 playing poker, when £1 for a round would have been manna to me. I must have been twenty-two years old before I was invited into the Ferndown clubhouse. And even when I was selected to play in the Ryder Cup match of 1953 I felt odd about using the place. I suppose I was still considered 'the boy', a fixture at the club, and I began to think I had been there too long.

And yet, as I was to realize, more golf professionals in my time have been ruined by being allowed into the clubhouse than were ever ruined by being kept out. It is the old business of privilege and prohibition. Often, like children, we want something simply because we cannot have it and, when we do get it, we find it simply was not worth all the fuss. The tradition of golf club members keeping the professional out of the clubhouse and 'in his proper place' is superficially medieval, and smacks of master and retainer. But the practicality of it is not half bad. I know the scene so well. It's winter time, perhaps a long winter with two or three months of bad weather, almost no play on the course during the week, very little action in the professional's shop, few lessons to give. There is the inevitable group of aged members, retired, down at the club every morning to read the free newspapers, drink a coffee, perhaps play a frame of creaky snooker, fugitives from the wives between breakfast and the six o'clock news. The pro is there of course and it's cold and miserable and: 'By God the heating's a bit low today – let's have a Whisky Mac.' So they have one, and another, and suddenly the pro is into the act, into the Whisky Macs, into the frame of snooker and the card school, and he's buying his rounds and he's one of the group.

Before long he is a regular, walking in uninvited, keeping pace at the bar with the others. But as the months pass, some of the members don't like the fact that the pattern is persisting, and soon it becomes, 'I say, don't you think old Bill is getting a shade forward?' 'Yes, just been thinking the same myself.' 'Mmm. Doesn't do much in the shop, doesn't have much in there. Always in the damned clubhouse, you know, drinking. Doesn't give many lessons. And when he does, always with Mrs So-and-so.' 'Quite right old boy. Suppose her husband is still working hard, travelling a lot, is he? Mmm.'

So the tide has turned. And often the members now criticizing the pro are the very people who insisted that he came in in the first place. Perhaps one is a committee member, and soon it is being discussed by the committee, the professional's reputation has gone and, not long after, he is gone. I've seen it happen so often I could write the script. But when I got back to Ferndown in 1951, aged twenty, I knew it all then. Pride was in the driving seat. After all, I had been out in the world, hadn't I?

Looking back from the watershed of fifty years, I have not changed my earlier feeling that the two dominant influences in the first half of my life were, first, simply that I was the son of my father, and second, the Ryder Cup match of 1953.

Only fairly recently have I made a close study of my father's playing career, which I now think was remarkable. His tournament career lasted really only from 1926 to 1939, and the first five of those years he spent in Germany. He would make an annual pilgrimage home to the Open Championship, and perhaps the Match Play Championship. Otherwise his playing career would be confined to the German Open, which he won for four successive years from 1926, and a few Continental events. He won the Italian Open of 1927 (I did the same just thirty-one years later) and again in 1935. He won the PGA Match Play Championship of 1933, was a finalist in 1935 (beaten by Alf Padgham), won again in 1937 and was a finalist in 1945, at the age of forty-nine, when he was beaten 4 and 3 by Reg Horne. He appears to have played some pretty good Opens, having had good chances at Prince's in 1932 when Sarazen won and again at Carnoustie in 1937 when Cotton won, but he putted abysmally. He finished fifth at Hoylake in 1936 when Alf Padgham won, and ninth at St Andrews when Dick Burton won. He played in the Ryder Cup teams of 1933, 1935 and 1937, having been banned form the team when he was in Berlin. Most of his contemporaries have now gone, but it is always a great delight to me to reminisce about him with people in golf who knew him, either personally or as a playing companion or opponent – people like Henry Cotton, Gene Sarazen, Dai Rees, Leonard Crawley, Gerald Micklem.

So there you had the famous public figure that anyone would relish having as a father. But that was only a small part of it. I was proud to be the son of my father the man, and I still have the most tremendous respect and admiration, and a very deep love, for the memory of him. In the fifties and sixties I was always being compared to him by people who remembered him as a player and loved to point out that the one thing that father and son had in common was that they could not putt. The references were scarcely calculated to improve either my view of life or my dexterity with the putter. The other obvious assumption that people make, and people do make a lot of assumptions, was that I had been intensively coached by him and that he had set out – must have done – to make me a super champion golfer. Not so. On the contrary I think he was concerned that I should do it on my own, stand on my own two feet. He merely told me to watch the best players, observe their swings and their rhythms, watch how they handled different circumstances – then practise.

Alas, I had little incentive to practise. There was no practice ground at Ferndown, and I had to practise at the side of a fairway without taking a divot! More importantly, I never really had any trouble in hitting the ball. I've always been able to hit the thing. By the time I was in my middle teens, I could cut the ball, hook it, fade it, hit it high or low. Father's main concern was that I always wanted to blast the ball into the next county, always hit it that extra ten yards which really made no difference to the playing of the hole. He'd say, 'You have a perfectly good swing – control it, and go out and use it.' One thing that he did insist on, very firmly, was that I change my grip. Until I was around fifteen or sixteen, my grip was like a bunch of bananas, left thumb round the back of the grip, right thumb resting on second finger of left hand. A Canadian lumberjack would have been proud of it. I cried myself to sleep for six months before the change worked.

Equipped for the game or no, I was soon into tournament action after National Service. The vast distance I clobbered the ball, and I suppose my name, meant that the writers paid me some attention, hailing me first as the new white hope, then suggesting that the white hope was becoming black despair, and why didn't I win something? I did, the

Assistants' Match Play Championship at Hartsbourne, and with it my biggest prize to that date, £200. The next year, 1953, the year of Everest and the Coronation, brought me close to a real breakthrough. I played in the Open Championship with serious intent for the first time, and finished in ninth place at Carnoustie behind the unique Ben Hogan. I finished third in the Irish Open, behind Eric Brown and Harry Weetman and eight strokes in front of Bobby Locke and the rest of them. After thirty-six holes, Leonard Crawley had declaimed in the *Daily Telegraph* that if I finished in the first three, my place in the Ryder Cup match would be assured. He was right. Sixteen players were invited for trials and I was one of them, and also one who survived the trials, to my intense delight and pride. At twenty-two years and seven months, I was one of the youngest-ever Ryder Cup players. Bernard Hunt, also selected, was a year older than me. Henry Cotton had played at the age of twenty-two. But it was young Alliss, going for Great Britain against the might of the United States, who made the headlines. The Alliss family had set a record which still stands as unique – both father and son could boast of being Ryder Cup players.

Here was to be the second major influence on my early life, although this time it was more of a happening, a happening that was to plague me for years as 'The Match That Alliss Lost'. Cotton was our team captain and a superb leader he was. He put us up at the Dormy House at Sunningdale, just a few miles from Wentworth, and made sure we had plenty of steaks and dairy produce, fresh fruit and vegetables, when such things were not easy to come by. Wives were banned, he kept us working strictly and seriously and, when the gun went off, we were ready to go. Lots of people, myself included, have written about this Ryder Cup match, played more than a quarter of a century ago, and there is no particular point in going over the whole ground again. The Americans led 3–1 after the foursomes, getting most of the luck but deserving their lead. In those days, the match comprised one-day matches of 36 holes' foursomes play, then a second day of 36 holes' singles play. Cotton put the youngsters Alliss and Hunt at the tail of the team, the last two on the second day. I was drawn against Jim Turnesa and all the others said, 'You'll be all right, Turnesa is no good.'

He was so no good that I went round Wentworth from those back Ryder Cup tees in 70 in the morning, and found myself one down. I was not convinced that he was any better than me, and battled through the afternoon, playing well and putting well, and holed a good putt at the 15th (the 33rd) to go one up with three to play. Turnesa's tee shot at the next hole was a wild slice, going miles to the right, over the hundreds of people in the gallery, but it hit an old lady who could not see it coming, and flopped down dead. If it had not hit her it would have been buried hopelessly in the woods. Turnesa knocked it out of the rough into a greenside bunker. I hit my pitch right at the flag, and in the air it looked quite perfect but in fact it was woefully short, into the bunker at the front of the green. The dead ground short of the green had rather foxed me. Turnesa, almost inevitably, splashed out of the bunker handily, and promptly holed a ten-footer for his four. I came out of the bunker four and half feet from the hole – and missed. I lost a hole I should have won, and right there, I realized later, I lost a match I should have won. That was the putt that won and lost my battle and that was the putt that lost the Ryder Cup match. But that was the putt that nobody remembered. The drama, which was to persecute me for years, and which I believe I threw off only a few years ago, was yet to come.

Jim Turnesa on the 17th tee was clearly nervous, fidgeting with his grip, but got a good drive away. I have described the events that were to follow in an earlier book, *Alliss Through The Looking Glass,* and I can do no better than more or less repeat what I wrote there. Wentworth's 17th is a dog-leg to the left, turning round some gardens at the angle, with the left side out of bounds. Taking the right-side route makes it a very long second shot to the green. I decided to aim at the left-hand corner, hit hard for distance and let the ball drift back into the fairway. I hit a real purler, but it did not fade back. It caught the very corner and stayed there, and there I was, out of bounds by two feet. I played a second ball, and made four with it, but with the penalty strokes that counted six. Turnesa was down carefully in five, and was one up with one to play – dormie, as we say. We were both now very tense, and it was his turn to miss the drive. He hit a massive slice, fully sixty yards into the trees on the right, while I hit a good one, exactly where I wanted it to be in the fairway. Hundreds of people were swarming around, in and out of the trees, and one of them came over and told me Turnesa was in a shocking place and could not possibly get out of there. Then there was a great deal of crashing and crackling around in the trees, gasps and sighs and shouts of 'Here it comes!' and the ball came reeling and staggering out on to the fairway. Next he hit a wood shot a good forty yards short of the green. I let go a pretty good 2-iron shot which finished almost pin-high and some fifteen yards to the left of the green. The ball had a little drag on it, caught the left-hand corner of the banked green and finished in a little mossy hollow. When I got there, I found it was rather close to the grandstands which had been built around the back of the green.

This was the moment when more than anything else I wanted some sound, mature advice. It did not come. Henry Cotton should have been there (all the other matches, with the exception of that between Bernard Hunt and Dave Douglas behind us, had finished). He was not. In fact he was on the other side of the green with his wife 'Toots' and a group of journalists. I learned later that Henry was about to fight his way round to me – thousands of people were milling around the green – when someone said, 'Oh, no, Henry, you simply cannot give blatant advice.' Cotton, it appeared later, was going to suggest that I play the shot with a straight-faced club and run it up to the hole.

The whole incident is almost ludicrous when I look back on it. The writers had a field day, describing how I had 'frozen'. Nothing of the kind happened. As I walked around the ball, even as I stood over it, my mind was full of nothing but feet, rows and rows of feet, and shoes – brogues, mocassins, sneakers, boots, shoes, spikes, rubbers – the shoes of the people in the front row of the grandstand which I could just see at the limit of my vision. In fact, the ball was within two clublengths of this grandstand, and in golfing law it could have been moved. The biggest pair of shoes belonged to Tony Duncan (Colonel Duncan, the former Walker Cup captain). Why I should notice that I'll never know. The thought of Duncan, Duncan's feet, and all those boots and shoes on the stand kept popping idiotically in and out of my mind.

The ground between me and the hole was not as simple as it may have looked to many people. It was rather mossy and fluffy. The answer was to swing my wedge well back and slowly and positively lob the ball on to the green. I had the fear that if I swung it back too far I might hit some of those damned shoes on the stand. I took a good steady swing at it, but at the last moment forgot about the ball – and bumbled the thing about a yard short of the putting surface. I had to play again. This time I ran it up to just about a yard from the stick, having played four. Turnesa was on, and missed his putt for five. Then, to square the match, and from that short range, I missed. For Alliss a ridiculous, incredible, childish, delinquent six, and the match lost by one hole. I don't quite know how I lived through the next fifteen minutes of my life. Next came Bernard Hunt and it was his turn to walk alone in the wilderness, isolated despite the thousands round that last green. He was at the back of the green in two, and needed only two putts to win his match, and tie the Ryder Cup. He three-putted, halved, and the entire Ryder Cup match was lost on that 36th green by the young ones, Alliss and Hunt.

I have dug into this eventful, if now distant, Ryder Cup match, not to justify what happened. I played the bad shots and missed the putts – no one else did. I have never much believed in going back in life. What happens happens once, for good or ill. But the events of Wentworth lingered over me for many a long year, and lingered with the critics and spectators. They were bitterly disappointed, and I was, and I respected their disappointment as coming from an ardent desire to win, to beat the Americans after many lean years. The narrowness of this match must have confirmed in many minds that we could indeed beat the Americans in our own country. Perhaps the failures of Wentworth were an integral part of the victory at Lindrick four years on. Perhaps if there had been no Wentworth, there would have been no Lindrick. Perhaps. What I do know is that over those last few holes against Jim Turnesa, I was a very young golfer. The putt on the 16th really lost me the match. The drive on the 17th, so close to being perfect, failed, but failed marginally by a couple of feet. Those were the real crises of the round for me, and not the 18th hole, and no doubt they reflected my lack of experience.

The Wentworth 'disaster' did nothing to help my game, to help my career, to eliminate a complex which was already forming over my short putts. It was a bitter moment for me and I cried. I had dearly wanted to win, dearly wanted our side to win, because my father had played in the last British team that beat the Americans. As we were going up for the presentation, he said to me, 'Come on now, chin up – you played very well, very well, go up there and stick your chest out a bit.' Neither Bernard nor I felt much like doing that. It was my first venture into the rarefied atmosphere of international sport at its highest level. I quickly decided that it was a man's world in which there was no room for boys, in which life was very real, very earnest.

It's a strange thing, criticism. You hear people saying that they don't mind criticism provided it is 'constructive', whatever that may be. I feel the expression is often misapplied, and know for sure that criticism is hard to take when one is on the receiving end. In a strange way, praise is sometimes even harder to take, especially lavish praise. In my time, I've had people come up and say, 'Great, great, you're the best, you're the greatest.' So I say, 'Oh, thank you very much, but perhaps not quite that.' Oh, yes you are.' So you say then, 'Very kind of you, but there are so many other people.' 'Don't tell me, son, don't tell me – I know . . .' I can feel the arrogance, the bolshiness rising up in them. The years march on, and there are not so many people left who saw the Ryder Cup match of 1953. Yet I had one, only a year ago, who came up and described my match including those last few holes, completely wrongly. He went through it all in detail, stroke by stroke, but had me totally confused with my opponent, Jim Turnesa, and had my game totally confused with that of Bernard Hunt. He insisted that I had three-putted the last green, instead of missing a chip shot and a short putt. After listening to this very politely, I said rather gently that it wasn't quite like that, it was rather like this. He looked at me most indignantly and said, 'Don't tell me, I was there!' I couldn't resist saying to him, 'And where the bloody hell do you think I was?' So that was the Ryder Cup of 1953. It put a brand on me – the man who lost the Ryder Cup. Nearly thirty years on, the brand mark has only just worn off.

CHAPTER THREE

Parkstone

In December 1953, Ryder Cup or no Ryder Cup, I married Joan McGuiness. It was a very nice wedding, and we had many good years together. We went off on honeymoon to Cornwall, and perhaps an omen of what was to befall our relationship was the fact that I played golf every day. Oh I was young, even younger than my twenty-two years.

My brother Alec came home from N'Changa, in what was then Rhodesia, to be my best man. I've long had the feeling that Alec has had the rough edge of life, certainly in his early days. When I say that, I realize there may be some selfishness in it, because I am sure that if he had been at home through all my teenage years, he would have had a positive and beneficial effect on my personality. As it was, he went off to the war and was a wireless operator on minesweepers. When it was over he came back, bent on a career in golf, to Ferndown. My father, in his kindly and occasionally misguided way, had told his pre-war assistant, Charlie Trickett, that if they all survived Charlie would have his job back after the war. Charlie had been a mechanic assembling Mustang fighter planes in Canada for a spell. When Alec came back, bright-eyed and no doubt as bushy-tailed as the average returning warrior, he found Charlie in residence, and my father saying, 'Well, look, Alec, there is just no business around at the moment, how can we work this out, what can we do, I'm afraid you'll have to move on, son.'

So Alec moved on, to Brighton and Hove GC, high on the Downs behind Brighton, in 1946, when there were no goods to sell, few lessons to give, the winter was cold, damp, foggy and very long, and altogether it must have been a depressing time for him as for so many other golf professionals. I was around fifteen when he had to go out and make his own way, and I was very much still at home. He moved on to Weston-super-Mare for some years, but the late forties, even the early fifties, were not really flourishing times in golf, as the country tried to draw breath and patch itself up and decide where it was going. (Around that time Dean Acheson, the American Secretary of State, said that Britain had lost an empire and not yet found a role, and I sometimes think that it still hasn't decided where it is going.) Alec then went to N'Changa, where there was a big and very busy club. He was single, on his own, but he didn't quite get Africa right. Perhaps he was not a real get-up-and-go man. In any event, when he came home for my wedding I said, 'Look, if we ever get the chance to work together, why don't we do that?' We agreed that, given the chance, we would give it a real go.

In the summer of 1953, there was a slight move afoot at Ferndown to 'allow' me to enter the clubhouse if I had been playing with a member or guest. It was suggested that in these circumstances it would be in order for me to go for tea, or to have a drink with my playing partner. I was quite shattered later to be told by a member friend that another club member had proposed that they should wait to see if I was selected for the Ryder Cup team that autumn, in which case it might be considered 'all right'. This nonsense did little to improve my thinking about Ferndown. It all seems ridiculous and almost medieval to contemplate now, but that was how things were. It was another demonstration of knowing 'one's place' in the pecking order. Now we are all free to do as we please, go where we please, or assume we are, but not then. Yet I was to come to appreciate that it is not a bad system for society, unfair or undemocratic as it may seem to some. If we all felt free to barge in anywhere – Buckingham Palace, No 10 – it simply would not do. At the time, I would not have been able to accept that. I had one or two offers to move from Ferndown, but I loved the area, loved Bournemouth and its hinterland, Poole Harbour and the rest of it. It was my patch, my corner of England, and I wanted to stay there.

Joan and I moved into the top flat of my father's house, paying a rent of around fifty shillings a week, which some weeks was damned hard to come by. In 1954 I buckled down to being a tournament player, carrying the cross of that Ryder Cup match and finding it a heavy burden. Three things lightened the year. I won my first man-sized tournament against all the big guys, I played for the first time in the Canada Cup, now the World Cup, and Gary, my first son, was born in Poole Hospital. The tournament was the Daks at Little Aston, and on the last day, when we played 36 holes, my partner was Bernard Hunt whose career has marched so much in step with mine, and who remains a staunch friend. We completed the 36 holes in 3 hours 53 minutes, and I scored 70 and 67 in two of the most light-hearted rounds of my life. Both Bernard and I seemed totally relaxed. I finished with 279 and a one-shot win over the redoubtable Bobby Locke. It was a critical break-through and the £400 first-prize cheque seemed like a vast fortune to me.

Earlier in the year I had made my first substantial trip abroad, to the Argentine with a team led by Alf Padgham and including Jimmy Adams, Tom Haliburton, Max Faulkner, Harry Weetman and Bernard Hunt. London to Buenos Aires was then forty-two hours in a BOAC Argonaut, four big props churning across the South Atlantic. We played Buenos Aires, Mar del Plata, then across the River Plate to Montevideo, in Uruguay. But the Canada Cup trip was quite different. Weetman and I represented England at the Laval-sur-le-Lac club, and we had a wonderful trip. Montreal, I thought, was a beautiful city of lovely squares and fine restaurants, very cosmopolitan. All told, the win in the Daks and the foreign travel to North and South America started me thinking that the game of golf had perhaps more to offer than I had imagined.

At home things were less clear-cut, and the uncertainty made me moody and uneasy. Perhaps the decade of the fifties was an uneasy decade. These were the years of the Korean War, the invasion of Suez, the uprising in Hungary; of Truman, Eisenhower, Eden, the last of Churchill as prime minister; of the Mau Mau in Kenya, and Ghana becoming the first of the newly independent, former colonial, states in Africa; of Harold Macmillan and his legacy of commercial television, bingo and legalized gambling; of Kruschev, Marilyn Monroe and the young Pele, and *Look Back In Anger*. Strange times, like all times. The year of my lost Ryder Cup was also the year of my marriage, a year of coronation and of the ascent of Everest. What could anyone make of all that?

It was soon apparent that Joan and my mother did not get along very well. There was something of a rift, and I would find myself making detours to visit my mother, which was rather childish, and because of the stresses and strains we moved in with Joan's parents to a rather smaller house at Wallisdown, a suburb of Bournemouth. I certainly didn't appreciate it or even recognize it at the time, but the requirements of professional golf tournament play obviously put pressure on any marriage. The pattern of my week was to leave home on Monday, sometimes quite early in the morning, for the tournament venue. If the event was in Scotland, that meant an all-day drive. Tuesday was given over to practice, and Wednesday, Thursday and Friday to tournament play. The two final rounds were played on Friday in those days, although by the end of the fifties we had Saturday finishes and even the beginnings of the Sunday finishes which are now commonplace. During the fifties the exhibition match, later to be supplanted by the

Pro-Am, was the fashion. This almost always took place on a Saturday or Sunday. Thus for most professionals, and certainly for me, one night at home per week during the season was the norm. Most of that time we would be living in hotels, a long way from home, with lots of time to get through, a few pennies in our pockets, most of us healthy and few of us relishing ugly, long evenings alone. The ways of temptation were many, and it was a ready-made formula for domestic stress. When son Gary and then daughter Carol came along, I was not at home for the arrival of either.

In 1955 it was already clear to me that the Ryder Cup match of 1953 had thrown a massive psychological curtain across my career and I would simply have to find a way past it. The 1955 match was due at the Thunderbird club in Palm Springs, California, and I was desperately anxious to be chosen for the team to mend the fences broken in 1953. I won the Dunlop Tournament at Wentworth (!), failed to qualify for the Open Championship at St Andrews – not my favourite course at the time – but finished fourth in the Dunlop Masters, behind Harry Bradshaw. I thought this was good enough to put me in the team, but the selectors thought it was not, and I promptly declared through my tears that I would never, never again play in their damned Ryder Cup team. At the age of 24, life is black and white indeed. Fortunately I didn't exactly broadcast this on the nine o'clock news, but said it privately, to friends. The Foster Wards of Little Aston bore most of the brunt of all that.

With the coming of the children, we plunged into a home of our own, in Branksome Wood Road. It cost £3200, we spent another £1000 on it, and as far as we were concerned, we had a palace. Then came yet another happening that was to change the whole direction of my life. In 1956 Alec came home from East Africa, and in the spring of 1957 the brothers Alliss jointly took over

Parkstone Golf Club, following the death of Reg Whitcombe. We were thus to succeed a former Open Champion, a distinguished member of a very distinguished golf family, who had been professional at Parkstone for the best part of thirty years.

Parkstone was an entirely different club, with a much wider cross-section of members. There were millionaires and plumbers, businessmen and carpenters – a marvellous club. The course, like Ferndown, was laid through heather and pine country, but was perhaps a little more rugged in appearance than Ferndown, with a fairly main road running through the middle of it. Parkstone is a rather short course of rugged beauty, interesting, varied and with the most lovely views over Poole Harbour and Brownsea Island, with the sailing boats scattered like confetti over blue water. The clubhouse is small and cosy, and to this day I take great delight in going back there, to a great atmosphere, after what turned out to be a stay of thirteen years. Alec and I knew perfectly well that comparisons with Reg Whitcombe's reign would be inevitable and we sought to forestall them by ripping out the shop, extending it, refurnishing it and putting in a comprehensive stock. We kept it open at all hours, much longer and later than the contract with the club called for. Alec and I made a pact not to go into the clubhouse and for the rest of the year we carried that through. Not only that, but I went off to the first tournament of the year, the PGA Close Championship at Llandudno, won it, and brought the trophy back to Parkstone in high style. It was the week of 1 April, All Fools' Day, a good start!

Many of the members and committee showed a positive interest in what we were trying to do, and altogether we found warmth and a splendid atmosphere at Parkstone. They all seemed to care. The Alliss partnership lasted five years. Then Alec met and married Joan Curry of the cycle and television stores family. She was the daughter of

Edwin, the chairman. There were several Curry brothers, and then Edwin died. Death duties took their toll, and a year or so later his widow, Joan's mother, died, which made a tragic saga.

Joan and Alec moved to Guernsey where Alec started growing roses, became a member of the local growers' co-operative, and shortly found himself selling his flowers for tuppence a bloom. By the time they were shipped to the mainland, went through the Covent Garden system and got out to the vase on top of the piano, they'd be selling for ten or twenty times that amount. Alec became disenchanted with the flower trade and dabbled in a few other ventures, breeding livestock and the like, and has settled into a gentle, insular way of life. After all these years, we have rather drifted apart. I am saddened by this, but it does happen in families. I speak to him about once a year now, and usually call him at Christmas.

After he had left Parkstone, things continued to go along pretty well. I had some excellent assistants there, among them Clive Harrison, cousin of George of Beatles fame, Roger Smith, Adrian Jordan, and Derek Khuller.

The late fifties and early sixties were good tournament years for me and I contrived to win at least one event each year. The big year was 1958, when I won the Italian, Spanish and Portuguese Opens in successive weeks. And as my playing career moved along, it was all reflected in materialism, the materialism of cars, the Jaguar, the Bentley, and in houses. We moved from Branksome Wood Road to a house on Parkstone golf course, then to what we thought was an altogether grand house in Leicester Road, one of the rather swank thoroughfares in Branksome Park, for which we paid £8500. Suddenly, in the early sixties, something very special, so we thought at the time, came along. The classic house on the hill, set in twenty acres of grounds – Crabb House, the former home of Sir Richard Glynn, MP, the whole thing looking across the valley to

Canford School. The house had all sorts of nooks and crannies and ups and downs and it was charming. I felt like the country squire, or someone who had cracked, at last, the world of the Sunday colour supplements, or *Homes and Gardens*. It was a fine address, there was a separate wing and Joan's parents came to live there. It seemed we had everything going for us, that we were really into the swinging sixties.

It was a convulsive decade indeed, of The Beatles and the Maharishi; of Jean Shrimpton and Mary Quant and Twiggy; of the death of Kennedy the young Lochinvar, and the death of Churchill the old Alexander; of Profumo and Vassall; of Dr Beeching and the World Cup of 1966; of Unisex and 'never had it so good'; of Vietnam and, at the end of it all, the Man *on* the Moon. For all of us, I suppose it meant finally the end of the British Empire, and, thanks mainly to the young, the end of much of the old hypocrisy. For me, there was nostalgia in that, since I could still, can still, weep at the Trooping of the Colour, the Edinburgh Tattoo, children singing, the Cenotaph ceremony – all these old boys swinging past, festooned with bits of coloured ribbon, shoulders back, head up, in cloth caps and duffle coats and bowler hats, with a bit of the old bull and swagger and that long, swinging stride the British use. They were all young men, once, and they did it. Some of their companions not in the parade gave their all, as indeed young men still do in Northern Ireland and other theatres of war. I sometimes think that British bones litter all the deserts and mountains and ocean beds of the world. And for what?

The decade was eventful for me, in almost every conceivable way. I won the Brazilian Open at the Gavea club in Rio de Janeiro, where Mario Gonzalez has been the professional for so long. I found Rio a magical, pulsating city, with its beaches, mountains, and gorgeously figured, elegant people. Muscular, sensuous, every shade of skin colour – they all seemed tremendous. I went back in 1965 and in the aircraft with me sat two very beautiful women and a man, and it turned out they were on a modelling trip. Who should one of them be but Pauline Stone, a staggeringly lovely model who even then was world-famous and who went on to marry the actor Laurence Harvey. She was charming. They turned up again at a party the British Ambassador gave for the golfers, and I carried her phone number around for a long time, but never called. Too scared, I suppose. A dazzling lady.

In January 1961 John Jacobs, Harry Weetman, Bernard Hunt, David Thomas and myself virtually burst into the offices of the Professional Golfers' Association, bent on reform. The offices, two rooms, were at 52 Leadenhall Street, in the heart of the City of London, which we thought rather a droll place to base a professional sports body. The organization was run entirely by one man, and a remarkable man he was, Commander Charles Roe, RN Rtd. In this quaintly Victorian place, with a roll-top desk and the assistance of a splendid secretary, Miss Coburn, Charles Roe ran all the affairs of the Association – club professionals, tournament professionals, assistants alike. During his naval career he had been cast away, marooned, torpedoed and shipwrecked. Yet from the time he joined the PGA in the thirties for an annual pittance until he retired in the sixties (he lived on well into his nineties) he did everything, including the organization of all tournaments and Ryder Cup and other international matches. He signed cheques, mailed cheques, made rulings at the tournaments, organized the order of play and presentations – everything. At that time, the PGA was run through a huge committee, laden with club professionals, and we felt that the tournament players should be in control of their own separate destiny. Now of course we have two separate organizations, for club professionals and tournament players, and I just wonder how much better it is. Certainly there are more tournaments, certainly there are perhaps three hundred more players entering each event, and certainly there is a more integrated European factor in the annual schedule. But, I wonder . . . However, twenty years ago we were bent on modernizing the whole concept of tournaments in the UK and Europe, and on paying a top executive a top salary to do it, but we were obviously ten years ahead of the game.

In 1964 I played in the tournament at Turnberry Hotel sponsored by Braemar, in which we were restricted to using seven clubs. I had a hole in one at the fourth hole. In the air, it looked a pretty good shot and we thought it would be close. There were a few people around the green and as the ball landed one man raised an umbrella rather nonchalantly. When we got up, there was no sign of the ball. Must be over the green. No, dammit, it was in the hole. We just moved on to the fifth tee without any fuss or excitement. No house, no motor car to be won in those days, but it made number six on my hole-in-one list.

We played many exhibitions then, mainly for the Lord Roberts Workshops and Forces Help and chased up and down the country between tournaments, doing perhaps twelve or fourteen of them each year. It was tiring work, but good fun. We raised more than £100,000, usually playing England v Wales – Alliss and Hunt against Rees and Thomas. One international exhibition match I remember clearly, at Blackpool North Shore. It was arranged by Sir Charles Abrahams of Aquascutum for the Duke of Edinburgh Awards Scheme, in the presence of the Royal Personage. We lined up for the arrival of Prince Philip by helicopter and there was the usual curtseying and bobbing and weaving. At the end of the line was the Lord Mayor of Blackpool, a lovely Lancashire lad. He walked straight up to the Prince, stuck out his hand, and said, 'Now then lad, it's nice to see you, 'ow you goin' on then?'

Let us now enter briefly the department of 'How times

have changed'. Expenses for the German Open of 1962 were £52 18s 6d. That included the return air fare to Düsseldorf, food, drink, taxis, caddies, etc. It should be said that in those distant days the local golf federation would take care of accommodation for 'foreigners'. Expenses for a Lord Roberts exhibition, including two nights in a hotel, would be around £15. Expenses for the 1967 Open at Hoylake, won by Roberto de Vicenzo, were: hotel for the week, £26 18s; tips, £4 6s 6d; incidentals, 8s 6d (!); caddie (Jimmy Cousins), £25. I paid Jimmy a guaranteed £25 per week throughout the season.

I made my first and only visit to South Africa in 1963. I went, I hope, with a fairly open mind and I thought the country was superb, physically very lovely and dramatic. And from what I saw I could readily understand something of the attitudes of the South African whites. They made the country what it is, warts and all, no doubt about that, and their lifestyle was quite dazzling. Most important of all, they have been there for three hundred years. No point in saying 'White man, go home' to a South African. He is home. Home for him is South Africa, not Holland or England. The South Africans' international public relations over the past twenty-five years have been abysmal, and clearly their policies of apartheid are now slowly being relaxed, but the fact is that when I went there the coloured folks, if they wanted to defecate, did it in the street. If they wanted to urinate, they just did it against the side of a car. I know. It happened and I saw it. You could say that the white folks made them what they are, which is only partly true, but one thing is certain – the white South Africans are not about to surrender, in spite of the problems the rest of this century will bring them.

The sixties brought me several experiences, even exercises, in introspection. I played in the World Match Play Championship for one thing. By the middle of 1965, the first symptoms of putting disease were apparent if not diagnosed, and by the autumn, at the Dunlop Masters event and the Ryder Cup, I was putting cross-handed, right hand above left, and doing it very well. With great help from Christy O'Connor I took five points out of six at the Ryder Cup match, my best ever, and it won me a place in the World Match Play Championship. This event, started in 1964 and sponsored then by Piccadilly cigarettes, survives to this day and must be one of the most successful commercially sponsored sports events anywhere in the world. The concept was intriguing. The winners of the world's four major championships, the US Masters, US Open, British Open and US PGA, were invited. Four other players, assessed on current performance and career status, were invited, and all eight set to in 36 holes of elimination match play. Arnold Palmer won in 1964 and got the event off to a thundering start and the list of subsequent winners reads like a roll of honour of the modern game – Player, Nicklaus, Charles, Weiskopf, Graham Marsh, Hale Irwin, David Graham, Isao Aoki and the others. The field was later extended to twelve players, but with so few competitors the sponsors were still able to treat them and their wives lavishly.

Each player had a suite at the Savoy Hotel – later a private house on or near the Wentworth course – a chauffeured limousine, private dressing-room and dining-room at the club, and there were dinners, gifts, shopping and theatre expeditions to London for the wives – altogether grand treatment. I was down to play Tony Lema in the first round and, as so often before, I did not properly prepare myself, mentally, for the match. I wasn't sure in my own mind that I was going to win or make a major effort to win. It was a problem of either lack of sensitivity or oversensitivity, of not being sure that I deserved to be there, or wanted to be there. Perhaps I thought that in some way I had not really earned a suite at the Savoy. Perhaps it was the peasant in me coming out, but I spurned all the glamour and elected to stay at the Berystede, the old familiar hotel only five miles from the course, and to drive my own car. I should have gone into the thing feeling that I was as good as any of them, that I would have the suite at the Savoy and the limousine, just like Palmer and Player and Lema, and got my head up and shoulders back and made it clear to the world that I was going to beat the lot of them. An illustration of the same silly muddled lack of thinking was that at the lunch break, when the match was still under control, instead of having a light sandwich, I went through the card at table, and felt heavy and stodgy in the afternoon. And Lema beat me comprehensively.

I also went to the US Masters at Augusta for the first time. Over the years, as a member of the Ryder Cup teams, I had had plenty of invitations. My first appearance was in 1966, and it was a total disaster. I have never felt so tiny, so insignificant, so alone. The way people cheered, the stands, the noise, the bustle, the colours, the blinding sunshine, the sheer Americanness of the whole thing – I just felt completely out of it, a very small fish in an enormous ocean. It was like playing in four Cup Finals on successive days. My putting was creaky. I played one round with Gene Littler, and took five putts from six feet at the 11th hole. Shattering. Ever since then I have had the most tremendous admiration for people who go there for the first time and do well, or even do well there at any time. Maurice Bembridge's record-equalling 64; Peter Oosterhuis leading after three rounds; Peter McEvoy, our young amateur champion, playing all four rounds a couple of times – these are real achievements. It takes a very special type of person to go out there, put it all together and play well.

In the sixties television matches, that is to say golf matches filmed for subsequent showing on television, were highly fashionable. The Shell company created the 'Shell Wonderful World of Golf', a series of matches played on either the historic courses of the world, or on courses of surpassing beauty and dramatic quality. Two international players would compete, for reasonable fees and all first-class expenses, with people like Jimmy Demaret and Gene Sarazen doing commentaries; several hours of film were then edited down to television proportions. They were very successful for several seasons. I had one against the late Tony Lema in Bermuda, where he missed a winning putt of less than four feet on the last green and we halved. That was in April. In July, Tony and I were godparents to the twins of Ian Mitchell, then golf manager of Slazengers, to which company both Lema and I were contracted. Sadly, about a year later Tony and his pretty wife Betty were killed in a light aircraft crash. This was a staggering loss to the world at large, for apart from being a quite brilliant player, Lema was a striking personality – handsome, with great style and a very attractive, outgoing attitude to life.

In May 1967 I played another Shell match, at Penina in the Algarve, with Doug Sanders, another close friend who had enormous talent for the game, and had a very successful career, but who will be remembered for one of the classic 'misses' in sport, when he failed with a three-foot putt on the last green to win the 1970 Open Championship. This tied him with Nicklaus, who went on to win the play-off. I always think of the Sanders putt as another Devon Loch in the Grand National, or Don Fox, in the last minute of the Rugby League Final at Wembley with a match-winning penalty shot in the rain, slipping as he kicked, muffing it and losing the Final. I don't know what you could say to a man after that kind of thing.

Sanders pipped me at Penina, and I began to think these TV matches were not for me, although they were great fun. We virtually opened Penina, and it was in a rough and ready state. It had been built on an old rice paddy field, the trees had not grown and in short it was pretty bloody. Now it has matured, and thanks to Henry Cotton's beavering publicity over the years is very well established with, of course, the Penina Hotel which is quite lovely close at hand. There was another match at Gleneagles, with the dreaded Tommy Bolt, and one at the Tryall Club in Jamaica in which Dow Finsterwald and I set what must be a world record for filming 18 holes of golf – we took two and a half days. What with bad light and bad weather, including fierce storms, we took two and a half days and three hangovers to get the thing finished and Finsterwald beat me. Since the shows were basically for American consumption, I rationalized these defeats by thinking it was a good thing for the good guys, in this case the Americans, to win.

In November of 1968, my mother learned of her cancer. She had surgery on 5 December 1968 and she lived one more year, dying on 3 December 1969. In the midst of all this, my marriage was crumbling.

Joan did nothing wrong. Her great saying was that she loved me too much. She was a smashing housekeeper, the children were always fine, she didn't swear or drink, she wasn't promiscuous. She was a shade older than me and her parents lived with us for a spell, which may have put a strain on the relationship, but I daresay it was all down to me. Looking back, I don't think I was a very good father. I was young, too young to appreciate and know what the needs of children were. I was never a great one for 'doing things' with the children – I was away from them a good deal – and I've always been rather envious of parents who can take their children fishing, or make them models, or fly kites with them and have time and patience for them.

I was that much younger than Joan in all respects, but contrary to the gossip in 'the trade' – and the world of professional golf can be a small world indeed – I was not really the great pick-up lover man. In fact, when it came to the casual pick-up, the lady would almost always have to make the first move. Perhaps I was just a typical Pisces – romantic, wanting everyone to like me and love me, and not understanding when they didn't. So I would try to flatter people, charm them, as much to let them see their own strong points as to impress them with Alliss's. But no doubt all my sexual inhibitions, and I had plenty then, were a throwback to my youth. Many of them derived from silly things – like never seeing my parents without clothes. My mother, for all her waspish sense of fun and games – she could be a good, honest-to-God vulgar comedienne at times – was very prim and strange in her attitude towards sex and nudity. I have always been attracted, of course, by women. I admire them as I do flowers in a garden, or a painting, but it always took a long time for me to make a move. I always needed encouragement, some indication that the lady was interested in me. I suppose I flirted and canoodled around the country throughout my first marriage, but there was always the terror of putting the lady in the family way, or of disease – 'Cupid's Measles' as the jokers had it. Inhibitions were the contraceptives of my day and the Pill was not so commonplace as it is now. So, contrary to what seemed a widespread belief, I was not in fact the world champion of the seduction stakes. But there were lots of people only too anxious to put it about that I was. I suppose Joan and I might have soldiered on, as so many people do, if it had not been for something that happened in 1965. That was when I met Jacqueline Grey.

At the Senior Service tournament at Dalmahoy, near Edinburgh, in 1965, I was aware of Jackey's presence for three days before I spoke to her. I was in the bar with David Thomas and Guy Wolstenholme when she walked in, and all of a sudden she was with us and we had bought her an orange juice. Jackey had been to a finishing school in Switzerland, and she was doing interpreter work at the golf tournament. She seemed my kind of lady, small, dark, round, a pretty, cuddly girl then only twenty-one or twenty-two. I was attracted. The other two went off to play golf, and I found myself saying, 'Would you like to come out for a meal this evening?' She agreed, and we drove out ten or fifteen miles, had dinner and just never stopped talking. She then lived in Birmingham, I in Bournemouth and I remember saying when I dropped her at her hotel, 'Good job you don't live any nearer, because I could fall for you.' That was in late summer, and we had no further communication until early the following year and that was a fluke meeting, in Manchester.

Jackey seemed to me to be an entirely different woman to any I had met. Her strength of character never ceases to amaze me. She is in many ways one of the most confident women I have ever known, yet she is basically a non-competitor, which was one of the main attractions. She didn't seem to care what the Joneses had and she didn't. Nothing was too much trouble for her. She was bright, kind, attractive, a giant. She listened to all my stories, rode through all my moods, black and white. She speaks French and German fluently, types, cooks beautifully, is an able seamstress, passed her advanced driving test first time, wants to learn to fly an aeroplane and fancies having a go at parachute jumping. Remarkable. Her family, from Birmingham, has been remarkable too. Her grandfather, Sam Grey, was Lord Mayor of Birmingham in the thirties, in fact at the time of the abdication of Edward VIII. Her father, Geoffrey Grey, CB, CBE, DL, MA, was a rowing man at Oxford, a lawyer, prominent in the Territorial Army especially after the war, when he commanded the West Midland Divisions. He came out of the war, having got through the Normandy beaches, the battles around Caen and much more, when he was pushing thirty. He was married with two young daughters and no firm prospects. He had married Betty Trimmingham from Bermuda, where her family had been for centuries, no doubt producing a normal cross-section of clerics, pirates and villains in the early days but later becoming most respectable and very influential. Their children, Sally and

Jacqueline, were born during the war. When Geoffrey came home, he found himself in something of a Percy Alliss-Alec Alliss situation. His father, a staunch Baptist, indicated that he had better get out on his own. He entered the local legal practice that is now called D. G. Dawkins and Grey, a very successful and highly respected firm in Birmingham.

My romance with Jackey wasn't an explosive, whizz-bang thing. It just grew and grew. We met in 1965, as I have said, and it was more than three years before we made love. Jackey had her own flat in Wimbledon, worked for Clarkson's Travel, earned £1000 a year, had her own MG car saved for and bought, and was her own woman. She had been engaged briefly to a young fellow in Birmingham who seemingly had done nothing for her self-confidence, and now was making her own success in business. But our affair had an explosive dénouement, at the Ryder Cup match of 1967 in Houston, Texas. David Thomas and his wife Robbie were involved in the sense that they knew of the relationship between Jackey and myself, and Jackey had written to me care of Robbie in Las Vegas, where the Ryder Cup team had moved on to after the matches. One of those silly mischances brought the whole drama to a head. Joan and myself and the Thomases were at the hotel reception desk when the clerk handed the letter to me instead of to Robbie. I pushed it into my pocket quickly and made nothing of it, but Joan, like the good detective she was, found it later. No doubt in any case she had some suspicions by this time. All hell broke loose. It was Joan's birthday that week, on 25 October (Jackey's is on 24 October). We had booked for dinner and a show, there were torrents of tears and Joan flew home a couple of days later, devastated. She was much comforted by Bernard Hunt and his wife Margaret, especially Margaret. In these matters, almost all women take the part of the lady spurned, and it is almost always the man's fault. I'd done plenty of things to get me in trouble. I'd been selfish and promiscuous. Now I was ridden with guilt at having involved valued friends like the Thomases and the Hunts. And I was guilty about the break-up itself, and reacted by giving Jackey a hard time. I kept going back to Joan and throwing Jackey out, then going back to Jackey after squabbling with Joan. In turn, Jackey had enormous support from the Thomases and from Roy and Beryl Beckett, Bournemouth friends. My mother thought the whole thing was dreadful, particularly for the children, but she had never been comfortable with Joan, whereas she liked Jackey very much. Our son Gary was around fourteen when it happened. Carol was eight, and both had as hard a time as anyone involved.

The divorce took a long time to finalize. Crabb House was sold, in 1968, for around £18,500. There was around £20,000 for the sale of the land, some of which was zoned for development, and by the time all the bills were paid, all the settlements decided, it was all gone, and I was about £9000 in the red. Anthony Reid, who had been the family bank manager at a little branch in Ferndown, and later Barclays at West Southbourne, kept me going virtually without any assets or collateral. Joan was later courted by Michael Lee whose family owned garages in the Bournemouth area and who was a very well-known figure around town. I was paying some £98 per week in maintenance, school fees and the rest at a time when I was earning £110 a week – goodness knows what would have happened if Joan had not eventually married the man. In due course they sold up in England and moved to Alderney in the Channel Islands to make a new start. Joan, who had been in the fashion business in her early days, found a job in a dress shop, but since Alderney is about the size of four football fields and must be altogether too inhibiting for anyone not born there, it didn't work. They parted company. Joan took a flat in Bournemouth, and it was all over.

So, as the decade came towards its end, I took stock and

the stocktaking was none too encouraging. Parkstone Golf Club was fine. My tournament career looked likely to draw peacefully to a close – the putting was definitely crumbling. I was pushing forty, overdrafted to hell, with a new, lovely lady, but cut off from my children. What was to become of us all? I had lost my mother, and my father was ageing. As so often in life, the next stanza in the Alliss odyssey arrived from nowhere, from a telephone call with Irwin Bellow, later to become Lord Belwin of Leeds, saying in effect, 'Come to Moor Allerton.'

CHAPTER FOUR

Moor Allerton

Moor Allerton Golf Club in Leeds is one of the oldest Jewish golf clubs in Britain, if not in the world. Having said that, I had better qualify it quickly by saying that there really is no such thing, at least in our country, as a golf club that is exclusively for Jews. Gentiles can join, and do. This is probably because Jewish people have been persecuted for so long that they think they cannot be seen to be prejudiced against anyone. Consequently there is a marvellous cross-section of members at Moor Allerton.

I'm not saying they are all super guys – I've never known any club where they are all super guys – but they do behave and ask other people to behave and, for example, dress in a neat and tidy way. There are no strange restrictions on dress at Moor Allerton. The fact is, there are jeans and jeans, slippers and slippers, T-shirts and T-shirts. If a member or a visitor wears a well-cut, neatly pressed pair of jeans, casual, clean moccasin shoes and a decent sports shirt during the day, they see no reason why he should not be able to go to the bar for a drink, or go in to lunch. Restrictions at some clubs about ties, blazers, cravats, and so on do irk me on occasion. Any club has a right to make its own rules, but a good deal depends on the ambience. You would not expect to go into Muirfield or Royal St George's in jeans and a T-shirt – if you ever got past the car park, that is. But at Moor Allerton they have good sense about dress and of course there is the intrinsic 'sartorial elegance' about Jewish people, and the desire to dress more smartly than the average. You'll find it happens at other 'Jewish' clubs such as Coombe Hill, Dyrham Park, Hartsbourne, Dunham Forest.

In the sixties the Moor Allerton course, then inside the city boundaries, was sold for development and the club found another site, out of town. The price was confidential, but the talk in Leeds was that it was at least £500,000 and might have been as much as £750,000. The club resolved to spend it in the grand manner, with an altogether splendid course and clubhouse. They commissioned Robert Trent Jones, the famous American golf architect who, if not the best in the world, then surely was the most commercially successful, and who was addicted to excavating huge lakes and water hazards, moving vast quantities of soil, building enormous, very fast and sloping greens, spending great wads of money in transforming the entire landscape. He did all that at the new Moor Allerton, building 27 holes. The clubhouse provided really splendid facilities: superb locker rooms, dining-room, lounge and card room, a two-table billiards room, bars, toilets, car parking for all – everything a member could wish for.

When the call came from Irwin Bellow, I was at a low ebb, and Bellow I think knew this. He said in effect, 'We have this marvellous new club and course. We'd like you to come and help us get it moving. I believe things have not been too good with you, so what about it? Could be a fresh start for you.' Alf Sanders, the Moor Allerton professional, was retiring after many years' service, and Bellow, who had led the club out of the wilderness of the old course into this new and promised land, obviously felt my status in the game, whatever that might have been, could put some polish on the project and move it along.

My marriage was all but gone. I had resolved to withdraw from international team play. My domestic life was a disaster as I bounced between Joan and Jackey. I had a flat in Admiral's Walk, Bournemouth, paying £6 10s a week which I could not afford. There was not too much of a tournament career ahead of me. On the other hand, I knew the Leeds area well. I had lived as a boy in Scott Hall Road when my father was professional at Templenewsam and I had played often in the old *Yorkshire Evening News* tournaments at Sand Moor and Moortown. I could see myself settling in at this very nice new club, joining a few Alliance meetings in the area at some of my favourite courses – Alwoodley, Moortown, Pannal, Starbeck, Oakdale. Incidentally, my idea of an Alliance meeting was a fun day out with someone you liked to be with. You'd be out for the entire day. You'd play your 18 holes of Greensome or Stableford golf, or whatever, have lunch which was invariably steak and kidney pudding, go out and play a bit more, then everyone would stay for a rather raucous prize-giving in the evening, and no doubt a toddy or two. In the South, individual golfers would join their local Alliances. In the North, the clubs would join and could enter as many members as they pleased. The result was huge fields, everyone playing four-ball better ball, and if you started early, virtually at daybreak in the winter, you'd be finished before noon and simply clear off home. Often, in fact, when it was dark at around four o'clock, the late starters would not finish their rounds. So what with professionals, assistants and regiments of amateurs all playing off an assortment of handicaps, it proved rather a hodge-podge. Pity. I still enjoyed playing and still played well enough to enjoy playing.

David Thomas, with whom I was becoming more and more involved in business, in particular the golf construc-tion business, was only an hour's drive away in Cheshire, and I was in no way put off by the fact that the club was predominantly Jewish. I had had lots of experience of Jewish holidaymakers and visitors to Ferndown and Parkstone and had some notion of their sense of humour, their sense of the ridiculous, the fact that they were inclined to make a lot of noise and be very demanding at times, but that underneath it all they had one saving grace – they demanded service, but were entirely prepared to pay for it. All told, the move looked right.

All of this happened in 1969. Early in the year I drove Joan up to Yorkshire. We stayed with Marshall and Carol Bellow (Marshall is Irwin's brother) and went to have a look at Moor Allerton. I thought this was the last chance for our marriage to survive, and that success or failure would depend on Joan's reaction to the people and the place and the club. Driving home, I finally knew it was all wrong, that it would no longer work, and I said so. It was a tearful, arduous journey. I felt I was touching rock bottom. One or two things, one or two people, helped. Anthony Reid, the bank manager, kept me afloat. My future father-in-law, Geoffrey Grey, said, 'What are you worried about? I came out of the services, aged twenty-eight with a wife and two young daughters, no job, no money, no prospects. You at least can always go out and give golf lessons for immediate ready cash.' That spurred me a bit, made me feel I might turn the corner. At about the same time I heard a Harry Secombe song, entitled 'And yet, and yet . . .' The thrust of the lyric was that if you felt past the prime of life, had reached an age when it was time to be quiet and sensible and still, 'and yet' there were still many bridges to cross, many places to see, much wine still to be drunk. This impressed me enormously, and I have made it the epilogue to this book. Above all of course I had the support and courage of Jackey, who knew my entire life history and every facet of my personality, yet wanted to be with me.

So off we went in 1970 to Moor Allerton, heads up, shoulders back, hopes high. The first problem was where to live, with house prices even then starting to move up. Suddenly an old farmhouse on the Moor Allerton course became available. When the club bought the land for the new course, this farmhouse came with it. It had been derelict for four or five years and had been completely vandalized. This is another aspect of life I find quite extraordinary. The vandals had torn out the bathtub and thrown it through a window. Every loo was smashed, floorboards were ripped up, and fires had been lit, fortunately only in the grates. We asked the club if we could resurrect this place, and they agreed. They would not sell it to me, but would allow me to organize the work, which they paid for, and live in it. The structure was about two hundred years old – no damp course and salt still coming out of the stone in some places, but we added an extension in time, and it turned out to be a very happy house for us. We had almost no furniture, but then Jackey was never a girl who needed a David Hicks house. She picked up attractive old Victorian furniture, chairs, settees, mirrors, for £10, £20 here and there and gradually got it all together.

The ten years we were to spend at Moor Allerton were amongst the happiest of my life, and we made marvellous friends. Jackey and I were warmly welcomed. There was never any vandalism on the course, such as they had had at the old Moor Allerton, where swastikas were carved out of the greens and all the other terrible, idiotic, pathetic, sadistic rubbish that people inflict on each other. In the past there had been some kind of vigilante patrol organized by the Jewish community in Leeds, which had been one of the flashpoints for Oswald Mosley and his Blackshirts in the thirties. One Moor Allerton member, an incredible man called Jack Fineberg, was one of the 'minders' of Jewish youth in those days. Jack, who must be pushing seventy now, was not tall, perhaps five feet nine inches but about the same in width, and there are terrifying stories of him laying out four or five toughs at the occasional dance-hall fracas. There was a good deal of Jew-baiting in Leeds in those days, which the Jewish community handled one way or another, and Moortown corner was a favoured spot for the yobbos.

The Jewish members were certainly remarkable for their resilience. It seemed no particular disgrace to go under in business, to declare bankruptcy. The thing was just to get up, dust yourself off, and get on with it again. And all the stories of Jews rallying round and sticking together and bailing each other out were not entirely true. Just because you were a fellow-Jew did not mean that people would hand you large dollops of money. One old member there, Doddy Aber, who insisted on calling me 'Mr Alliss' for about four years although he was a good twenty-five years older than me, used to tell me these tales. We'd sit around for hours discussing things, and he told me a great deal about Jewish folklore and attitudes. He'd say, 'Don't believe people who tell you that all Jews are good businessmen. If they say that, they don't know much about Jews. Jews are no smarter than anyone else – it's just that they are prepared to work longer at it.'

One thing I did particularly like about Jewish people was their attitude to the family, to family life, to holding the family together come what may, also the custom of having everyone round the table on Friday evening. They took special care of young people and the old. Old people can be a burden and so often, if a family has a bit of money, the old are simply pushed off into a home. But I found that those Jewish people who were able to take a broader view of such things were tremendously kind. In fact, if it isn't too Irish to say so, some of the finest Christians I have met have been Jews. My time at Moor Allerton gave me a strong insight into religious thinking, not just Jewish religious thinking, and brought me face to face with many characters, as you would expect from such a club with around 1800 members. One in particular, Bob Fox, dubbed 'The Store Detective', would walk straight up to a stranger and ask if he had paid a green fee, who he was, what he was doing and where he was from. With some 1200 voting members, it was perhaps difficult for some of the elders to accept strange faces and green fee-paying guests around the club. Perhaps it was an indication of the insular side of their nature, that they felt that it should be a members' club only and that nothing should interfere with the pleasures and desires of the members. This was probably reflected too in the 'failure' of the course to take off fully as a commercial venture, which is a great sadness.

Of the 27 holes of golf there, the first 18 were designed as the best of it, but in fact I think holes 10–27 make the best 18 for tournament play. The course was perhaps a shade difficult for the older members. It was a bit of an assault course, although they did become accustomed to playing the 'top' nine, which looks hilly but once one is quickly 'up' it mainly runs gently and slowly 'down'. The course produced a lot of good young players, too. Incidentally, the subscription in 1970 was £37 a year, and in 1980 almost £200. There's inflation for you.

Looking back, I think the businessmen who commanded the move and the new development got it wrong. Much of the capital was poured into the construction of the clubhouse, and not enough money held back to develop the course after its completion; maintenance lapsed and the whole thing almost crumbled away. After ten years, the club should be reaping a very healthy income from major tournaments, since sponsors will now pay a club £10,000 or more for the use of the course for a tournament. And having been brought up at Ferndown and Parkstone clubs, which take in thousands of pounds a year in green fees, I was fully aware of how profitable this can be.

However, club managements can do bizarre and unthinking things. At Ferndown, for instance, there used to be a very big Christmas Alliance meeting each year. It generated a good deal of income in food and drink for the club. However, the Ferndown club got greedy, and decided to start charging green fees, whereupon the Alliance simply moved the event away, to the Isle of Purbeck Golf Club at

Studland Bay. So how much can you expect to take on 8 December without an Alliance? Ferndown soon found out. A pity, because it was a super place for that meeting.

Moor Allerton is virtually in the centre of the country, close to the motorway network, with excellent rail and air communications, huge parking areas, an extensive, fully-equipped modern clubhouse and all the services of a major city at hand. It should be vying with Wentworth and Sunningdale as one of the most sought-after venues in England. This hasn't happened. Ironically, their most recent big offer was to stage the 1980 Haig Whisky Tournament Players' Championship. But the dates coincided with the Jewish New Year, and the club had to say no. It went to Moortown instead.

In the early years there, I was still playing the occasional tournament and becoming more involved as a television commentator, so I needed help at the club during these absences. I thought of Bert Williamson. E. B. Williamson I had almost idolized when I emerged into tournament golf around 1947. He came from a famous old professional family in Nottingham, had been through the war as an infantry captain and was a fine player and teacher, and, I thought, a person of some stature. We travelled the circuit a good deal in the early days, and I enjoyed it because at the end of each day Bert wasn't too obsessed with going over the day's round, stroke by stroke, but was inclined to talk of other things. He had been club professional at Kingswood in Surrey, but was now at Olgiata in Rome, a very fine, modern club where the Canada Cup matches had been played in 1968. There had been some internal political squabbling there, as there is in almost every walk of Italian life, and perhaps they wanted Bert out in favour of an Italian professional. Whatever it was, he became something less than senior professional there, in fact something of a floater at the club, giving a few private lessons. He was married to a charming Italian girl, Carla. I wrote to him with such high hopes, giving him all the details of this fine new Moor Allerton course and club, perhaps making it a shade flowery, saying come on, we've been friends for years, this can be very big, and what about it. He replied with the opening line: 'Dear Pete, that noise you hear is my helicopter landing on your roof.' I thought, how tremendous; he's coming here with a happy heart. Alas, it didn't work.

The plan was that we would put in equal amounts of capital. Bert never did put his money in. I brought all my stock from Parkstone, and it was all valued by Bert. In my absence, Bert was responsible for the ordering of stock. It was one of the big disappointments of my life. He did not seem able to adopt an attitude that was broad enough, flexible enough, to be acceptable to the members. He disliked bartering, which Jewish people love to do. If Bert wanted to sell something for £1, he would mark it £1 and that would be the end of it. He would demand £1 and never think to mark it at £1.25 and sell it for £1 after a bit of light-hearted chat. Everything was black or white. There were no in-between shades. Although a small nucleus of members adored him, as I was to discover, he appeared to me to be offhand with them in general, in spite of being an excellent coach and a very fine player. The club seemed to grow gradually more and more disenchanted with Bert, and in time Jay Harris, the chairman, summoned me to his office, the first time in my life *that* had ever happened to me. There was a good deal of table-thumping, and 'Bert must go and you had better tell him.'

So how was I to break such news to a very old friend, that the club didn't want him and that I had been ordered to sack him? Right there I made one of the notable mistakes of my life. I did not go to Bert that very moment and do it. Instead I started to think of just how it could be done, and how I could let him down lightly, and I took too long over it. I realized later that if anything in life simply must be done, and ther is no avoiding it, you'd better get on and do it right there and then.

David Thomas and I were very involved at the time in building a new development at Alicante, in Spain, and I thought Bert might want to go there. I started planting the thought with him, that his wife would enjoy the sunshine, good place for his daughter to grow up, 36 holes, big club, great potential, and after five or six weeks I thought I had it about right, since I clearly didn't have the courage to say baldly to him, 'You're fired.' Finally I got to grips with it. I was half-way through my speech when a smile spread slowly over his face, he put his hand on my shoulder and said, 'You can stop right there Pete. I'm taking over the shop on my own – you're the one who is leaving.' Stunned silence. End of story.

With Bert going, I had been planning to spend more time at the club, take on a new assistant, involve myself more closely with the day-to-day activities, and suddenly there it was, the tables had been turned. I suppose I could have called it a rub of the green, or standard business practice, but I could not find any way of rationalizing this sort of conduct. Bert took over, although I remained publicly associated with the club. I reckoned I still had a public relations role to play for them, and whenever I could, in my writings or on television, I gave Moor Allerton a plug. Because of my friendship with so many of the members, because of the high hopes I had had in going there, and in bringing Bert to the club, and I suppose of my own notions of proper behaviour and moral and business integrity, I felt obliged to do what I could. But I hardly ever went into the club again, and eventually Bert left at the end of his contract. Altogether the whole episode was rather messy and disappointing. Fortunately, Peter Blaze was to take over in due course and has done a splendid job for the club.

There is much I miss in the Leeds area – the lovely country within half an hour's drive; the frankness of the people; and the restaurants – Mario and Franco's, Pool Court, The Spice Box at Boston Spa, Harry Ramsden's famous fish and chips, and the Box Tree at Ilkley, one of only five restaurants in Britain with two Michelin rosettes.

Through the seventies I was getting deeper and deeper into the media, as my tournament appearances ran down, although it all happened in a rather casual and certainly uncalculated way. I wrote a column in Mark McCormack's *Golf International*. As the years passed I became more and more involved with ABC TV in America and in 1976, for example, I did three events in a row, the Bing Crosby, the Hawaiian Open, the Los Angeles Open. All this emerged from more and more BBC exposure and I found it fascinating to observe how one thing grew out of another. There was *Pro-Celebrity Golf* from Gleneagles, and *Around With Alliss* which we can look at more closely later. I went on *The Generation Game* with Larry Grayson, did *Games People Play* on the radio with Pete Murray and another programme with John Dunn. There was *Call My Bluff* on television from Manchester, and *Two's Company*, a late night record programme on radio in which I had to choose six or seven favourite records – not so easy when you have to produce a good reason for each choice. I went on the Michael Parkinson show, quite an experience also. I was getting so much exposure that people actually started to recognize me in the street. I found myself amazed when this happened. I feel privileged about the whole thing, mindful of my good fortune, particularly over the past ten years, when I have travelled the world at someone else's expenses. I think I have tried to be honest and sensible, tried to do a good day's work for the money I have been paid. Of course, I don't always achieve the highest standards. Simple failings sometimes intrude, but, on balance, I would be happy to meet my Maker.

The eighth day of April 1979 was a black day at Moor Allerton. My young son Simon was involved in a car crash.

He and a little friend were being driven home from a birthday party by Mrs Turner, a fine lady who looked after the children for us when we went away. It was a commonplace accident, someone turning right and suddenly bump. The children were unhurt, but thrown about and rather hysterical. Mrs Turner cut her leg severely, broke an ankle and was badly bruised. It made a big family drama, and it made me realize that the old saying 'in the midst of life we are in death' was becoming for me more and more true. Early in 1980 Sam Leitch and Paul Lang, two top boys in Thames TV sport, both ex-BBC men, died within a week or so of each other. Leitch was 52, Lang 33, each of them leaving families. You can imagine the pattern, working very hard, socializing hard, going home, perhaps jogging several miles each night to keep in shape for it all, but suddenly gone, leaving children and wives and all the rest of it. So you wonder at it all, you wonder why, you wonder at the unfairness of it all. Despite religion, God, the Bible, life's all so unfair. People persist in expecting life to be fair, and perhaps that's the mistake we make.

You are driven to the conclusion that the only people who matter, the only people who really matter, are your own people, your loved ones, your family – as Jackey and Peter Alliss were to discover, with Victoria.

CHAPTER FIVE

Victoria

Soon after Jackey and I settled in at Moor Allerton came Sara Elizabeth Jane Alliss, Jackey's first-born, the first child of my second family and a source of deep joy to us both. Then came Victoria, our second daughter. Victoria was born with massive brain damage. She sits or lies, and indeed is now, at the age of eight, waiting to come to the end of her life. Expectancy in her case is not much more than eight years. She needs constant care and attention every hour of the day and night. She has never been with us, and in all her life to date has been out of hospital for some three weeks.

We noticed, shortly after she was born, that she was not responding to the world around her, to light, dark, noise, movement. We took her back to the local hospital in Leeds, where a highly-qualified lady rang bells and tinkled things and shone lights in front of her, and said, 'Oh, Victoria is just a little backward, take her home and give her plenty of love and affection.' After a few more weeks of the recommended love and affection, there was no change, and I said to Jackey that this was not working and we needed a second opinion. Off we went to the famous Hospital for Sick Children at Great Ormond Street in London, a remarkable institution. There they did very extensive tests and took samples of blood fluids and tissue and drilled into the child's head. They came back with the chilling, honest verdict that they did not quite know what it was, that it was probably a genetic thing, and they had only three or four cases a year. They felt it might happen again and that we ought to think very carefully before having any other children. Victoria was brought back to Leeds, where she had the most devoted care and kindness at St James's and Seacroft Hospitals and later she went to the Oaks School at Boston Spa. For a time, Jackey was almost destroyed by this – she could not understand the unfairness of it all. But then no one can, and she quickly took command of the situation, visiting the child each day, talking with her although Victoria plainly did not understand, fondling and loving her. And we went through all the thought processes that afflict any family in such circumstances. We thought of thalidomide babies, and the parents saying, 'Why us? Why us?' But of course there is no answer. There is no explanation. Neither do I believe it is something sent by God to try us. I don't believe in that. If He wants to try us, let Him find a better way.

In this situation I became an ostrich as far as Victoria was concerned. I couldn't make myself visit the child. I turned my back on her, spurned her, tried to pretend that she didn't exist. It was the 'Why me?' syndrome again. I thought of spastic children, those tragic little figures, and reasoned that they could be coped with, that no matter how crippled or deformed they might be, if the brain functioned they could learn, learn to read, learn to speak, learn to communicate, somehow, and maybe in time even learn to do something with their lives. But when the brain is totally gone, as in Victoria's case, I decided that any such child should just quietly slip away. Yet as time passed, it came to me that in these appalling circumstances the danger is that those of us who are involved can wallow in self-pity, the most treacherous of all the vices, and completely forget the sick, the victims, the dying, the very people who deserve all our strength, all our energies, all our love. Jackey was offering all this to Victoria. She saw. She knew.

There were people who said they were sorry, who said, 'We know how you feel.' But nobody, nobody, knows how we feel. They were like those people who go to the funeral of someone they know only slightly or distantly, and it is little more than a social obligation. Like the people who have visited the sick in hospital a couple of times, and have seen people grieving, and try to tell them they know how they feel. I became very disenchanted by all that, for they were talking of Victoria, *our* child, created in great and sublime love by Jackey and me. What did they know? Then there were the others who said Victoria should be at home, surrounded by the 'love of the family'. Jackey and I discussed this very deeply and decided that this could very easily mean the 'death of the family'. If Victoria had been at home I doubt if she could have lived very long, in spite of the love and devotion that Jackey would have lavished on her. It would have destroyed Jackey. And it would have torn the heart out of the family, as it has done to many other families with a child less afflicted. The parents just give everything to the afflicted child, even if the case is hopeless, and it puts a tremendous strain on the other children. They can grow away from each other, and from the parents, and the whole love and structure and entity of the family can be destroyed because of a misguided priority which almost becomes a penance on the part of the parents. Anyway Victoria had to have medical attention one hundred per cent of the time, and it was impossible to have her at home.

Jackey became pregnant again. Her gynaecologist, Theo Redman, was very anti-abortion. However, after long discussions, it was agreed that it was not worth the risk, and Jackey was to have an abortion in St James's Hospital. We were conscious of the rather disapproving eyes of some of the staff, they no doubt thinking, 'Huh, wealthy woman – must be, wife of him on the telly, the golfer, must be rich, probably just an inconvenience for her to have the baby.' Little did they know it was the one thing, the one and only gift that I wanted to give to Jackey at the time. It could never have been a total replacement for Victoria, but it would have been marvellous for Jackey to have had another child just then. The operation was carried out successfully and Jackey was home in a few days, and I think by then the atmosphere in the hospital had improved – probably word had got round to the staff about the real motive, about Victoria.

Before Victoria, I thought Jackey was a giant. After Victoria, I knew she was. I could not accept, could not handle the situation for a long time. But I began to realize just what this kind of thing can mean to a mother. It made me more and more conscious of other people's feelings and problems, more tolerant, not to worry if they walked past, or ignored me, or didn't smile or say hello. It helped me to see that everyone has a private grief, a private hell, whether it is losing a purse, being fired, an old granny dying, a dog run over. There are hundreds of reasons why one can seem aloof or indifferent to a situation. But when things seem beyond one's control, one simply must face them, square up, look them in the eye and do the very best one can. And be more ready to forgive what one takes to be other people's shortcomings.

A couple of years went by, and Jackey and I had been back to Great Ormond Street with Victoria, and she was being well cared for in Leeds. We talked endlessly about it, then decided to try again, when Sara was about three. Jackey became pregnant, went back to St James's to have the baby, and when Simon arrived, oh, there was the anguish of looking at arms and legs and fingers and toes and eyes, and the immense joy of knowing that all was well. In the eyes of Simon Peter Grey Alliss there was light, and life.

CHAPTER SIX

The Ryder Cup

The Ryder Cup match goes back to 1927. It is played between teams of professional golfers from the United States of America on the one hand and Great Britain and Ireland on the other (since 1979 GB and Ireland have become 'Europe', to take in the Continental players). In 1921 and 1926 there were informal matches between US and UK professionals, before the existing trophy was presented by Sam Ryder. Ryder had a seed business in St Albans and it is said that he made himself a millionaire by being the first man to put seeds in a packet and sell the packet for sixpence. He was a golf nut and at one period in the twenties had the famous Abe Mitchell retained as his personal professional.

I didn't much care for the whole thing in 1953, when I made a rather soul-destroying début in Ryder Cup play. By 1955, when the next of the biennial matches came round, I thought I had done enough to be selected and was bitterly disappointed when I was not. Then in 1957, for the match at Lindrick, I was back in the team and, miracle of miracles, was in a winning team this time. But even that left me with a sour taste – with Bernard Hunt, I lost my foursomes match 2 and 1 to Doug Ford and Dow Finsterwald, who played some very good golf, then lost my singles against Fred Hawkins in infuriating circumstances. Hawkins and I were at the height of our battle, the match finely balanced, when Dai Rees, our team captain, came rushing up shouting, 'We've won, we've won, don't worry, it doesn't matter!' Oh yes it did – it mattered a helluva lot to me, after my 1953 fiasco. But the news of the team's overall victory took all the stuffing out of me, and I lost 2 and 1. Oddly enough, Harry

Bradshaw was the only other British player still on the course when the result was decided, and all he could manage was a half, with Dick Mayer. Great celebrations, joy unconfined, dancing in the streets – but for Alliss, this famous victory was a little bitter-sweet.

The 1959 match was scheduled for Palm Desert, in California, and I qualified comfortably for the team. We crossed the Atlantic on the *Queen Elizabeth*, which was a notable, if not memorable, experience. I am not a sailor, and on the whole you can say that in these matters I prefer the jet aircraft. I certainly would never pay to travel on one of these huge transatlantic liners. Little chance of that now – there are few of them left. They do creak and groan, you know, these great ships. Aircraft wings flap a little and the designers and engineers will tell you that if ships don't creak and aircraft don't flap their wings, they are about to disintegrate. Maybe so. I found that voyage simply boring.

The match was eventful for me, because I was paired for the first time with Christy O'Connor. It was to be a fruitful foursomes partnership and one which I enjoyed immensely. I had complete faith in Christy. I felt that no matter what trouble I put him in, he would play the shot, and get us out. We were paired in the foursomes against Art Wall and Doug Ford, both winners of the US Masters, Ford a PGA Champion in his time, and each of them famous as consistently magnificent putters, which we were not. We putted the eyes out of them, or rather Christy did. When he holed a fifteen-yard putt to win the match, they simply could not believe it. When we shook hands and thanked them for the match, the expressions on their faces were unbelievable. In my singles, I halved a good match with Jay Hebert, and although we lost the match overall, by 7–2 with three halved, I was unbeaten and felt that there was perhaps some sugar to be sipped from this Ryder Cup after all.

It was around this time that I realized that there were lots of players who simply did not have the stomach, the bottle, for the thing. Some fellows had a fierce pride in winning, they wanted to win more than anything – people like Dai Rees, Ken Bousfield, Eric Brown, and more recently Bernard Gallacher and Brian Huggett. Some fellows were a bit 'come day, go day' – if they won, they won, and if they didn't, it didn't matter. But I thought it mattered, mattered like hell. This whole attitude has contributed greatly to our failure to win the Ryder Cup over the past twenty years. We should certainly have won two or three times on home soil in that time.

I had this emotional, patriotic thing that helped me along. I wished I could have done it in tournament play because I holed putts from all over the place in these matches, some I had no right to hole, but I did it with sheer bloody-minded willpower and pride. Maybe it was because my father had played, and played well, before me. Memories of the Ryder Cup will stay with me forever – the great moments of cameraderie, the late nights, the nervous tensions, the flag-raisings and the anthems, the travel, the grandeur of it all. In the 1961 matches at Royal Lytham I was drawn against Arnold Palmer and I could almost hear sighs of relief from the others. They had avoided Palmer, then at the height of his powers. They were terrified of losing 7 and 6. But I made up my mind that nobody was going to beat me 7 and 6. If he hit the fairway, I'd hit the fairway. If he hit the greens, I'd hit the greens. If he holed the putts, I'd hole the putts. If I had to steel myself to get the ball in the hole, I would bloody well do it.

In this year, the format of play was changed. Instead of 36 holes of foursomes and 36 of singles on successive days, we were to double up, with one 18-hole match of each type on the same day. In morning foursomes play, O'Connor and I put it all together against Gene Littler and Doug Ford, and won going away, by 4 and 3, with Alliss storming everything into the hole. In a much more scratchy match in the afternoon, we were beaten by Art Wall and Jay Hebert, by one hole, with Hebert holing from at least twenty-five feet for a winning birdie.

Next day it was to be Alliss against the great man, Arnold Palmer, with Alliss quite determined that, come what may, he was not about to be slaughtered. It was Arnold's first Ryder Cup match, and needless to say, he had already won both foursomes, paired with Bill Casper. I have written about the match before, in some detail. Suffice it to say that Arnold putted one straight into the hole from behind the 7th green, chipped in from off the green at the 10th, and holed a bunker shot at the 15th. Three times he holed out from off the green, yet we came to the 18th green all square, Alliss twenty inches from the hole in three, Palmer thirty inches from the hole in three. Arnold conceded my putt then settled down to his. Suddenly, as he was crouched over the ball, something made me say, 'That's all right Arnold, pick it up.' He looked up, picked the ball up, and there was an absolute storm of applause. As we shook hands, I said, 'We've had a good match, let's leave it like that.' Lots of people came to me later and prattled about this splendid act of sportsmanship and so on, but I found myself wondering – wondering what would have happened if I had had Palmer's putt, and missed it. That would have been Wentworth all over again.

Even then I was not finished with Arnold in the Ryder Cup. The next match, 1963, was scheduled for the East Lake Club, in Atlanta, Georgia, the home club of Bobby Jones, and again the format was changed. This time it was to be over three days with foursomes, fourballs, then singles, with two sets of 18-hole matches each day. O'Connor and Alliss in the first morning's foursomes came out against Bill Casper and Dave Ragan and were beaten by a birdie on the last green, Ragan holing from fifteen feet across the very severe slope of the green on the long, par-three hole. Beaten by only one hole and – we couldn't

believe it – we were dropped! On the second day I was
paired with Bernard Hunt, and we halved with Julius Boros
and Gene Littler in the morning, and lost by one hole to
Tony Lema and Johnny Pott in the afternoon – one hole
again, but two very good matches.

I had not been playing too well, all my problems
stemming from poor driving. The singles draw came out,
and there it was again, Palmer v Alliss, a repeat of Royal
Lytham two years earlier. Arnold at this point had won two
Open Championships, three Masters titles and the US
Open Championship, and it was not unreasonable to say he
was the best golfer in the world. Off we went and there was
the usual whoopin' and hollerin' from the crowd – 'Go get
him Arnie, kill him, Arnie!' – all the way round, the usual
volatile, exuberant American gallery. That is how they are
and in those days it didn't bother anyone. No obscenities,
of course. Good fun. I was driving with a 2-wood, rather
chopping at the ball, not turning properly, making rather a
bitch of a swing at it and moving the ball from the tee not a
lot more than 200 yards down the fairway, but fairly
straight. Arnold of course was nailing the ball some 260
yards right down the middle every time. At the 17th, and
one up, I got the ball in the fairway about a 6-iron distance
away, and hit my second about fifteen feet from the hole.
Arnold hit an 8-iron three feet from the hole. When I got to
the green, although I hadn't been putting too well, I
thought, 'I really must do something here, must get this in
somehow.' I struck the ball straight into the middle of the
hole. Suddenly it was Palmer left to hole his putt, to stay
alive. He did. On to the 18th, Alliss one up.

Time for negative thoughts. They crept in. 'Worst I can
do is halve the match, if I lose this last hole. At least I'll
have done that with the great man, both home and away.' I
hit a long iron to the huge green and caught the front right
corner of the putting surface, a long way from the hole on a
very fast green with a good eight feet of borrow on the putt.

However, I trundled it up and across the slope and the ball stopped five inches from the hole! Arnold's tee shot was about 15 yards above the hole and he gave it his usual death or glory charge in an attempt to save the match, and ran the ball a good six yards past the hole. All over. I had beaten the man on his own ground. In the afternoon I played Tony Lema, the late Tony Lema, a close friend of mine and a lovely man. We halved for the only British point scored in that session. In a later book, Lema quoted me at one hole, when I had knocked in a putt of all of twenty yards, as turning to him and rolling my eyes and saying, 'Oh dear, I am most frightfully sorry about that, Tony.' I don't believe I talk quite like that, but Lema was vastly amused.

In 1965, we were at Royal Birkdale, and it turned out to be a good year for me. Back with Christy O'Connor in the foursomes, we beat Ken Venturi and Don January 5 and 4, and in the afternoon beat Bill Casper and Gene Littler by one hole. On the second day, in fourball matches, we were drawn against Arnold Palmer and Dave Marr and were trounced 5 and 4. The afternoon draw put us against the same two Americans, and this time we won a quite marvellous match by one hole. After Day One, the overall match was tied 4–4, after Day Two it was UK 6 US 8, with two halved. Not bad, not at all bad, and everything still to play for in the last-day singles.

There are people, like Arthur Lees, for so many years the Sunningdale professional, who can remember shots played twenty-five years before. I can't, but I do remember well the 18th at Royal Birkdale, against Palmer and Marr on that afternoon. The two Americans, and Christy for that matter, were all over the course from the tee, and I had hit the best drive. Christy and I were one up, and I decided that none of the others could reach the green. It was October, there was virtually no run on the ground, and we were playing the small ball in those days. So I elected to go for the big shot that would clinch the match. Remembering something I had read in one of the John Jacobs golf-instruction books, I decided that the only way I could make the green would be to turn in the toe of my 4-wood slightly, hood it a little, aim slightly to the right, and let it rip. I did just that, cracking the ball right out of the middle of the club, hard as I could, and the ball did exactly as it was told, turning slightly right to left in the air, running on and stopping some twelve feet above the hole. A real winner – with that shot I was sure we must win. Even then, as we walked on towards the green, some kind of silly paralysis made itself felt, negative thinking taking over: 'What if I three-putt, no surely I can get down in two more from there, just roll it up to the side of the hole,' and so on. Ridiculous thoughts, really, considering my experience. Then Dave Marr had a chip shot, his third, and dammit he almost holed it. Just shaved the hole. Palmer came out of a greenside bunker, not very well, and suddenly golf balls were being picked up, they gave me my two putts to win the match, and it was all over. I've seldom been more relieved in my life.

In the morning singles next day, I was against Billy Casper. By this time I was putting cross-handed. I had started this – left hand below right hand for a right-handed player – at the Dunlop Masters tournament a few weeks earlier at Portmarnock, that magnificent links course near Dublin, and now I was really rolling them in from all points. There is a marvellous piece of film, which I hope is still in the BBC archives, of my performance on the last green against Casper and with a five-foot putt to win. When we got to the green, Casper had very kindly pointed out that my ball was resting on a spike mark. Was that sportsman-ship, or gamesmanship? I don't know, and I didn't know. But I thought to myself, 'Screw Casper,' stood up cross-handed to the ball with the old George Lowe putter which I had, and went one-two-three-bump, and in she went, dead centre. I gave a sardonic little bow to the crowd, not meaning to be impertinent, but saying in effect, there you are, I've done it, holed a putt on the last green to win a match, and that's that. I was so pumped up by everything at Birkdale that week that when I went out in the afternoon against Ken Venturi, I just gobbled him up, 3 and 1.

The Ryder Cup matches in 1967 went for the first time to Texas, to the fairly new Champions Club in Houston, the creation of Jimmy Demaret and Jack Burke. Jimmy Demaret, a raucous character and a colourful dresser, had won the US Masters Championship three times. Jack Burke had won the Masters and the PGA, and if he had the unfortunate distinction of being captain of a losing US Ryder Cup team – at Lindrick in 1957 – he was to find some compensation in being captain of a winning team at Muirfield in 1973. Both of these fellows were very prominent on the US tournament scene in their time, but they were considered somewhat crazy to be building a big club twenty-five miles from the city. But a freeway was built, which went quite close to the club, and it turned out to be only a thirty-five-minute drive from downtown Houston. When they had finished, they had 36 holes – lovely courses in rolling, well-timbered country, with the inevitable 'creek' and spaciously elegant clubhouse, and they were set to make a fortune.

For the British, this was one of the least distinguished of Ryder Cup matches. We lost 21–6, with five halved, and that was quite miserable. After fourteen years with old Sam Ryder, it seemed like the beginning of the end for Alliss, too. I lost three times with O'Connor, once with Malcolm Gregson, and managed to win only one single, 2 and 1 against Gay Brewer, the US Masters champion. This was the period when my marriage was breaking up, and altogether I don't suppose I was in the right frame of mind for the thing. But if there were few golden moments in Houston, there was one memorable one. It held many clues to the personality of Ben Hogan, the American team

captain, and indeed to the American attitude to international sport. At the gala presentation dinner, before play
started, the teams were to be introduced individually to the
audience by their captains. Dai Rees, our captain, made
rather a meal of it, going on about the things each of us had
won and done. As we stood up in turn, there were polite
ripples of applause. Hogan then stood up, asked the
audience to reserve its applause to the end. When he had
finished, he introduced his team individually by name only
then, when they were all standing, said, 'Ladies and
gentlemen, the United States Ryder Cup team – the finest
golfers in the world.' Storm of applause, and the British
about ten down before a ball had been hit.

By the time the next match came around, again at Royal
Birkdale, in 1969, things were getting a shade dodgy for
me. I was getting deeper into television commentary by this
time, a major domestic change was on, and my putting was
decidedly creaky. Eric Brown was our non-playing captain.
I said to him, 'Look, I'll do my very best for you, but I'd
prefer to be excused in the afternoons.' Brown, to his
credit, never once asked me to play in the afternoon, but
looking back on it all now I have decided that this was
hardly fair to him, and not the best of attitudes to take
into the match. In fact it was perhaps a rather cowardly
attitude, and as one of the senior men in the team, widely
experienced by this time, I should have buckled down and
done much better for the team and its younger players.

The morning foursomes went well. O'Connor and Alliss
halved with Casper and Frank Beard, a very tough
character, in a good match. All the other British won. In the
afternoon, three were lost, one halved, and at the end of the
day it was 4–4; not bad. On the second day, we were split.
Christy went with young Peter Townsend and beat Dave
Hill and Dale Douglass. Brian Barnes and I tackled Lee
Trevino and Gene Littler and lost by one hole; in spite of
strong opposition, it was a match we should certainly have

won. At the end of the second day, the teams were tied again, and I felt we had a great chance of winning the match.

For one thing, I thought this was one of the weaker American teams. People like Dale Douglass, Miller Barber, Tom Aaron and Dave Hill were experienced players, but I felt that under the particular stresses of the Ryder Cup match, away from home, they might well crumble. In the last morning singles, I had the first, lead-off match, against Lee Trevino. In this match I hit the ball as well as ever I did in my life – God, did I play well from tee to green! But on the greens my putting was in tatters. I was an absolutely jibbering idiot on the greens. I actually missed seven or eight putts from six feet or less, right down to eighteen inches. In fact the word was out by this time, about Alliss's putting. No one would give me a putt of a foot, and even that was a tremendous strain on me. Enough was enough. I was getting more and more into television. My domestic situation was not yet finally settled, and the move to Moor Allerton was on. It seemed time for a major change in the direction of my life, so at the end of the match I made the grand Press announcement that I 'no longer wished to be considered for international match selection'.

I lost that match to Trevino, who by contrast holed a number of stiff putts, by 2 and 1, but the British took the morning singles 5–3, and things looked very good. In the event, the match was tied, for the first time ever, at 13–13, with six halved. We should have won, should have got the extra points early on in the piece, but people nevertheless thought that a halved match was an achievement. This was the year in which we saw Jacklin and Nicklaus in the last match coming to the last green all square, with the entire Ryder Cup match tied, and Nicklaus conceding Jacklin's putt of around three feet to halve their match. Jack put his arm round Tony's shoulder and said, 'If you had missed that, it would have been a helluva way for the Ryder Cup match to end.' Nicklaus always was the greatest of losers. I must say it occurred to me at the time what Sam Snead, the US captain, might have been thinking, and what he might well have said to Nicklaus. If Jacklin had missed the putt, Snead's US team would have won the Ryder Cup. But the really abiding memory of this match was of Huggett, with a putt of around four or four and a half feet on the last hole to halve his match with Casper, and with Huggett thinking this was the putt to win the Ryder Cup match. Steeling himself, he drove it straight into the hole. Brian Huggett was in tears, thinking we had won, then was shattered to learn that the match was still alive. His was one of the bravest putts I have ever seen in my life.

Since we are on the subject of putting in Ryder Cup matches, we might mention 'the yips', the well-known golf phrase which covers a multitude of ways in which golfers of all classes, including the very best of them, get to a point where they cannot strike the ball on the greens with any degree of certainty. Many great players have suffered from the affliction. Even Ben Hogan, probably the coldest and most rational champion golfer who ever lived, got to a point where he could not take the putter blade away from the ball, could not commence his *back* stroke, much less hit the damned thing. In the variety which afflicted me, in the late sixties, I convinced myself that I was going to hit the ball too hard, and that it would jump over the top of the hole. Even from six inches I was entirely convinced that I would hit the ball so hard that it would hurdle the hole. And that really is a joke when you think of the great days of Palmer, Player – Player in particular – and Nicklaus. These fellows just drilled the ball into the hole. It was ridiculous, so hard did they seem to hit it. More recently Hale Irwin does the same, even on twelve-inch putts he just draws back the putter and cracks it in. To someone in my state, that is frightening.

I've given so much thought to this. For a time, I thought

it must be physical, just the business of growing older for, after all, towards the ends of their careers, Hogan almost went out of his mind with it, Dai Rees was afflicted, Bobby Jones became a bit twitchy, Jimmy Demaret had it, Harry Vardon, Charlie Whitcombe, Henry Cotton – all dreadful putters towards the end, although I never thought Cotton was quite as bad as he said he was. When I write about it being physical, I don't mean in the sense of ageing in years so much as the cumulative effect of years and years of tournament and championship play, with its intense concentration. I remember hearing a neurologist who talked about a nerve at the back of the neck which controlled virtually everything, and how after long use it simply wore out, like a rubber band growing thinner. Nothing like breaking a spinal cord, just wear and tear. But there are so many different forms of 'yip'. Throw down three balls on a putting green, and when there is no hole to play to you putt perfectly well. It's easy – it seems easier to hit a chair leg than a hole more than four inches wide. The disease is universal, and there is no known antidote. Everyone gets it, of course, but when a professional gets it, it's like setting fire to money. Putting is his life's blood.

After a man has been putting professionally for years, he finds himself increasingly aware of all the things that can go wrong. In lining up the putt, professionals are deciding along which line the ball should run. Then they think of how much pace to put on the strike to get the ball to the hole. And finally, they think of the 'drop', visualizing exactly how the ball will drop into the hole – from the side, in the centre, one side or the other, dying into the hole, ramming into the hole. But there came a time for me when all I could visualize was the ball catching the side of the hole and spinning away four or five feet down the slope. Thinking negatively, thinking of all the things that could go wrong, instead of how you will positively make it go right – right into the hole. So there is a combination of anxieties – line, speed, and drop. Put them all together and nothing is clear and you are in a great hodge-podge of emotions, on a gigantic roller-coaster, now up, now down, and you don't know what the hell you are doing.

The paradox and the irony is that you think you do know what you are doing. Everything is crystal clear until you get over the ball, then something happens. I do not say that things go blank. You are there, in position, everything is fine, but somehow you are not thinking and even more suddenly you just know that you are not going to move that damned putter. You walk away, indulge in a little deep breathing, come back, and the sequence happens all over again. So then you go through a variety of different systems and approaches. The Harry Bradshaw method – blade in front of the ball, then behind the ball, then hit. Doesn't work. All right, try Fred Daly – twenty-seven waggles and twitches before you hit the thing. Doesn't work. All right, give Bobby Locke a chance – close inspection of the hole, then back to the ball, two dinky little practice swings and hit. Doesn't work. In fact, changing the procedure, or the grip, or the feet position often does work . . . for a time. But it doesn't last, I promise you. On reflection, I don't believe that all of this has anything to do with eyesight, or focussing ability, as has been suggested. Perhaps it is all a simple question of nerve. Perhaps one starts off in life with a supply of nerve, and simply uses it up. Unlike a car battery, it is not rechargeable. So perhaps after all it gets back to the simple business of age in the sense of having done it for so many years, under pressure, and having nothing left but the 'yips'. Of one thing I am certain. Once you get them, you've got them, and you always will have them. And perhaps your only consolation is in the Confucian precept: 'When rape inevitable, lie back and enjoy.'

The 1969 Ryder Cup match was my swan-song as a player, although, of course, the great event has been able to bumble along nicely without me. Yet, as I have said, I am tremendously proud of having had the privilege of representing my country and the memories of the greatness of the competition will stay with me forever. It really annoys me when young players, young boorish players who have very little to offer the world in their style of play, their dress, their conversation, their humour, their personalities, their posture, their knowledge of and appreciation of the media, and even their performances – not one single thing going for them, and yet they behave so badly, being rude at dinners and ceremonies and not wearing the team uniform and saying that it is all a load of old rubbish. Yawning through national anthems, taking no pride in why they were there and with no sense of the history of the event, and of the truly great players who have taken part in it, that's what bugs me. Walter Hagen, Gene Sarazen, Byron Nelson, Ben Hogan, Sam Snead, Arnold Palmer, Jack Nicklaus, Lee Trevino, Abe Mitchell, George Duncan, the Whitcombes, Percy Alliss, Henry Cotton, Dai Rees, John Panton, Bernard Gallacher, Tony Jacklin – great players like these have been proud to take part in these matches over the years.

I am talking, of course, of Ken Brown and Mark James in 1979, who turned up at the airport in London apparently improperly dressed, an overture to a sad trip to the Greenbrier in West Virginia where the match was to be played, and where their behaviour was apparently not much improved. I suppose we put all this down to the general attitude to standards and the lack of them, the changing face of things, the ugliness, the stupidity, the lack of pride and politeness. I was appalled, I must say, and not made to feel better when after the event there were articles written about them saying 'Are they misunderstood?' when they said, for example, that the US did not have any good food. This is nonsense. The USA is the most extraordinary country, busy, vibrant, incredible, with the best of everything, including food, although it may not be in the corner coffee shop. I don't feel vindictive towards these boys. They are popinjays, silly boys who want their bottoms smacked, or to be made to wear nappies. The whole business is rather like going on parade with filthy boots or unpressed trousers. You don't do that, you get up when the bugles blow and the flags fly, you get up and go. They really have to think beyond the ends of their own noses. We may not be the greatest people in history, but there is so much good, so much quality in our country, that we ought to be proud to be part of it.

In all of this, I felt sorry for John Jacobs, the team captain, and I indulged my continuing fantasies on the theme of 'If *I* were captain'. My own inclination would have been to send James and Brown straight home from the airport, before they got on the plane, and tell them to follow on when they were properly dressed, or, if they preferred, not to bother to come. And yet it is a difficult situation, and Jacobs was obviously in a bit of a cleft stick. Perhaps the attitude of Jock Stein, the Scottish international football team manager, is the right one. Apparently he believes that you take the young man aside and say something along these lines: 'Look, son, you have been a silly boy, and I would be quite justified in sending you home. But just think of the consequences if I did. It could not be kept out of the newspapers, or the radio and television. Just think what your wife would say, your parents, your friends, your children at school. And what would your club say to all that, you being sent home in disgrace? So go away and be a man and behave yourself.' That is probably the sensible way, although I'd have been inclined to say 'Go home, son.'

No doubt James and Brown will learn. They are not unintelligent. Yet I don't really know why they did flaunt authority, which is what they were doing. Let's hope it is personalities, rather than authority in the abstract, which bugs them. The irony of all this is that such people are against a system which allows them to criticize it, which allows them to survive. If there is no one in authority, no one in charge, no one holding the reins – whether it is a referee, a managing director, a government or the law – where do we go? What's left? Who gets the work done? Big questions, and these boys will have to learn, somehow, the hard way or the easy way. Only idiots learn the hard way, and I just hope they don't run into a dictator with my attitude, or they will find themselves in a very cold and damp place without friends and they will certainly not enjoy it very much.

Oddly enough, it was the two Spanish boys, 'foreigners' playing in the Ryder Cup match for the first time, Angel Garrido and Severiano Ballesteros, who got it right, and who would have done anything anyone asked of them. They were nervous, didn't win many points, but the spirit was there. As Ballesteros said, 'This is no for money – we play here from the heart.'

It is quite amazing to me that we have lost so many matches, so many individual matches, narrowly over the last few holes, even without the distractions of all this off-the-course nonsense. The conclusion is that the Americans are better, harder, finishers. I have never really believed that they are any better technically, that they know any more than we do about striking the ball, but they are all products of a tougher society, where success is the thing and success is hugely rewarded. They have a quite different way of life and attitude to life. They are creatures of competition, pressures, noise; there are more of them in competition, week in and week out all year round, and I think they are a whole lot tougher. And also, I suspect, they are more proud than we are, when it comes to the business of playing in these matches. So often they seem blasé about the match, there is not much money in it, they are missing a tournament week by playing in the team, yet so many of them have told me that when they get to the actual venue, and the opening ceremonies, and see their flag flying and the anthem played, they just want to get out and slaughter us for Old Glory, and they would go in against lions, barehanded. This is something we constantly forget about the Americans. We just don't seem to feel the same emotion about the thing. I've seen it in only a few of our players. Bernard Gallacher has it. Brian Huggett had it, he showed the most tremendous courage in that 1969 match.

If you are going to lose, I always felt you should lose in the grand manner, head up, fighting all the way to the finishing line, so that you could look the other guy in the eye and say, 'Well done. I tried like hell and you beat me fair and square and good luck to you.' But so many of our people lose without seeming to care too much, like Brian Barnes, for example. He wins lots of matches, but loses too many that he simply should not lose. Max Faulkner, for all his flamboyance, wasn't really a fighter. The real fighters were men like Eric Brown. Ken Bousfield was a quiet man, but an enormous fighter. Dai Rees, in a different way, was an enthusiast, tried hard, battled on even if he didn't win that many matches.

I think we have to change our attitude to these Ryder Cup matches. In modern professional sports, I think we have gone about as far as we can comprehend at the moment in terms of the physical preparation of the athlete, and the techniques of the sport in question. The remaining area of research and improvement is psychological, in putting the team or the individual into the contest in absolutely prime mental condition.

If I were given four years in which to win the Ryder Cup, I would certainly want some changes made, especially when I think back to my time, and the captains I knew. My first was Henry Cotton, in 1953, a time of austerity. Cotton was very good. His enthusiasm came through, he saw that we had the best food and accommodation. He was convinced that we could win the match, and the result in my début year was desperately close. For years I have thought it was a disastrous experience for me, but as the years pass perhaps I am not so sure. Dai Rees had boundless enthusiasm, bouncing and hustling around, with endless chat. Eric Brown was Eric Brown, the fiery Scot, or sometimes, when he made a botch of things, the 'fiery twot'. Eric has an unbeaten record in the singles, over four matches, which is quite remarkable, but sometimes he let his patriotism run awry, as when he gave orders that if the Americans were in the rough, we shouldn't help them find the ball! Harry Weetman was all right, but did not bring any particular flair or magic to the job. Johnny Fallon was debonair, experienced, a fine after-dinner speaker, but when he got to East Lake in Atlanta, and saw how big the occasion was, I think he was a little overawed by it all. (I had better say that I was on the PGA Committee at the time, and in fact proposed his nomination.)

I have been a shade surprised that other people have not been invited to captain – Max Faulkner for one. As a former Open Champion, I think he should have been. Max could be a bit wayward at times, but then on the American side Sam Snead and Lloyd Mangrum, for example, have not been exactly paragons of rectitude in their careers, and Hogan was a shade uncommunicative. Max, I think, has been disappointed by this. John Panton is another who should have been given the job.

Captaincy is an intriguing business. The captain has to give the team something. What that might be is the rub. I don't know if you employ the Brian Clough/Bill Shankly technique (I have never met either of them), which seems to be an amalgam of discipline, cynicism with the players, a certain passionate romanticism for the game, and above all a blinding honesty, even in public. Or perhaps you do it with the Bertie Mee technique, the manager of Arsenal in the early seventies, who was the CO who left it to his adjutants, and stayed aloof and quiet and very cool, almost in the background. It is a finely balanced thing, and a matter of individual opinion and personality, but there are certain things I would want to change. For example, I believe the teams should fraternize, should talk together, should exchange ideas and then go out and fight like hell.

I would want wives banned. The match has become too much of a social occasion, with cocktail parties and receptions and dinners, with wives at all the happenings. They do have an influence, the ladies, and it is not a good one – they get upset, nervous, edgy over trivialities and all this conveys itself to the players. The special frock she has bought for the occasion suddenly doesn't show up too well with the elegant gown *she* is wearing, the perfume or the accessory isn't right, they take a little longer dressing, the place at the table is not as it should be – all these things bubble and burst into a scene when the team really should be in retreat before the great day. Some players have even brought children. Eddie Polland, a migraine sufferer, had a teething child with him at the Muirfield match, and was getting only two or three hours' sleep each night. Then he and Bembridge had to go out and face Arnold Palmer and Jack Nicklaus next morning! Result? 6 and 5, *not* in favour of the British. And Bernard Gallacher went and ate a dozen oysters – a *dozen oysters* – and got what he deserved, food poisoning. You just don't do that on the eve of a Ryder Cup match. All these things are filed away in my mind, although I suppose it would now be impossible to reverse some of these social changes.

I think I would be a hard taskmaster. I would want to consult my senior players, informally, but I wouldn't stand any of the nonsense – 'I want to play with him, I don't want to play with him.' I really believe that if people got seriously out of hand, I would be able to say, 'You are not properly dressed, you are not behaving properly, so just pack your bags and get to the airport and get yourself home. You are no good to this team.'

There have been weak links, poor selection methods. We have carried lame ducks too often. Including the Europeans now, we have about ten players who are up to it. The Americans have thirty to thirty-five. They do not have a hundred, as some people say – that is nonsense. They have about twenty-five very, very good players, the fellows who earn $100,000–150,000 a season, and you have to be very good to do that. So our selection is critically important, and the best committee is a committee of one. I'd be happy to do the job. People in golf say I couldn't do it because I am no longer close enough to the game. Ye Gods, I work in television on as many as ten major events in the US, and I know more about American players and their methods and their thought processes than possibly anyone in Britain. And I am steeped in British golf. It is my life. And, oddly enough, almost all the captains I played under – Cotton, Rees, Brown, Weetman – have all had major battles with the powers that be.

We should also give a great deal of thought to the preparation of our course when the match is played here, as the Americans do in their country. Laurel Valley and The Greenbrier were very American – monster courses with narrow fairways in the driving zone, severe rough, very fast greens. We seem obsessed with links courses, and too often the rough is simply not severe enough, while the greens, contrary to common belief, are no longer really fast. Too often they are too heavily watered, too soft, too receptive, too easy. But, above all, I think what our teams need is a little more discipline, a little more pride. I believe I could give them these qualities, and I'd love to have a stab at it – beat the Americans first in this country, then go over and beat them on their patch. And if that isn't worth a knighthood, I don't know what is!

Above 'In an English country garden . . .' Father, mother and the lad at Two Gables, Ferndown, 1954 *(R. Saidman)*

Left With Big Brother Alec at Weston-super-Mare GC, 1951 *(Fox Photos)*

Below Carris Trophy, Moor Park, 1946 – just look at that James Galway grip! *(Keystone)*

First family – with Carol, 'Tannhauser of Merlin', Joan and Gary in Bournemouth (*Peter Alliss*)

Opposite Big blast against Cobie Le Grange in winning the Esso Round Robin at Moor Park, 1964. The record was: played 14, won 12, drawn 1, lost 1 – some of the best golf I have ever played! (*Sport & General*)

Sweet success – with the Spanish Open Trophy in 1956 (*Suarez*)

From the second family album:
Jackey with Simon and the godfathers, Bruce Forsyth, Henry Longhurst and Cliff Michelmore *(Yorkshire Post)*

Sara and Simon *(Peter Alliss)*

CHAPTER SEVEN

The Canada Cup

The Canada Cup was started in 1953. The plan was to bring together two professional players from every golfing nation in the world, at a different venue each year, and have them play four rounds of golf for team and individual prizes. The plan was put into effect then, and still survives, in spite of several hiccups along the way. The rationale was 'International Goodwill through Golf'. It was sponsored initially by John Jay Hopkins, presiding tycoon of General Dynamics Corporation, a vast American enterprise beavering away at the business of constructing nuclear submarines, space hardware, aircraft and various other items of military equipment for the US government. If Hopkins was a merchant of death, perhaps the goodwill part of the thing might have represented compensation, or sublimation, for John Jay. As I understand it, Hopkins had been persuaded to underwrite the whole thing by Fred Corcoran, a Boston Irishman and entrepreneur extraordinary.

Corcoran, who died in the late seventies at the age of seventy-two, had been – among other things – tournament director of the American PGA, four times their Ryder Cup team manager, personal manager to Sam Snead, and had started a tournament circuit for US women professionals. To organize the Canada Cup, he became head of the International Golf Association, an organization which still exists. The first two events were held in Montreal, the first, in 1953, being won by Tony Cerda and Roberto de Vicenzo for Argentina. The Canada Cup, which in 1966 became more grandly known as the World Cup, has gone on ever since, through good times and bad.

I first played in 1954, with Harry Weetman at the Laval-sur-le-Lac Golf Club in Montreal, and in these early years few countries were represented. I was to play ten times in all, and from that very first year I saw the event as a passport to the world. We were provided with air fares, hotel accommodation and a fee of $500. I didn't blow my money, but brought it home intact after paying the necessary local taxes. Before this trip, I had been to Paris and Buenos Aires, but here I was in Montreal, all expenses paid, money in my pocket, in an annual event that could take me to a different world capital every year! Montreal I thought a delightful city, very cosmopolitan, with lovely squares, trees, statues, restaurants, and its spicy French flavour which gives it a particularly different ambience. At that stage in my career, I thought this golf game was wholly marvellous – no-one had mentioned that putting, for example, might after all be quite difficult.

The Canada Cup took me to the Far East for the first time, to Tokyo with Ken Bousfield in 1957, and again with Tony Jacklin in 1966. It also took me to Australia for the first time, to Washington, Mexico City, Puerto Rico, Buenos Aires and Hawaii.

My chief impression of Japan was of its being like an ant's nest. I discovered that all the kamikaze pilots did not die in World War II – here they were driving taxis in Tokyo, hurling cars all over the place. I've always thought that the Place de la Concorde was a shade hairy, but traffic in Tokyo had to be seen to be believed. Such a perplexing country, with so many faces. True Japanese-style homes I thought were charming – shoes off at the door, bamboo screens, matting floors. How sensible to take your shoes off at the door. Our way is nonsensical – you're entertaining, just had the new carpet fitted, it's deep snow or hissing with rain outside when the guests come in, shake their umbrellas all over the hall, leave them in the wrong place, someone rubs a shoe on the new settee and all the boot polish comes off and they say, 'Oh, I've marked your settee, most terribly sorry,' and you say, 'Oh, doesn't really matter, just an old thing,' while inwardly you are absolutely seething! How sensible to take off shoes, and put on little paper slippers.

But I never did get to grips with the Japanese breakfast. Bits of raw fish and some seeds, it seemed designed for a cross between a sea lion and a canary. I could not see that it would ever replace the Great British Breakfast.

I first went to Melbourne in 1959 and found quite marvellous golf courses. The composite course for the Canada Cup at Royal Melbourne was simply majestic. This was the first time I had ever seen blue gum trees, koala bears, first time I had rubbed a leaf between my hands and smelled eucalyptus, first time I had seen such a collection of all sorts of Victorian architecture, houses with verandahs, iron and concrete roofs – strange recollections. It seemed a wonderfully tranquil, sedate, Anglo-Saxon city. I went back in 1979 and found changes, changes. For one thing, I discovered that it had the largest Greek-speaking population outside Athens. Before there were virtually no high-rise buildings. Now there were buildings thirty or forty storeys high. Melbourne is much changed. Now it is like any European city, much more cosmopolitan than it was. There are really not so many 'okkers' around as the Australians would have you believe. Going there is not like going to a Commonwealth country in the old sense. The New Australians have little allegiance to cricket, the Queen, or Botany Bay. But, old or new, I do love Australia.

One of the greatest achievements in golf took place in the Canada Cup matches of 1958, in Mexico City, when Christy O'Connor and Harry Bradshaw won for Ireland. Bradshaw, the roly-poly Portmarnock professional, two stones overweight, the most unathletic figure you ever did see, with a grip like a bunch of bananas, suffering dreadful nose-bleeds because of the altitude and quite unwell, helped O'Connor win for Ireland and tied for the individual award with Angel Miguel of Spain. In the 18-hole play-off, he simply ran out of stamina. Even so, it was a remarkable performance.

I went to Mexico City, in 1958 with Bernard Hunt and again in 1967 with Malcolm Gregson. There I saw the most unbelievable poverty. The gulf between rich and poor was staggering. I had seen a little of it in Rio, in Brazil, a magnificent country constantly being raped by bad government or the Army. It does seem to me to be dreadful that the rich, or governments, or dictators come to that, don't seem to be able to look after their own people, *all* their people, even if modestly, and in the same way fail to produce sane, sensible societies.

So if the Canada Cup was my window on the world, my passport to romantic places, it also let me see, and start thinking about, the dark side of things. As the tournament evolved, it changed in unpredictable ways. John Jay Hopkins died in 1957, and was succeeded by Frank Pace, Jr, who was inclined towards platitudinous speeches about 'uniting against the Communist menace', which I thought a shade naive. Players were scattered around various hotels, they played in national pairs throughout the event when I thought they should all have been under the same roof, and thoroughly mixed up on the golf course. And there was no doubt that the Americans got privileged treatment, but then, unlike some countries, they always sent their best players.

There was also increasing criticism of the event. In 1964, it went to Maui, Hawaii, one of the early Robert Trent Jones courses at a magnificent hotel and property development. The almost complete absence of spectators rather defeated the object of the exercise, and there was a good deal of adverse Press comment. General Dynamics Corporation faded out, and multi-sponsors came in – American Express, Time-Life, Pan Am, Rothmans and others. They used the event to entertain and influence key figures in government and business in the host country from year to year. Peter Thomson, after twice helping Australia to victory in the early years, abandoned it on the grounds that the IGA and the sponsors were using the players for blatantly commercial purposes without proper compensation, and American golf managers like Mark McCormack increasingly came to the same view.

Over the years, with tournament golf becoming more and more international and huge prizes to be won almost everywhere, the impact of the World Cup has diminished. It has become less important. And it came to a critical point in 1979 with the match scheduled for Glyfada, near Athens. At the very last moment, the government of Greece, under pressure from a United Nations sub-committee, would not permit the South African team of Dale Hayes and Hugh Baiocchi to play. For a time it looked as though the entire event would be cancelled. The United States team of Hale Irwin and John Mahaffey seriously considered withdrawing, and eventually took part with golfers from some forty-five other nations, only after making the following statement:

'We find it deplorable that politics and governments must concern themselves so deeply about the participation of South African athletes in world events. We entertained the thought of withdrawing from this tournament in protest. But we found little to be gained by this action. We instead chose this message to express our regrets, and hope that our fellow players will agree with us. Our sincerest best wishes to the players from South Africa, for they are indeed gentlemen. We hope that these kind of situations will cease to appear in the future.'

The United States won, and Irwin won the individual award from Bernhard Langer of West Germany and Sandy Lyle of Scotland. The same UN sub-committee had tried the same caper in 1978, when the World Cup was played in

Hawaii, and that time failed because, I suppose, the US government has a good deal more muscle in these matters than that of Greece. There were rumours of sanctions, yet this same sub-committee has given little thought, apparently, to the good the event might be doing for the competitors and competing nations. Countries like Yugoslavia, Rumania, Singapore and some of the African states take part. It gives their players a chance to mingle with the supermen of the game, and to travel abroad. As Irwin said, 'This is the one time we can all join hands, and be one. I would just as soon see the World Cup disbanded before succumbing to political pressure.'

I played for England ten times in the Canada Cup/World Cup, from 1954 to 1967. Perhaps the early years were the best years. The future certainly seems clouded for the event. All I can say is that I was proud to be part of it, and took great pleasure from it. In retrospect, it was certainly good while it lasted.

CHAPTER EIGHT

Golf People

The Superstars

Throughout my life, perhaps the most amazing single thing I have noted about this remarkable game has been the number of different ways there are to play golf well. One can almost say that no two players are alike in their actions and that would certainly be true of the 'superstars' of my time.

There has been a handful of them and defining the word superstar, now in fairly common usage, is much more difficult than recognizing them. I would say that they are the people who have set new records, have made singular marks in the sport, who have enriched the game, who have been in the golfing sense larger than life, and who have made all such impacts internationally. Examples from other sports come easily to mind – Muhammad Ali, Bjorn Borg, Lester Piggott, Pele.

In my time in golf, my list would be Ben Hogan, Arnold Palmer, Gary Player, Jack Nicklaus, Lee Trevino, and now I don't believe I can resist saying young Severiano Ballesteros. Come to think of it, I had better add Tom Watson. The next stratum of players runs them close, and would include Sam Snead, Peter Thomson, Bobby Locke and Roberto de Vicenzo, and possibly, just possibly, Tony Jacklin.

Hogan I never really knew well and never saw much of as a player, but from what I have seen and known of him in the few times we have met, I am left with the impression that he is a secretive, perhaps introverted man. His life story, which was filmed with Glenn Ford playing the part, is well known. He started as a caddie, had hard early days on the tour (existing briefly at one time on cheap oranges). There was an awful and near-fatal car accident. By sheer will power he had evolved a golf swing that was simple, powerful and repeating, and it took him to the heights of the game, both before and after his accident, and left him with a unique place in golf history. Yet I have always had the feeling that he must have so much to leave behind him, still has so much to offer, that he should be out and about, spreading the gospel according to Ben and still active in and contributing to the game in some way. It seems a pity he did not become a television commentator, a media man of some kind, since he must have the most exceptional insights. Ben should be the oracle of the game, but he remains rather withdrawn from it all.

Apparently he still goes to his club every day, still hits balls every day, has the odd drink, watches golf on television and to that extent is still the pundit. If he sees something, and says that is good, that is bad, that is indifferent, people accept it, and he is still quoted occasionally. I am just sorry that no one knows more about him. But then, perhaps he has hidden his memoirs, buried them in capsules which will be opened when the Martians get here in about five million years, and they will discover the Thoughts of Chairman Ben, Golfer.

There are lots of Hogan stories, some of which may even be true. Gary Player is supposed to have telephoned him and asked for advice on his swing. Hogan said, 'What equipment do you play?' Gary replied, 'Spalding, Mr Hogan,' to which Ben said, 'Why don't you ask Mr Spalding?' Then there was the friend and club member who left Ben practising 3-wood shots while he went to play a leisurely nine holes of golf on a warm summer day. When he came back a couple of hours later, Hogan was still on the practice ground, still hitting 3-wood shots. His friend went over and said, 'Hell, Ben, what do you have to learn about hitting 3-wood shots?' Hogan said, 'I want to discover how well I hit them when I am tired.' Jimmy Demaret told of how he partnered Hogan in almost the perfect round of golf in which Hogan had not made one single mistake and had birdied six or seven holes. When they finished, Demaret went straight to the clubhouse for a sip, Hogan went straight to the practice ground. And when Demaret was leaving, an hour or more later, Hogan was still practising. Demaret went over and said, 'For Chrissake Ben, nobody can play any better than you did today – you can't birdie every hole, you know.' Hogan gave him the coldest of stares, and said, 'Why not?'

Hogan's game had the quality of a certain coiled, spring-like power, and above all was marked by a compelling accuracy. His immediate successor was Arnold Palmer, and no more unlikely successor could be imagined. No two players could be more different. Arnold was the complete extrovert in the sense that he was the world's sweetheart, open, friendly, amiable. Televised golf in America was just beginning to happen in the fifties, Hogan's decade. It really took off, and became a major televised sport in the sixties, coinciding with the age of Palmer, and perhaps Palmer was responsible for it. There were two main reasons for this. One was that Arnold was just about the most exciting golfer anyone had ever seen, anywhere, and the other was that Arnold became, almost overnight, 'The American Hero'.

His swing was not elegant, but it was ferocious. He crunched through that ball with such intensity that it seemed like a war game. He sniffed, he rolled his eyes, he hitched his pants, he smoked cigarettes with the same intensity that he hit the ball, he strode down the fairway as though he couldn't wait to get to the ball, he always knew which television camera was live, and on him, and above all, he charged, and he won! He charged the course, he mauled the course, he wrestled with the devil, and made the birdies. He came from behind and won. In the US Open of 1960, his final round was 65, his outward half was 30, and he won after being a handful of shots behind. It is quite difficult for any non-American to appreciate how much Arnold captured the public imagination, how much he was idolized in his own country then. American sports writers made him 'The Athlete of the Decade'. Tommy Bolt used to say, 'Everyone's out there whoopin' and hollerin' for that son of a bitch, when they should be cheerin' ol' Tom.' Bolt considered himself superior to Palmer (as a shot-maker I daresay he was) but then Bolt considered himself superior to everyone. But Palmer got the crowds out, the television ratings up.

His gallery of worshippers was dubbed 'Arnie's Army'. They wore buttons to that effect, and carried 'Go, Arnie Go!' banners along the side of the fairways – never been known in the old game before! Palmer was flamboyant and powerful at a time when America was flamboyant and powerful in the world. He smashed and crashed his way around the course, often in the woods and in the rough, from which he played the most spectacular recovery shots. He squandered as many tournaments and championships as he won – he should certainly have won a few more US Opens and Masters championships – but he loved it all and the galleries loved it all. He loved 'the smell of the greasepaint, the roar of the crowd'. He never refused to sign an autograph. He mingled with kings and presidents. For a spell, it was 'Palmer for President', 'Palmer for Governor', 'Palmer for the Senate'. I am not sure he could have handled any of that, for he is a simple man, with simple tastes, a beer, a Scotch, a cigarette. To extend the dictum of Peter Thomson that the ultimate thrill in golf is the flight of the golf ball, Palmer's shots seemed to have a distinctive flight all their own. They didn't, but sometimes we thought they did. For Arnold, come Sunday night and the end of the tournament, only one place mattered – the winner's. Arnold would just as soon have been 32nd as second. Winning was all. And it was not golf which was

Arnold's great love – it was competitive golf. He loved to beat all the other guys, and all told I suppose he made a greater contribution to professional golf than anyone since Walter Hagen, forty years earlier.

Golf was very lucky to have Palmer, Player and Nicklaus, the 'Big Three', at the top for so long in the sixties. In retrospect, it looks like a golden age of golf, and these were the men who made it so, even if it is easy to pick them to pieces. Jack Nicklaus, for example – now what do you say of a man who has broken all the championship records of golf and broken all the prize-money records in professional golf? You could talk of his awesome power, his meticulous measuring of the course, with everything calculated in advance and nothing left to chance, his rather upright swing with his right elbow away from his body, crunching down on the ball, a not-particularly-elegant-at-all-swing.

Jack in a sense has had several lives. He was a prodigy, no doubt about that. He won the Ohio Open Championship, against all the state's professionals, at the age of fifteen. He was US Amateur Champion and a Walker Cup player at the age of nineteen, and almost won the US Open as a young amateur. He did win it just seven months after he turned professional. He changed from being the fat goose, blond, crew-cut, overweight and physically quite unattractive, to the handsome swan, his hair longer and styled in contemporary fashion, his body leaner and trimmer, his wardrobe rendered rather more elegant. I suspect the death of his father Charlie some ten years ago had a very profound effect on Jack, and provoked a complete re-think of his entire life style. Unlike Palmer, who was the son of the late 'Deacon' Palmer, a professional-cum-greenkeeper at a modest course in a small town in Pennsylvania, and who therefore had a modest early life, Nicklaus had a prosperous, if not entirely rich, upbringing. His father was a pharmacist with several shops in Columbus, Ohio, a substantial city, and, as I understand it, the Nicklaus family lived very comfortably, and Jack had immense encouragement in his golf.

As a young man, Jack had all the arrogance of the early Lester Piggott – he would keep people like Hogan and Snead waiting on the tee without a blush, then just as likely go out and beat them handily. He has not yet lost all of that. I have heard journalists say to Nicklaus, when he is in with a 64, 'Did you play well, Jack?', and he has given them the very steely look and a dismissive 'I scored 64 – I must have done something right.' End of conversation. The arrogance that lingers in Jack sometimes gives one the impression that he is a complete expert on anything – the design and construction of golf courses and golf clubs, not to mention clubhouses and greenkeeping and grasses and how the greens should be cut; the rules of the game; cars and aeroplanes, flying and fishing; how slacks should be cut; the buying of wine and the bringing-up of the family. Rather frightening. But I am sure this is all a product of a supreme belief in themselves which these fellows have, the simple fact of being 'the greatest'. Before the exceptional events of 1980 when Jack won both the US Open and US PGA Championships, I had the feeling that after twenty years at the top, grinding and smashing away up and down and across the US, and all over the world, Jack was showing the first signs of being tired with it all and of being a shade over the top. Now I am sure his 1980 achievements will stimulate him to go on for a few more years, and I am even more sure that Jack William Nicklaus has not yet finished with the great championships of the world.

So, as Palmer succeeded Hogan, Nicklaus has succeeded Palmer, all very different animals. Hogan is still involved in the game with his own-name golf clubs but has seemed perfectly content to abandon the public side of it, and in that sense is almost a recluse. Arnold Palmer, now in his fifties, plays on, and I think will shortly have to face the major problem of what to do with the rest of his life. He has ample business interests, but I suspect he is an action man, a physical animal who has to be on the move, and what he will do from here on, I just do not know. Nicklaus on the other hand will be able to walk away from the competitive game, I am quite sure, when the time comes, and without much anguish. He seems very interested in course design, and gives every indication of being a man of parts. One thing that does strike me about Hogan and the 'Big Three' is that they have all had exceptional women behind them in Valerie Hogan, Winnie Palmer, Barbara Nicklaus and Vivienne Player.

Now, marching in parallel with the two great American players, and not one step behind them, has been a man whose story I have always thought to be one of the most astonishing in all sport – Gary Player. Gary was born in Johannesburg, where his father Harry was a superintendent in a gold mine, working for much of his life underground. Gary's mother died when he was six years old. At the age of seventeen, Gary left home to cross the city and become an assistant golf professional at the course of Jock Verwey, who in time became his father-in-law. By the time he was twenty, he was ready for the first assault on the UK with a wardrobe of two pairs of slacks and not many pennies to put in them. I must say I was one of the wiseacres who said in effect, 'You'll never make it son, go home and get yourself a sensible job.' Gary's grip was appalling, his stance all wrong, his swing pattern a disaster. But the next year, 1956, he was back and had the effrontery to win a five-round Dunlop tournament from Arthur Lees on Arthur's home course, Sunningdale. Two years later, he had finished second to Tommy Bolt in the US Open, and the year after that he had won the Open Championship. An astonishing career was launched. By 1979, Gary Player had won three Open Championships, three US Masters, two US PGA Championships and one US Open; twelve South

African Opens, seven Australian Opens and the World Cup, team and individual; five World Match Play Championships and more than 100 tournaments all over the world. He had scored a round of 59 in a national championship (Brazil Open) and had won the 1978 Masters with an inward half of 30 in a final round of 64, eight under par. We may now pause for breath.

Gary is the little guy from the little country (in the golfing sense) who went to the big country and all the big guys on their own patch. When you consider how difficult it is for an *American* player to win a tournament in his own country, and realize that for a period of twenty years Gary averaged one US tournament win per year, that is the measure of the man. He still lives in Johannesburg, some 12,000 miles from his 'place of work'. I've heard of long-distance commuting, but this is ridiculous. When Player started out on this road, South Africa in international golfing terms meant Bobby Locke and no one else, but now there are a dozen South African players playing worldwide and each year a couple of new ones appear who are just as likely to win events anywhere.

I have watched Gary play for twenty-five years, and in that time have seen him play a good deal of rubbish, but I have also been impressed at how he can get round the course and hold the whole thing together and get in with a score when his swing was not working for him quite as he might have wanted. He has such outright tenacity, such blazing determination, such a total conviction that nothing is impossible for him that although there are times when you just cannot make sense of him, cannot follow his logic, cannot begin to agree with him, his enormous ability and the sheer achievement of the man override everything. Gary is a never-say-die man. Seven down with seventeen to play against Tony Lema in an early World Match Play Championship, and winning, is well-known and is in the record books. But in a first-round match in the 1979 World

Match Play Championship, at the age of forty-four, he was four down with eleven to play, and won, which is just as impressive. And scoring a final round of 64 in the US Masters, to win, then going on to win the two following tournaments to make it three in a row – the man is almost preposterous.

Drama and controversy have been meat and drink for Gary Player. He has produced marvellous material for the writers over the years. He has played sixteen times in the seventeen years of the World Match Play, and in almost every case, on the morning of the first day, there has been a Gary Player story heading the golf page. When he won the Lema match at the 37th hole, he sat down at the side of the green and, by his own testimony, passed out for thirty seconds or so. On the same green, the 37th hole of a match with Jacklin, he stopped when over a putt and turned and rebuked the gallery when someone is supposed to have called out, 'Miss it.' Not too many people heard this, but everyone, including Jacklin, heard Gary's lecture to the crowd on the subject of sportsmanship. Jacklin promptly three-putted and Gary won the hole, and of course the match.

Gary Player is an exceptional match-play merchant. He grinds away at his man, niggles him, upsets him both with the quality of his own play, and his capers. He is rather like a boxer, leaning on, holding, pushing, shoving, smothering. There was another World Match Play incident at the 35th in a tight match when he suggested that Graham Marsh had teed his ball in front of the markers. Another year, he irritated Johnny Miller by taking an inordinate time to rake the sand in a bunker while Miller waited to play. Gary might be appalled to read this or any suggestion that he does not play according to the spirit of the rules. He uses a great set speech whenever anyone beats him, which is not too often. He says, 'I always take my hat off, look the man straight in the eye, shake hands firmly and congratulate him.' In all, Gary is a remarkable fellow. I am not sure I would like to be one of his children. He can do everything better than they can – running, jumping, riding, table tennis, swimming, bunker shots, everything. I think I prefer Spike Milligan's attitude – if he is tackled by a seven-year-old, he falls down to let the child see that it can win sometimes.

Always fiddling with his game, always looking for gimmicks is Gary. For years he was a rap putter, giving the ball a short, crisp clip. Then he discovered stroke putting. Then he was back with rap putting. In his earliest days, he had a wicked hooker's grip, which he modified. He used to drop his hands noticeably at the top of his backswing to get 'inside' the arc of his swing, but he has always had a very wide, big-swing arc for his height, giving him enough length to keep in touch with the sluggers of the game. One year at Wentworth he said he was being plagued by a hook which he wanted to get rid of, and he invited a crowd on the practice ground to spot his fault. A police inspector (!) identified the fault, it is said, and Gary thereupon declared that he would never hook the ball again, never again, in his entire lifetime. He then proceeded to the first tee where his opening drive was – hooked.

So my opening point remains – there are more golf swings, Horatio, than are thought of in any teaching manual and, the greatest players included, no two swings are exactly alike. Take Lee Trevino, now what would you make of him? If Trevino came to you and said, 'I'm 14 handicap, I would like a lesson,' and set himself up to the ball, you would agree that his handicap could not be any lower and that everything, with one exception, was a complete disaster. The ball is teed three or four inches forward of his left heel, his whole body seems open, the club is picked straight up on the backswing, dropped at the start of the downswing, there is a huge dip of the right shoulder down and through, but oh my! in the hitting area everything is perfect! Lee gets down to the ball, stays with the ball, goes through the ball fairer and squarer than almost anyone you care to mention, and the ball goes out, under perfect control, with the slightest of fades.

The old John Jacobs teaching dictum that the object of the exercise is to deliver the face of the club to the ball in line with the target, at speed, is never better illustrated than by Lee Trevino. The man is a genius, and I say that knowing how overworked the word is. He is a conjuror of golf shots, a master manufacturer of the shot required for the situation. I have never seen any other player do it as he can.

The one exception you should spot on first seeing Lee Trevino is his grip – firm, solid, correct. In fact that would be the one thing, perhaps the only thing, that the great modern players have in common. There are virtually no bad grips, or even unorthodox grips, today. The Whitcombe brothers, Charlie, Ernest and Reg, famous in the thirties, all had interlocking grips, with thumbs sticking up and out and all over the place. Not seen today, that kind of thing.

Trevino's personal story is bewildering. His father, it is said, was a Mexican gravedigger. What is certain is that Lee grew up in the West Texas town of El Paso, which is certainly not the most prosperous corner of the United States, and there were few cents to spare in the early days. The country around there is poor and sandy and scrubby, and so are some of the par-3 and municipal golf courses. Trevino hustled around these courses, picking up an income, if you could call it that, where he could. He reached a point when he could play with a big soft-drinks bottle, heavily taped, and he would take on all-comers with this freakish implement, and beat them over short courses. And there was born and developed his talent for manufacturing shots, and for controlling the golf ball as well as anyone who has ever played the game.

He reached the status of assistant professional in El Paso and played in his first US Open, his first national appearance of any substance, in 1967. This was at Baltusrol, in New Jersey, and featured a majestic duel between Palmer and Nicklaus, with Nicklaus winning in the end, but Trevino finished sixth, and took home $6000, a huge sum for him. And he left thinking, 'Why didn't they tell me about this?' He was a good deal more brash then than he is now, and thought this US Open game was just the thing for him. So he went back the next year, to Rochester, and won it. How he won it over the two closing holes make my point about how he fashions shots, and fashions them out of trouble. On the 17th, the 71st hole at Rochester, he cold-topped his second shot and was well short of the green. He pitched the ball twelve feet from the hole and holed it. On 18, the 72nd hole, he drove into the rough, advanced the ball in the rough, then pitched it out four feet from the hole and holed it – and tied the US Open record at 275.

Three years later he put together one of the unique achievements in the history of the game. He won three major championships in not much more than twenty days. He beat Jack Nicklaus in a play-off for the US Open at Merion. He beat Art Wall in a play-off for the Canadian Open, then came to Royal Birkdale for the Open Championship, and held off 'Mr Lu' to complete the transformation of the country boy who had made the long trek from El Paso to New Jersey in 1967, into a true superstar, who apart from anything else knows a good deal more about the history of the game than people give him credit for. Of all the players we have mentioned, no-one has more respect for the game of golf, and the riches it can offer a man, from whatever background. Trevino's story is a fairy story ranking with that of our next superstar.

Severiano Ballesteros is the wonder of the age. Consider a boy born on the rain-washed northern coast of Spain into a family of brothers, his father a farmer. They live near the Pedrena golf course, now fifty years old and built before the Spanish tourist-based boom in golf of the last twenty-five years, built at a time when golf in Spain was for the few, the rich, the aristocratic. Then also consider that by the time he was twenty-three, this boy has won the Open Championship and the US Masters; won the first event he ever played on the US tour; headed the European Order of Merit three times; helped win the World Cup for Spain twice, won tournaments and championships in the UK, USA, Europe, East Africa, Japan and New Zealand – five consecutive events in five starts in five different continents. Can it be true? It is true. How could it happen?

There is the classic set of circumstances – uncle Ramon Sota who was an international player in his time, two brothers who became golf professionals, his youth spent caddying, learning the trade behind the caddie shed with an old inherited 3-iron, hustling around, scuffling for golf balls, playing and practising whenever there was the chance. Without privileges, a youngster can learn all the skills, acquire the resolution of a champion and still know the value of things. There is a story which I like very much of Severiano signing a huge contract for Slazengers, and in a photo session for them in Spain hitting out lots of practice balls. When they had finished, Severiano was seen scratching around in the rough. The son of one of the Slazenger representatives went over and asked him what he was doing. Severiano said, 'I know there is one more ball here somewhere. No like to lose ball, even practice ball.'

Of all the young players in world golf today, Ballesteros has the most going for him. He is very good-looking, which is no drawback when it comes to endorsements and appearances. When he puts himself out, he is very good with people. In the last few years, his command of English has improved strikingly. He wears clothes well. In general, he handles the Press well. And above all he swings the club and plays the game with such dash and élan that it is Arnold Palmer come to life again.

The Americans rather put him down after his Open Championship win at Lytham, saying that he had hit only two fairways in the last round and not one single fairway from the 11th onwards and had only one two-putt green over nine holes. What they missed was that over those closing holes Ballesteros always failed to hit the fairway on the right side, that is, the correct side that gave him a more open shot to the green, even if it had to be played from the rough. His great strength made that no particular problem for him, and they did him an injustice. They may have realized this at the 1980 Masters, when he spreadeagled the field, faltered a little in the last round, then rallied to be the totally undisputed champion. He is a thrilling superstar, no doubt about that, and the best thing that has happened to European golf since Tony Jacklin's great days of ten years ago. My only worry about Severiano would be his physical fitness. It cannot be too comforting to have back trouble at his age, but if his back and the rest of him hold up under the stress of his ferocious shot-making, the future is unlimited for Severiano Ballesteros.

Tom Watson, with three Open Championships and one Masters Championship so far, is rather like Ben Hogan in my group of seven in that he has really played only in the US and UK. But his record to date is hugely impressive, with some $2 million won in half a dozen years. He looks a Huckleberry Finn figure to me, blond, boyish, but as Nicklaus said after the unforgettable Open of 1977 at Turnberry, when they battled each other stroke for stroke through the third and fourth rounds, right down to the 72nd hole, 'Tom Watson knows where he is going – and that is straight ahead.' In singlemindedness, Watson can give all of them a shot or two. In 1980, he won seven official US events and more than $500,000 in official prize money, which is almost indecent. Tom has a simple swing, straight back, goes straight through, but he gets an exceptional shoulder turn which gives him deceptive length. He is very, very long when he wants to be. The only thing that can go wrong with his action is tempo, and his only visible fault is that he can get a shade too quick betimes.

Tom had a chance to win the 1974 US Open at Winged Foot, but took 79 on the last round, and let in Hale Irwin to win. In 1975 he had a chance to win the Masters, and again the US Open but took 77 on the last round, and the Americans quickly had him dubbed as a 'choker', a man who would blow up under pressure. What they had perhaps overlooked was that Watson in 1974 was only twenty-four, and had played the tour over there for only three years, not exactly a mountain of experience behind him. But his performances at Carnoustie in 1975, at Augusta in 1977, Turnberry in 1977, and at Muirfield in 1980 have put all that far behind him. Carnoustie I have often thought was for Watson a triumph of willpower and moral courage and doggedness as much as shot-making in a low-scoring championship, clearly demonstrated at the finish of the championship proper against Jack Newton, and again in the play-off with Newton, particularly after two US Open disappointments.

Then in 1977 he won the Masters from Nicklaus by two shots scoring 70, 69, 70, 67, and repeated that in the unforgettable Open Championship over the magnificent Ailsa Course. And at Muirfield, he simply shattered the field, a marvellous field which included Lee Trevino playing his best golf, and had the championship won with nine holes to play. Tom's background could not be more different from say, Trevino's. He actually played in a club exhibition match with Arnold Palmer when he was a teenager. He is a graduate of Stanford University, California, one of the better US 'schools', where he majored in psychology.

Here again, there is a wife to be reckoned with. Linda
Watson is a strong, positive character, and I suspect she is
something of a business woman who knows what is going
on, rather like Henry Cotton's wife in his playing days.
Given his all-round game, and his cold, clinical attitude to
the work in hand, Watson may well reach Gary Player's
total of nine major championships and get closest to the
Nicklaus total, although Ballesteros has some seven years
in hand on him. On the other hand, it is beyond my
imagination that anyone in my lifetime can pass the
Nicklaus total of seventeen major wins in championships,
plus two US Amateur Championships, which is where he
stood at the end of 1980. But different times, different men.
Hogan's career was interrupted by war and accident.
Palmer did not turn professional until he was twenty-five.
Nicklaus was playing competitive golf at the highest level
in his teens. Player lived about 12,000 miles from his main
place of business, and for Ballesteros and Watson all is still
to play for. There is no point in drawing lines and awarding
marks and saying A is better than B who is not quite as good
as C. All of these men have enriched the lives of all of us
who have seen them play, and who care about golf, and
champions and championships. We should rejoice in that,
and remember that diamonds are diamonds, rubies are
rubies, pearls are pearls.

The Stars

Peter Thomson was a very great player. Indeed in his
time he was the dominant golfer everywhere the small
ball was played, which meant everywhere in the world
except North America. And although it is not widely
known, Thomson was successful in America. He did not
much care for the American way of life, the hamburgers,

the hot dogs, the raucousness of the American style, and he did not much care for American golf courses, and their sameness. Yet he never went to America without making a profit, he won tournaments there, and he had a good chance at the US Open of 1956, won by Cary Middlecoff, in which Thomson finished fourth. He came to believe that our way of golf was the best. He was very much an Empire man. Although he had a keen awareness of Australian history and the fact that the British had left just as many scars there as throughout the rest of the world, on the whole he reckoned the British had left several good things, not the least of which were cricket and golf. He particularly loved Scotland, and I believe there was a grandparent from Aberdeen somewhere in his story.

Peter made the game look ridiculously simple. He hit the ball straight, from A to B. His approach to it all was that of the wholly rational man. The jaunty stride, the confident, casual look, the simple, unerring straightness of his stroke-making, with white shoes the only bright splash in a conservative wardrobe. All this in fact disguised a very tough, steely charachter. Thomson could be as hard as any Australian games player you could mention. The logic he applied to the game was clear. He came to accept that golf in Britain, with its wide variety of links and other courses, and particularly Open Championship golf in Britain, always played on links with all their humps and hollows, freakish bounces, hidden bunkers and winds that could reverse their directions in an hour, was to be taken as a fact of life, accepted, and not complained about. He accepted the old Bernard Darwin view. When someone complained to Darwin that 'It isn't fair, it isn't fair,' Darwin replied, 'No – but then it isn't meant to be fair.'

This may have emerged from the fact that in Thomson's home town many of the courses are on sand bases, and are about as close to links golf as you can find; moreover, many of them were designed by Scottish and English architects towards the end of the last century. Certainly Thomson's credo for golf in our country – and at this he was a master – was that the great thing here was simply to 'keep the ball in play'. This was the advice he gave to every young Australian golfer bent on making his first trip to the Old Country.

His own experience in the Open Championship was quite remarkable. In his very first Open, at Portrush in 1951, when he was but twenty-one, he finished joint sixth behind Max Faulkner. In his second, he finished second to Bobby Locke at Royal Lytham, only one stroke behind. By this time I suspect he was beginning to see that it was entirely feasible for him to win the championship. In 1953 at Carnoustie, he was joint second behind Ben Hogan, and by this time I am quite sure that young Thomson was convinced he could win. He thereupon won the next three in a row, at Royal Birkdale, St Andrews and Hoylake. In 1957 he was second, again to Locke, and in 1958 won at Lytham after a play-off with David Thomas. And in 1965 came perhaps his crowning success, his fifth Open Championship against a field which included Palmer, Player, Nicklaus, Lema, de Vicenzo, Nagle.

I was invited to his new home in Melbourne in 1979. For many years he had lived in a grand old mansion there, but that had been sold and he moved into a rather stark, single-storey ranch-type place, and as far as I can remember there was not one single memento on view of his career in golf. Five times Open Champion, he won three Australian Opens and nine in New Zealand; played eleven times in the World Cup and twice in winning teams; took the Open Championships of Italy, Spain, Germany, Hong Kong, India, the Philippines, and tournaments galore in the UK and Japan – yet I do not recall seeing one single ashtray. How different to, for example, the amateurs Michael Bonallack and Joe Carr, who have yards of wallspace covered with cabinets full of hundreds of bits of silver.

Thomson was awarded the CBE, and when he declared
in 1979 that he had now retired from championship golf no
one need have been concerned that Peter would have too
much time on his hands. He was already an established
success as a journalist and commentator, and a golf-course
designer, with many courses built through the Far East. He
has a positive interest in politics, which I suspect he will
pursue, and with success. If you walked in on Thomson at
home, unannounced, you'd be just as likely to find him
reading Arthur Koestler, or listening to Gustav Mahler. A
well-rounded man is Peter W. Thomson, and, on second
thoughts, I have to promote him to 'superstar'.

The last of his championships, the finale to the
astonishing career of an Australian hero, was strangely
low-key. It was the Australian Open of 1979, at which I was
a television commentator, and I looked down on the last
hole, the last green, that Peter Thomson would play in
championship golf. He was not of course in contention. I
don't suppose the gallery round that last green was more
than about fifteen people, perhaps half of them children.
There were two promotional girls there splendid in white
jeans, long black boots and white T-shirts (no bras, of
course) and they were quite distracting – almost more
interesting than watching Peter Thomson hole out. I got
them out of my mind and looked down at Peter from the
commentary position. He holed out, neat and jaunty as
ever, with just the suggestion of an extra chin coming,
and walked off, tossing the ball to a little boy in a red T-
shirt.

In years to come that boy might say, 'This is the ball, the
very ball, with which Peter Thomson finished his
championship career –thirty years of championship golf.'
Or perhaps he would kick it about in the street, or knock it
round a golf course and lose it in the rough, or a pond. In
the old days, players used a new ball each round. Now they
use one on each hole. If I had won an Open Championship,

for instance, I would never have thrown the ball away. But Peter Thomson probably did not give it a second thought – he always was more rational, less emotional, than I.

Arthur D'Arcy ('Bobby') Locke would have to have a place in any golfing hall of fame. He was an outstanding amateur, just before World War II, and won the South African Open twice as an amateur, in a total of nine wins. He was twice leading amateur in the Open Championship before the war, then dominated it in the first post-war decade, with four firsts and two seconds. In the same period, he won a dozen or so tournaments in the US, was third in the American Open a couple of times and was second leading money-winner there in 1947, a notable achievement for a non-American. Locke really launched South Africa as a force in world golf. Before him, Sid Brews is about the only name I recall, and he was never really an international player. Locke paved the way for Gary Player and the host of young South Africans we have seen in the past twenty-five years.

As the years slipped past, Bobby grew more and more portly, and as he did so his shots became rounder and in the end he seemed to be aiming off 100 yards to the right, and drawing the ball enormously back to the fairway or on to the green. He did everything at a careful pace, moving sedately down the fairway in his 'knickers', as the Americans called the plus-fours he wore, for all the world like some strolling bishop. But no golfer was ever better balanced than Locke, no man was a more deadly judge of distance from 100 yards in, and surely no one was ever a better putter, with his familiar, unchanging system. A very close scrutiny of the hole and its immediate approaches, back to the ball, two practice strokes and bump, away she went – and as often as not into the hole, from whatever range.

Of all the people I listed earlier as the stars and superstars of my time, the next two have perhaps the most elegant of swings. Roberto de Vicenzo from the Argentine is a lovely man with a lovely swing and a lovely strike through the ball. Every time I meet the man I do long to be able to speak Spanish fluently. In English, his sense of humour is sharp enough, but my Spanish friends tell me that in his own language he is hilarious. I almost said that Roberto was not the toughest of characters, but dammit, the man has won more than 230 events, they say, and at least forty national championships around the world, and no one can do that without being tough. But Roberto is a gentleman in the best, old-fashioned sense of the word. I seem to recall that he lost all his money in a Mexican mining venture at one point, and at the age of forty simply buckled down to life and golf all over again, and apart from many other things became the oldest winner of the Open Championship at the age of forty-four, in 1967.

He has always been considered a suspect putter, but there again, how can anyone win all those events and not be a fine putter? Despite what they may say from time to time, every champion is a first-class putter – you can't have one without the other, as the song goes. Roberto de Vicenzo had one thing in common with Bobby Locke. He was the trail-blazer for a whole generation of players, he and his contemporary, Tony Cerda. Before Roberto, there had been few South American golfers. Jose Jurado from the Argentine was prominent in my father's time, and I remember Enrico Bertolini; Eduardo Blassi who in the early fifties used to putt one-handed with a putter some eighteen inches long; Ricardo Rossi, who became very big with Dunlop South America; Leopoldo Ruiz who, like Eric Brown and Christy O'Connor, came so close to winning the 1958 Open at Lytham; Fidel de Luca, and others. And there was Mario Gonzalez of Brazil, outstanding both as an amateur and a professional, from the Gavea Club in Rio, where I won my Brazilian Open in 1961.

But to have done what de Vicenzo has done – winning everywhere, missing a tie for the US Masters on a scorecard technicality, coming from a distant land which had so little previous impact on the golf world – has made his achievement substantially the greater.

In the Masters of 1968, Roberto finished one stroke behind Bob Goalby, the winner. The last day was Roberto's forty-fifth birthday. He started it two strokes behind the leader, Gary Player, and one stroke behind Bob Goalby. On the very first hole, Roberto holed out his second shot, a 9-iron, for an eagle, to share the lead in the tournament, and as he walked on to the green to fish his ball out of the hole, the crowd broke into a chorus of 'Happy Birthday, Roberto.' It was a perfect day, a perfect day for scoring, the course benign and true, the greens holding any and every kind of shot. There were eleven scores under 70 on that last day, against a par of 72. Goalby scored 66, and Roberto scored 65 – to tie, we thought, but no. What happened at the end of that Masters was one of the truly tragic happenings in championship golf. On the 18th hole, Roberto, seeking a par 4 for, it seemed, a 64 which would have won, pulled his second wide of the green and eventually missed from five feet for his par. Perhaps still annoyed at this, he signed his card rather hurriedly, and left the area of the last green. Roberto in fact had birdied the 17th hole, but instead of the figure 3 being written on his card, it was 4. Roberto had signed the finished card, his playing partner Tom Aaron had counter-signed and it was a wrong card, showing a 66 which should have been a 65. The Rules of Golf say that when a card is signed, the total on the card becomes a fact. If the player signs for more strokes than he has taken, that total will stand. If he signs for fewer strokes than he has taken, he must be disqualified.

A gallery of thousands saw Roberto score 3 on the 17th hole, and a television audience of millions saw Roberto score 3 on the 17th hole. His birdie there was a fact, an indisputable fact, but he had signed his card for a 4. Under the Rules of Golf, a 4 it had to remain. And also, under the Rules of Golf, Goalby and de Vicenzo had not tied. Goalby was first, de Vicenzo was second.

In the US PGA Championship of 1979, at Oakland Hills, a long and tiring course, Samuel Jackson Snead scored 288, four over par, the equivalent of four rounds of 72 – *at the age of 67.* The swing, in its time one of the wonders of the game, was perhaps no longer entirely impeccable. There was perhaps a suggestion of groping or reaching for the ball and a little extra shoulder movement through and after the ball, but time and again Snead rifled his iron shots at the flagsticks, and with his peculiar side-saddle putting method got in a few putts and returned, as I say, the equivalent of four 72s. I make this a totally staggering performance, almost without comparison to anything I can think of in any sport.

Snead has won eighty-five official US Tour events. He won the first of them in 1936, the last of them in 1965 and since then has dominated seniors' golf. His early great contemporaries were Byron Nelson, Jimmy Demaret and Ben Hogan, his latest the most recent batch of professional products from the US college golf-scholarship system. With the exception of the American Open Championship – he was second four times – he has won everything worth winning in the game, and with it a vast fortune, much of it tucked away before the days of Arnold Palmer and Jack Nicklaus and high taxation. The stories of his fortune, and his fondness for retaining every dollar, are legion. The late Fred Corcoran, his manager for many years, told me a long time ago that Snead before World War II had bought vast tracts of land in Florida for ten cents an acre or some equally ridiculous price. He had sold off pieces for huge profits, but still owned much of it, and has kept pretty quiet about the whole thing. He must certainly be one of the wealthiest sportsmen in the US. No one could ever call

Sam Snead the most gracious man in the world, but with the straw hat, the athletic walk, the arrogant stride and the broad hillbilly accent – he comes from West Virginia – he is an exceptional person, and a helluva golfer.

The Meteors

It may not be entirely correct to title this chapter 'meteors' if you want to consider the word in its literal context as meaning pieces of matter that flash into the earth's atmosphere and glow for a few seconds, then vanish forever. That would be an overstatement in assessing the careers of the people we now look at, some of which have been quite lengthy, but I am simply trying to illustrate the difference between them and those that have gone before, the players who shone strongly and brightly for so long at the very top of the firmament.

I have always considered players in two loose categories – those who have rather dissipated, or not made the most of, their natural given talents, and those who have capitalized on what may not have been initially a very massive talent for the game. You might well put me in the first category, even if I did have my moments of glory. And moments of glory are ultimately the whole object of the exercise. I had twenty-one tournament victories in events that would now be considered major, without of course winning any of the world's major championships. Yet every champion needs a supporting cast. Consider the thousands of golfers who have competed in the Open Championship since it all began in 1860, and consider further that in that long time there have been only sixty or so Open Champions. The supporting cast makes the existence of the champion possible. Infantry and artillery, what the Russians call 'the god of war', and not the General Staff, win all the wars. The fellows who go out and die win wars. I know – I have died often enough on the golf course.

And when you take what I hope is a reasonably detached view of a life encompassing fifty years, thirty of them on the golfing scene, the squabbles and the feuds and the quarrels one may have had with one's fellows seem less and less important and in hindsight all the happenings, all the personalities, all the places one brushed up against made a mark, enriched one's life and deserved their place in the pattern of things, if there is a pattern.

Dai Rees has been a remarkable man of my time. Now pushing seventy, he was of an earlier generation but he still cracks on, ebullient as ever, busy as a sparrow on a dung heap, no longer playing tournaments but furiously active and involved in writing, conducting clinics and golf weeks, immensely loyal to the PGA and all its affairs and still, as he has been for so many years, professional at the busy South Herts club in London. Dai is a fervent Welshman who could never see the slightest sense in Welsh separatism. He thought the whole idea of separatism in the British Isles was quite ridiculous. If you wanted to speak Welsh, fine, you should have an opportunity to learn. He loved his country, but his country was Britain, and he just happened to come from the Welsh part of it.

Dai has never worried himself overmuch about the affairs of the world, or if he did he kept it all to himself and went on his way blissfully, loving the golf, the travel, the challenge, the silly clubhouse conversations, the wispy flirtatious chat on the golf course which we have all experienced. In his early days, Dai with his two-fisted grip was not all that good technically, but he was a demon putter and he made the most of it. His greatest asset was and is his enthusiasm for the game in all its aspects. Brilliantly flamboyant, boyo – pity he never won an Open Championship. He deserved one.

Max Faulkner was one of the most brilliant shot-makers

I have ever seen in my life. Sadly, he rather drifted out of golf when his competitive playing days ended, and I believe he is now not too fit. Sadly, because he is now at an age – the mid-sixties – when he might still be making a handy income from golf clinics, exhibitions, dinners, speeches, and giving a lot of people a lot of pleasure. Max I fear never really made the most of his talents. If ever there seemed to be a natural for television, and for so many other things, it was Max Faulkner, colourful character, colourful dresser, extrovert. He should have been the Jimmy Demaret, the Doug Sanders, of British golf. But perhaps the truth was that Max, like so many apparent extroverts, was never quite as colourful as he seemed. I often thought there was a rather lonely figure in there, longing to get out.

The same was true of Fred Daly, a meteor who flared for a few brief, brilliant years, from 1947 to 1953. Fred was seen as the cheerful, whistling Ulsterman, with very small hands and immensely long clubs including a driver weighing $17\frac{1}{2}$ oz. Although he was a small man he hit the ball miles and was magisterially straight. But I often wondered if he was as cheerful as the public thought. There had to be a reason for anyone taking more than twenty (they were counted) waggles before striking a putt. Fred had the Red Hand of Ulster emblazoned on his brown leather golf bag, and back in the forties and fifties this was not considered outrageous. He and Harry Bradshaw from Dublin teamed up in happy harmony and were a great double act, which is some kind of comment on our present times.

Ken Bousfield made the very most of what he had and was a very steely and occasionally strange man. He had been a colour sergeant in the Marine Commandos during the war, but in golf he never was a man for making great decisions, never an activist, never a committee man, in fact rather a loner to the point of being secretive. Yet he was generous in deed, gift and spirit, and that is worth all the rest of it. Ken was never a long hitter, but always a tenacious competitor with the most exceptionally delicate touch around the green, famed above all for his pitching with a long, leisurely deliberate backswing. When Dick Burton passed from the scene, Ken took over at the swank Coombe Hill club, near Kingston, but he didn't seem to want to play the part, wasn't really into the business of the income tax and accounts, stock and stocktaking, recruiting and controlling assistants, displaying the goods and generally running a top shop. Ken didn't really enjoy that. Yet he was kind, and he was fun.

This generation of players contributed very little to the structure of the tournament scene, off the course. They never did seem much interested in change. Charlie Ward didn't do much, nor did Rees, Sam King, Dick Burton, Arthur Lees, Fred Daly, Harry Bradshaw – they all seemed content to leave the organization of tournament affairs in the hands of Commander Charles Roe, secretary of the PGA, who ran the events like an ayatollah from his Victorian office in the City of London, while the club professionals ran the affairs of the PGA through huge, bumbling committees.

Things have changed. Around 1961, John Jacobs, Harry Weetman, Bernard Hunt, David Thomas and myself were determined that there should be reform, even revolution. We felt that the organization needed modernizing, that we should market our 'product' more professionally, that we should get more sponsors and do more for them, and that we should resolve the differences that then existed between club professionals and tournament professionals over how the PGA should be run. In the event, it took almost ten more years before it happened and the man responsible for it, in large part, was John Jacobs. John was literally born into golf at the lovely Lindrick club, near Sheffield. I remember him going to the Gezira club in Cairo as a professional, a long time ago, and I thought at the time that this was altogether terribly grand. For me, he has always been a good friend, a good fellow. As an administrator, I have thought him a shade stubborn, difficult to sway when he had formulated his own position. He often thought it had to be done his way or not at all. This I am sure emerged from his experience with big business. He told me once that when he went to his first board meeting, rather awed by the tycoons present, he deliberately kept quiet for half an hour, until he suddenly realized that no one was talking much common sense. Most of it in fact was waffle. And he realized then that common sense does cut through a lot of the world's nonsense. Subsequently he did a very great deal, as Tournament Director of the PGA, to expand the schedule of tournaments, to create the separate Tournament Players' Division, later extending this to the European Tournament Players' Division.

Not many of my contemporaries got anywhere in the business world. The earlier lot, the Whitcombes, Padgham, Duncan, Mitchell, Robson, my father, all departed this world as they had started, as professionals at golf clubs. They never thought of doing anything else. When I left Moor Allerton and got more into writing, television and golf course construction, plus an interest in a wholesale glass and china business in Bournemouth, any urge I ever had to spend the rest of my life as a club professional was long gone. (The Bournemouth business, by the way, is in partnership with Roy Beckett who played for Stoke City in the days of Stanley Matthews and the Mountfords, then later with Port Vale.)

Of my own contemporaries, Eric Brown and Harry Weetman were the naughty boys of the day. The late Harry Weetman, the Shropshire lad, was an interesting case – son of the soil, father a Shropshire gamekeeper, he was a powerful man, slow, but with a droll sense of humour. Harry thundered the ball from the tee, thundered the ball off the fairway with mammoth crunching blows, but had the most delicate of putting touches. Weetman and Brown, like Cotton and Rees, had many brushes with the PGA in their time, yet all were eventually appointed Ryder Cup captains. Funny old world.

David Thomas never quite made the most of his great talents. He was a magnificent striker of the ball, but he probably spent too much time looking around, taking in the world at large, the cars, travel, food, smelling the flowers along the way. But I think when you have lost a play-off for the Open Championship (against Thomson in 1958) and finished second by a stroke (to Nicklaus in 1966), then some of the zest for the whole thing leaves you. David in a sense is perhaps the unluckiest player in the world. If he had won that Open against Thomson, it would have changed his entire life. He lost it so simply that you sometimes start to think about fate and outside agencies. David hit a mid-iron shot a shade too heavy to the 17th green in the last round, making five instead of what would have been four. He and I have been staunch friends for more than twenty years. I can't think of two more opposite people, yet there is a chemistry which makes it work, like Morecambe and Wise, Laurel and Hardy, Mutt and Jeff if you like, and it is precious to me. He is completely into golf course design and construction, and finds fulfilment in that.

Bernard Hunt I make one of the very finest of my or any generation, a complete professional on and off the course. He was very active with us in trying to make changes to improve the tournament scene. Bernard was a player of very high calibre, with his short, distinctive backswing. In one year, 1963, he won six tournaments and took home, at the end of that year, not much more than £3000. A man can now earn that by finishing tenth in one event.

Christy O'Connor was very close to being a genius in golf. I have always had an enormous amount of time for him. He can be a difficult man, and when he has had a few glasses of the dark stout, he may not be the world's sweetheart. He has strong Republican tendencies, as any Irishman may think he is entitled to have, but he has been a player of extraordinary talent. If he could have putted better, putted in fact as well as any middle-of-the-road player, he could have won anything several times over. Of course he did have spells with that flippy, flappy, wristy style when he would hole it from everywhere, anywhere. Ballesteros and O'Connor have a good deal in common. Christy was a much straighter hitter. Ballesteros is perhaps a mixture of O'Connor and Arnold Palmer, with all the charge of Palmer. But Palmer never could play the short shots that the two others do. Christy's was the real caddie's style, opening the blade of the club to cut it up, bending it round and up and over trees exactly as Severiano can do. These fellows can virtually pitch a ball up in the air with a 3-iron – wonderful talent.

Of the players still active, we must start with Tony Jacklin. How to categorize Jacklin is a problem. He is unique. He held the Open Championship and the US Open Championship at the same time, a singular achievement for a British player, and whatever else he does or does not do, whatever is done to him, for the rest of his life they can't take that away from him. In those golden days, as we turned into the seventies, he had a lovely rhythm, like a powerful car accelerating smoothly away, most striking when he won the championship at Royal Lytham in 1969. In recent years his swing has become a shade quicker, particularly on pitch shots, and those little thirty-yarders, over a bunker, perhaps from a tight lie. The knees go a little and he looks a shade ungainly by comparison with times past.

I've always been a great supporter of his, although he may not have known it. Tony as a youngster was a touch cocky and bumptious, even a know-all. Some people didn't like him then, don't like him now, so perhaps he hasn't changed. What I did like about Jacklin was that he so obviously enjoyed his success. Some of his moves were very theatrical, the Rolls-Royce car, the mansion in the country. There was a good deal of criticism of the McCormack organization, which managed his affairs, but it is very difficult to stop someone buying things and spending money when the money is there. The McCormack people are very hard-nosed and I am sure they pointed out Tony's extravagancies, but the purchase of 'Langley', the huge mansion in the Cotswolds, may have been simply an ego-trip on his part. The cost of the whole operation – he filled the place with thousands of pounds worth of Spanish furniture – is said to have run to around £250,000. It was subsequently divided into lots and sold, and I daresay he lost money on it.

Now he seems settled and well-established in Jersey. He has been immensely lucky with Vivienne, his wife. I must say that when the money is flowing in, when there are the complimentary limousines, the first-class air tickets, suites at The Dorchester, exhibitions and appearances in exotic places, showers of household goods, the cashmeres, the perfumes, the jewellery – this is sometimes hard to handle. Both of them are from humble backgrounds and I think Vivienne probably coped with the success better than he did, and so helped him along. He had a dark spell in the seventies, but I think he has worked his way through that and may now be moving on to other things. I think he could be very successful in television, for example. What has impressed me most about Tony is that he did enjoy his wealth and success. Of his golden years, the 'worst' was said to have grossed him £250,000 and there is no doubt that he dished out thousands on this and that. But he has never cried over it. He learned a lot about life. We were talking about this whole thing at Wentworth, during the 1980 Suntory World Match Play, and he really amused me by saying, 'You know, it won't be long before I am saying I was born ten years too soon!'

In contrast to the sometimes theatrical Jacklin, Neil

Coles is the quiet plodder, the studious professor, the balding one with the wispy hair, the man of no words – not true, absolutely not true. Here is a perfect example of the totally false public image. Coles is a singular man. He is rather quiet, rather modest, but he also happens to be a big winner in European golf, with £250,000 in official prize money from twenty tournament years and a good thirty tournament wins behind him. He has a very clear idea of what he wants from life, and sets about getting it without trampling on anyone in the process. The only way the name Coles will ever appear in the newspapers will be concerning how Neil plays golf, which he loves and at which he is an artist in pacing himself, his shots, his game – and that is why he has gone on so long. Contrary to the general belief, Coles has a neat sense of humour, and one distinction. He was probably the first British player to be a tournament golfer only, with no club professional responsibilities, as my lot had. He decided at the beginning that he wanted to be a tournament player only, that he could exist on his tournament prize-money and he has gone ahead and done just that, creating a shining example for all the contemporary players in the process.

I have but one criticism of Coles. He declined to captain the British team against Europe in the Hennessy Cup matches at Sunningdale in 1980, and said he did not want to captain any international side on the grounds that he would not know how to talk forcibly to his team. I think that is rather sad. Coles is vastly experienced in international golf, and is much respected by all the players. I think he owed it to the game to be captain, and I think he dodged a responsibility there.

So many of the modern tournament players no longer have any significant connection with golf clubs. They played endorsed by hotels, insurance companies, even engineering companies. Part of the joy of the job, in growing through into manhood as I did, was in having to go

back to the club and face them when you had done a pair of
82s and failed to qualify. There would be the old club stiffs
saying, 'What went wrong with you? Buggering about, I
suppose?' Likewise if you had done well, there would be
the over-fulsome pats on the back. Very educational. But
the club was a base, it was roots, it was what we were
brought up with. Few of the young players have experienced this. I cannot imagine where they practise when
they are not out on the road. Perhaps they each know a
benevolent local club which lets them hack about on a
practice ground.

Let us now consider Brian Barnes, a very interesting
man. I was vastly amused by his remark about how
appalled he had been by the happenings during the 1979
Ryder Cup team's visit to the Greenbrier. Well, Brian has
been in a few scrapes in his time – putting back-handed,
one-handed four or five times, tossing a tee box into the
bushes, and a few others. He has committed plenty of
indiscretions in his time, but I must say has never done
anything to my knowledge when he has been representing
his country in a Ryder Cup match. He has not always been a
man to think before he spoke, and this is precisely what
happened at the English Classic at the Belfry in 1979. He
was quite outspoken about the condition of the course,
saying it would not be ready for tournament play for in
effect several centuries, and of course he said this to the
golfing journalists and it was all widely publicized. Almost
immediately golf bookings at the Belfry dropped by fifty
per cent with people calling in to cancel reservations.

This was quite terrifying to the Belfry Hotel people and
is another illustration of how professionals must be made
aware of their responsibilities to sponsors, host clubs and to
the public. Without them, professional golf does not exist
and the players' organization must show more control over
this. Above all there should be a greater awareness by the
professionals that golf does not owe them a living. Nobody

owes anyone a living. They should all look, and think a little, before they open their mouths, think perhaps of how people like Neil Coles get through life very nicely.

Brian Barnes has had a very successful career. I think in a way he has made the most of his talents, because he seems to be lacking in rhythm and poise, just lumbers along. The backswing is almost too slow, too deliberate, the downswing a now-familiar shoulder heave. Brian in fact is a very good player who could see them all off quite comfortably but for one basic shortcoming – he does not have enough respect for the game of golf.

The kind of thing you can imagine him saying would be at a match play championship. The chairman of the sponsoring company has been talked into sponsoring the event by his PR whiz-kids. Brian wins. Picture the scene at the prize-giving. The chairman, handing over the cup, says, 'Congratulations, Mr Barnes, what do you think of our championship, do you like match play?' 'No,' says Brian Barnes, 'I'd rather be fishing.' So the chairman goes back to his PR whiz-kids and says, 'What the hell is this? What are we doing in this kind of sponsorship? I don't need this kind of thing – forget it.' And we have lost a sponsor.

All this is not too exaggerated. It represents a simple lack of proper thinking on the part of our players. You see it so often in their scoring at the Open Championship. They'll start with a 69, then score 78 and just make the cut. Then it will be 71 and 68, and all the talk will be if only they had not had that bad round, that one bad round. But players who are going to win the Open just *don't* have the one bad round. I can talk from experience for I have done a bit of that myself. And it's all *fear*, it's not bravado, because they are really not all that good. You see it in cricket, too. This young boy David Gower looks a beautiful player, but he is careless, he has to knuckle down and concentrate. Players have to work hard and do their best on *every* shot. So often it is not super shots, majestic shots which win champion-ships, it is the absence of stupid shots.

I know quite a bit about Brian Barnes from people who taught him at Millfield or who played golf with him in his younger days, and I have some interesting letters, delightful letters, sharp letters from his father Tom, who lives down at Burnham. Brian has great power, and a lot of talent. I used to think his nerve was suspect, because his seemed to be the classic case of the one bad round, and a devil-may-care attitude. Yet he steps out and beats Jack Nicklaus twice in one day in a Ryder Cup match. And you can be sure that Nicklaus was trying – he tries his hardest every time he plays. And Barnes slaughtered Johnny Miller in a Double Diamond even at Gleneagles when Miller was on top of the world. You would think these things would spur Brian on, but he has never really threatened any of the major championships.

Perhaps there is a bit of the bully in there. When Brian is on top, everything is fine. When he is down, he'd rather go fishing. Perhaps it is all a matter of nerves, or machismo, or ego-polishing. Golf at his level is a very, very demanding game. Perhaps it is all just his peculiar nervous release. As I say, he could see them all off if he had a little more respect for the game.

Barnes and Bernard Gallacher, ageing not in years but in experience, have been a fine partnership in Ryder Cup play, and they would always be in my team. Bernard tries all the way, from the word go. In the team that went to America in 1979, these two were giants. Gallacher in particular was magnificent, kept the whole pot boiling and was quite superb in his contribution to the team. Now he is quite rightly one of our most respected players, well settled in at Wentworth with the sensible, attractive Lesley to help him.

Peter Oosterhuis – now there is a man who has really made the most of his talents, and the greatest of his talents has been temperament. Oosterhuis inside Jacklin's technique, inside almost anyone else's, would have been a worldbeater. If I had had the Oosterhuis temperament, I would have been disappointed not to have won ten major championships, because I could always hit the ball. Peter also has a lovely short game, which I never did, and above all that enviable slice of determination. When he does get a little cross with himself, he is still in control. And he has an armoury of the most fantastic recovery shots. In one round in South Africa, he made eight birdies from the rough. I just wish he had been a slightly better player, and I just wish he had had more success in America. Conversely, in many ways I wish he would come back to Europe and do very well here again. It would be exciting to see him week after week going after Ballesteros, Jacklin, Barnes and Lyle.

Brian Huggett and Maurice Bembridge often appear to me to be two of a kind, rather the barrack-room lawyer type. Huggett, small in stature, stocky and strong, a fiery competitor, has in fact seldom stood up to be counted, and when he did, perhaps didn't choose his ground wisely. I am thinking specifically of the Ryder Cup match at Lytham in 1977, when he captained our team and was a shade too outspoken about Tony Jacklin and others in the team. I didn't think that helped the cause all that much – no doubt his fierce patriotism and Welshness were getting out of hand.

Maurice Bembridge has always been better than the average player, but got to a stage in the seventies when he could not hit the ball at all and had no idea of what he was doing. In the opinion of most of his direct contemporaries, he seems to have been rather a moaner; perhaps with Maurice the glass was always half empty rather than half full, the classic description of the pessimist rather than the optimist. Much of his attitude came from the conviction that playing conditions here were rather prehistoric – old-fashioned courses, ill-prepared courses, the game held back by the rather non-professional attitude of administrators and prompters. He always suggested that things in America were better, although he never did what Oosterhuis did, and go out and join them. Yet he did work through his bad patch and in 1979 romped off with the Benson and Hedges event. He used to play extensively in the Far East and Australia, and now floats freely around the world with his pretty American wife, Suzie. Perhaps he just enjoys warm weather.

Tommy Horton I have always seen as the very best type of professional golfer, a latter-day Bernard Hunt. He is always immaculately turned out, never likely to say stupid or compromising things to sponsors, always has a strong feeling for what you might call the dignity of the game, and takes a very active interest in all the affairs of the European Tournament Players Division of the PGA. He seems perfectly able to combine a very active tournament life with running his club, Royal Jersey, successfully, and is a very fine player, balancing his lack of power with careful positional play and precise shot-making, and on his best form he is a very good finisher. He has played very determinedly in Ryder Cup matches and, all told, I have a lot of time for Tom.

Malcolm Gregson I thought might have climbed a shade higher up the ladder. I played with him in World Cup matches in Mexico when he was a youngster, and thought he had a chance to be really good. Malcolm, I am sure, has had a thoroughly pleasant life in the game, but he might have climbed a couple more rungs.

Peter Butler, now out of tournament play and apparently contenting himself with a club job at the RAC, Epsom, his home area, was a prime example of a man who made the most of his talents. Not a very long hitter, he played much of his golf off the back foot, the ball usually blocked slightly from left to right, with a low, running flight. He was very straight. He would be in the Alliss team, in the UK, if conditions were right for him, and I could select the course.

Peter Mills was a very good tournament professional, and distinguished himself more than at any other time in the winning Ryder Cup team at Lindrick, when he disposed of the American captain, Jack Burke, in the singles. Peter rather slipped out of the game, went to the Channel Islands where he was in the wine business, and then in 1980 sought and was granted reinstatement as an amateur.

Several other players had short spells at the top, true meteors, people like Hugh Boyle, Alex Caygill, Lionel Platts, Ralph Moffitt. Some of them were no doubt content to move on to the life of a club professional. The going of Harry Bannerman I always thought was a loss to the game. He was cocky, cigar-smoking, rather larger than life, and he could play. Harry was sometimes as objectionable as Scots can be, and Hugh Lewis once said, 'Nothing wrong with Harry that a couple of 83s won't put right.' Sadly, because of a bad back, Harry had to leave the tournament scene.

What we are all inclined to overlook from time to time is that competitive tournament golf is a very, very rough game and when people turn forty, much of the glitter goes out of it. One striking exception to that rule would be Brian Waites, who insists on calling himself a club professional – indeed played in the club professional team against the Americans until the EPTD put the block on him in 1980, ruling that he was too much a tournament player. Certainly he has been sneaking out often enough each season to win a good five-figures in official prize money and a bit more from overseas events. In fact, in five or six weeks towards the end of the 1980 season, Brian tucked away a good £20,000 from half a dozen events. Yet he did not become a national figure until a few years ago, when he was already forty.

The newer breed? Well, I just don't know, there seems to be something odd about them. They don't seem able to smile easily. Nick Faldo, for example, had something of a meteoric rise, and apparently because interested in the game, and even learned it (!) from watching television. He had a good amateur career, then won the PGA Championship of 1978 at Royal Birkdale going away. Defending at St Andrews a year later, he had the Old Course by the throat but couldn't quite hold on. He always looks unhappy, miserable. He needs to change that, since he is a good-looking boy. James and Brown? I think I have probably said enough. There were positive signs through the 1980 season that Ken Brown was certainly making an effort.

Sandy Lyle looks to be a great prospect. I saw quite a bit of him when he was an amateur, when I thought he swung the club almost too slowly. His rhythm has speeded up a little since then. He has a good nerve, is a pleasant lad and appears to enjoy it all, but just needs to build a little more personality into his work if possible. What these young fellows must accept is that the professional game is not golf alone, it is show business. It can be said that no one needs personality if they play fantastically well. It is a moot point. Hogan said, and very good stuff if he ever did say it, 'My clubs speak for me.' But it makes all the difference if you can be very good *and* do it with a smile.

Peter Townsend I think might have made more of his talents, which are considerable, and may still do so. He has won in Europe, South America, the West Indies, Australia, Morocco, but only once in the UK. He has a perfectly sound golf game, is attractive in personality – lots of bonus points, really, and he does smile. This is where Michael King scores in a quite sensational way, but God is he nervous – he'll fall apart at the seams one day if he doesn't calm down. If he could just relax a little, be a little steadier, he really would be a winner. He has lots of plusses going for him – tall, very good-looking, dazzling smile, man-about-town image of pretty ladies and gran turismo cars, and the rather posh background of Sunningdale and the City. If Michael gets a few more wins behind him, he will find the game will be very kind to him. His win in the Tournament Players' Championship at Moor Park in 1979 brought a breath of fresh air to the tournament scene. The game needs his type badly.

Of the very newest recruits, who will get to the top? That really puts us into the guessing game. Illness, injury, disenchantment, lack of real ability, bad luck – all these things can affect young men in their careers. Perhaps Brian Marchbank has as good a chance as any. The pedigree is right – father is the long-serving professional at Gleneagles Hotel and the boy has been brought up in a wholly golfing environment. Brian had an outstanding career as a boy and youth golfer and played very well in his Walker Cup match. He turned professional in August 1979, and had an encouraging first year in 1980 without quite getting into the top sixty at the end of the season. He chased Bernard Gallacher hard in the John Haig Tournament Players' Championship at Moortown, Leeds, in September, before blowing up in the last round. When he learns a few more tricks of the professional trade, we shall hear from him.

Mark McCormack

Mark Hume McCormack is an American lawyer, educated at William and Mary College and the Yale Law School. He is around my own age, married with three children, and lives comfortably in one of the better suburbs of Cleveland, Ohio. Please now be assured that all of that is bottom-line stuff as far as McCormack is concerned, because he also happens to be almost certainly the single most influential man in professional sport in the entire world, Kerry Packer and the Hunt family of Dallas not excluded.

Mark played for his college golf team and in a match against Wake Forest met a young fellow by the name of Arnold Palmer. When McCormack had qualified, he joined the Cleveland law firm of Arter, Hadden, Wykoff and Van Duzer, one of the most successful and conservative in the state of Ohio. He was a good enough golfer to compete in both US Amateur and Open Championships, and maintained his interest in the game by helping to arrange exhibitions, on a casual basis, for such young professionals as Dow Finsterwald and Palmer, in the fifties. Palmer had won the US Amateur Championship in 1954 and turned professional, promptly winning the Canadian Open in 1955. More and more he needed McCormack's help in making the arrangements, and by the time he won his first US Masters title in 1958, he had asked Mark to handle all his business affairs. Next to enlist with McCormack was Gary Player, who had already won the Open Championship of 1959. Within a few months of joining Mark, he won the 1961 Masters. In the same year, after an outstanding career as an amateur, Jack Nicklaus was contemplating turning professional, and he asked McCormack for his advice. Mark told him, 'Come with me and you will certainly make $100,000 in Year One.' Nicklaus did, in December 1961, and six months later had won the US Open Championship. Thus Mark was manager of what became 'The Big Three' of golf, the men who dominated the world game through the sixties and into the seventies, all of whom were enriched beyond anybody's wildest dreams by the shrewd dealing of Mark McCormack.

McCormack was lucky, of course, to have such clients in golf. But what his critics persistently overlook is that he started from nothing, and he has done it all himself. Now his empire includes a dozen offices around the world, homes and apartments in Cleveland, New York, London, Florida and I don't know where else, and hundreds of people working directly or indirectly for him. He told me a good half-dozen years ago that it cost him, then, $1 million just to open the doors of his various offices each year before he took in one dollar in fees and earnings. And his empire has extended beyond golf, beyond sport. His influence is immensely strong in television and he acts in this respect for instance for the Royal and Ancient Golf Club of St Andrews, the All-England Club for Wimbledon, the US Tennis Association, the International Ski Federation, and many other organizations. His Trans World International, the company which handles all film and television work, has made movies and created sports events specifically for television, such as the *Superstars* series. His management embraces financial and investment advice for his clients, who now include, for example, in addition to Palmer, Player, Jacklin, Nancy Lopez and many other golfers, other stars such as Jackie Stewart, Bjorn Borg, Virginia Wade, Jean-Claude Killy, Angela Rippon, Michael Parkinson and in some areas Muhammad Ali. And there are various American sports people, in American football, baseball and basketball, of whom I simply have not heard.

I suppose I've known Mark for some eighteen years, though for most of them rather casually. Before we talked formally in the autumn of 1978, when we arranged that he should act for me in certain areas, I imagine I put more work his way than he did mine. People would come to me and say that they wanted a golf movie made, and where did they start. Then as now there were two production companies pre-eminent in the field – Creative Film Makers Ltd run by Michael Seligman, and Trans World International, run by Phil Pilley, in his time a BBC television sports producer. I had done work for both, liked them both, and I always gave people both names and said, 'See them, talk to them, and make up your own mind.'

In autumn 1978, around the time of the World Match Play Championship at Wentworth, and after I had put in a few years of covering American events on television, I had a conversation with Mark in which he said he had heard my work on the US Open, thought it was very good and he could tell me that the top brass of the US Golf Association, the then-president Sandy Tatum and the executives P. J. Boatright and Frank Hannegan, also liked it. Mark said, 'You really ought to be getting a contract there.' Then he said, 'When does your BBC contract run out?' I told him 1 January 1979. He said rather casually, 'If you'd like me to take a look at it for you, I'd be only too pleased.' He did, and in time set up a new contract with the BBC, and with ABC, the terms of which, in each case, were mind-boggling. This is not to say I became an instant millionaire. There seems to be a public notion abroad that everyone who appears on television is awash in money. 'Tain't so, or it certainly isn't in my case. Only now is a better flow of compensation working its way through, and I hope it will continue. McCormack probably knew a good deal more of the background to all this than he cared to reveal to me at the time. It seemed that ITV were keen to take me from the BBC. And ABC in America, nudged no doubt by these USGA officials, wanted me on contract. ABC had a very strong relationship with the USGA which they were anxious to foster. They had rights to all the USGA events, indeed to all the major world events, with the exception of the US Masters, which was 'owned' by CBS. They were planning to drop out of covering the weekly run-of-the-mill professional tournaments in favour of the big international championships, and they were well aware that Dean Beman, Commissioner of the PGA Tour, which controls these events, was planning to ask for greatly increased television fees. ABC were quite happy to back out of his events and leave them to their rivals at CBS and NBC, the other big American networks. McCormack was therefore able to go into action on my behalf with quite a bit of firepower.

In fact the entire concept of the series *Around with Alliss* emerged from Mark's attempts to extract more money for me from the BBC. To justify what he asked for, the BBC were obviously casting around for additional ways to use me, for another Alliss 'vehicle', and the concept came eventually from Bob Abrahams, a BBC sports producer who suggested that a programme, or series of programmes, which combined a bit of tuition, bit of play, bit of chat with a celebrity, at pretty places, would make sense. It did. The series was very successful.

One odd thing about Mark is that he has never given me the impression that he is hustling. Over the past few years, when we have had business meetings, he is never surrounded by masses of paper; never behind a huge desk; never smoking outsized cigars (he doesn't smoke); never playing the classic show business-type tycoon which he undoubtedly is. There is no yelling and screaming down the phone, although I daresay a ration of that goes on elsewhere in his offices. With me, he keeps it quiet and cool, and as often as not we'll be sitting in armchairs, and the whole thing is softly, softly. That may not apply with his staff. If he has done a new deal for me, he'll talk round it for a while, keep it at arm's length, then perhaps say, almost as an afterthought, 'By the way, we got a fifty per cent increase on that – I think that's quite good under the circumstances, and on that other deal we discussed, I think it is going through, and that really will be pretty good.' In fact he has probably already clinched the thing. Then he'll say, 'Well, it's nice to see you, we'll keep in touch, I have to go.' And he's up, and off. And I'm outside on the pavement asking myself why the hell I drove all the way to London when it could have been done over the phone. But that isn't his style. I think he likes to be face to face with his clients, as often as possible.

For many people, McCormack seems to be a monster, an ogre, a ruthless businessman who will grind people into the dust just to make a deal. I have no experience of that, and I have tremendous faith in him. I believe he is hard, but I believe he is an ethical man, a man of integrity, a man who does not tell lies, which is a rare compliment. He has enormous influence throughout the world of sport, in television and with events, but I believe he is as fair to everyone as can be. Being a manager or agent with as many superstars as he has must be immensely difficult. The perfect situation for such a manager would be Colonel Parker with Elvis Presley, or Brian Epstein with The Beatles – just one 'property', and quite enough for any man to handle. I've seen something of the pitfalls which Mark must have faced. Let's take the Australian golf scene as an example, and the business of golf manufacturers' endorsements and contracts for his clients. If you tell the interested party that you have Gary Player, Arnold Palmer and Tony Jacklin, for example, and you can sell only two of these three, who is to be the odd man out? And what will he say when he learns about it? Or perhaps in New Zealand – do they want Bob Charles? Well, after all, he is a New Zealander, winner of the 1963 Open Championship, and he has won the Canadian Open, the Swiss Open and lots of other events. But perhaps no, he's a local boy, too local, we'd rather have Arnold Palmer. So how does Bob Charles feel, and what does he say to McCormack?

These are hypothetical, rather simplistic illustrations, and McCormack does not work that way. He always has a very clear picture before he goes into a meeting of just what the meeting should achieve, and how he is going to manipulate it, and he very seldom loses. He is quite masterful at controlling, even dominating a meeting, and he is very, very persuasive. But since jealousy is a fact of life, he must have had many such problems with his clients. He has had them for twenty years now, and I must say he has resolved them better than anyone else I could think of. Of course, no manager keeps clients forever, and the most famous of Mark's 'losses' must have been Jack Nicklaus, who decided he could do it better himself.

I remember Gary Player telling me once that, over the years, he had paid Mark an absolute fortune in commission, but he also said that the day he met McCormack was the most important single day in his life, in business terms, and that if he had to do it all over again, he would pay him double commission, even fifty per cent, quite happily and would never have left him. And, of course, McCormack's ventures with Arnold Palmer alone have made both men quite rich.

One could argue with some justice that he has too much power. You could say, as many players do, that if you are not a McCormack client, not in the McCormack 'school', you don't get a fair crack of the whip with invitation events, and spots on his many television shows. Possibly true. But Mark was there first, and created so many of these happenings, and his track record is enormous. His organization makes the occasional boob, and one of these I have always thought was when Tony Jacklin was allowed to buy his manor house in Gloucestershire for an enormous sum. Perhaps there was nothing they could do about it. Perhaps it was a Jacklin ego-trip. After all, at the time, the early seventies, the money was pouring in for Jacklin. So one wonders just how much influence Mark has on the personal life of his clients. There are rumblings and grumblings from other people, of course, like, for example, Hubert Green, who is not a McCormack client. He gets very sore from time to time at not getting the recognition and the invitations he thinks he deserves. After all, he will argue, he has won the US Open Championship and made mountains of money in tournaments with his rather unorthodox style. The sheer existence of the McCormack empire is bound to get through to these fellows after a while.

Mark lives in comfortable style quite close to his club, the Cleveland Country Club, which I visited during the US PGA Championship of 1979. His family I think has drifted a bit, two sons and a daughter, Breck, Todd and Leslie. For one thing, they are growing up, with the boys getting into their twenties and Leslie very much a teenager; and for another, Mark's lifestyle of constant international travel perhaps makes it inevitable. I remember his wife Nancy saying something which I thought was rather touching. I met her when she had changed her hairstyle, and I went over, gave her a big kiss, and said, 'Nancy, how nice to see you, you're looking well, the hair is sensational,' and all that jazz, and she looked at me with those kind but rather tired eyes, and said, 'Oh, it's so nice to be recognized for myself.' Based in Cleveland, I would guess that Mark is in New York twice a month, Los Angeles once a month, London half a dozen times a year, then there would be trips to Australia, Japan, and from time to time to Europe, and possibly South America in the last few years.

About five years ago he collapsed in the street in London, and was swept off to hospital as an emergency case. The diagnosis was a blood clot that was exerting pressure on his brain, and he had surgery which I am sure was both sophisticated and, for him, scary. He was in a National Health hospital in Maida Vale for many weeks, and to his credit he has never stopped talking about, and acknowledging, the marvellous and totally free care that he got there. I daresay a similar experience in his own country might have cost him $25,000 or more.

I think he enjoys Britain, certainly Scotland, since he brings the family over every summer for several weeks at Gleneagles or Turnberry, when I am sure he could afford any swank resort in the world. He never looks particularly tanned or particularly well. Standing a good bit above six feet, he has a rather sloppy, scuffling, unathletic walk, but he works at his general health and fitness, and has a mind that can shred you. He is quite an extraordinary drinker, that is, he does not drink in any ordinary way. Most people have a favourite tipple to which they stick, but Mark drinks everything, in an experimental way I hasten to add, when he is in an expansive mood. I've been with him in Hawaii, when he'd say we should try a Mai-Tai, then a Sunrise, then why not let's have a Banana Daiquiri? All this would have no effect on him. He is not a big drinker – I have never seen him drunk. He is a picker, and he'll do the same with food. If you are having something new, or he fancies it, he'll simply snatch a forkful from your plate and give you the verdict on it.

I've never seen him drive a car, don't even know if he can drive a car. I wouldn't know about his religion, and have no desire to find out. I wouldn't begin to know anything about his annual turnover or income, or his take-home money, and again I have no desire to find out. I must say, though, I would like to know the whole extent of his business and investment interests. I learned, early in 1980, when gold had rocketed to more than $700 an ounce, that Gary Player sometime earlier had gone in against a lot of solid advice, and bought gold heavily. The story was that Gary had sold at the right time, and 'made a million' on the deal. If Gary did, I am sure Mark would not have been far behind him.

Henry Longhurst

Henry Carpenter Longhurst, journalist, author, broadcaster, television commentator, sometime Member of Parliament, was a product of Charterhouse School and

Clare College, Cambridge. His family was successful in the retail trade, with department stores in Bedfordshire. He was born in 1909, and so essentially was a between-the-wars man, brought up in the twenties and thirties in a prosperous and even privileged middle-class setting. These I believe were the basic factors in the forming of his character and personality, although I also believe he thought of himself as an Edwardian. Anyone who knew Longhurst over a period, and took a rather subjective, left-wing view of him might have dubbed him a fascist. He was certainly an Imperialist who would not have rejected a 'them and us' philosophy, because if in his time the British Empire was crumbling slightly, it certainly existed through Longhurst's formative years and he was to travel and enjoy vast areas of it throughout his life. And he was entirely convinced that in spite of all the villainy, in spite of the fact that for every pound we may have put in we took out one thousand, nevertheless he was persuaded that on balance we the British had been good for the rest of the world with our empire.

Longhurst as a young man was a good enough golfer to have won the German Amateur Championship of 1936, and finish second in the French Amateur a year later. The first of his very many glimpses of the United States came in the early thirties, when he captained a team of Cambridge undergraduates on a tour there. America made a tremendous impression on him and forever more he loved to visit the United States. He was a great communicator, working professionally all his life in the media of the written word and the spoken word in radio and, over the final two decades of his life, in television as a golf commentator. His greatest single talent was as a talker, a raconteur and after-dinner speaker, and, as the Scots would have it, a man who loved a 'blether'. The Scottish word contains a hint of criticism, but with Longhurst it was all good stuff. Like Somerset Maugham, he was a marvellous storyteller, if not

a teller of marvellous stories. His greatest single achievement, I suggest, was a weekly article of eight hundred
words or so for the *Sunday Times* which he sustained for
twenty-five years without missing one single issue. Anyone
involved in newspapers will recognize that as a massive
achievement. I came to know him very well only in the last
ten years of his life, and he became possibly my closest
friend. When I was active in tournament golf, I never did
get close to the higher echelons of golf writing, where
Longhurst was clearly placed, with the possible exception
of Leonard Crawley of the *Daily Telegraph*. My early days,
of course, were rather before the era of televised golf which
we now enjoy.

Crawley seemed to like the way I held the club and hit the
ball, and was always a great supporter – indeed he is
godfather to my first-born, Gary. I think if Leonard could
have awarded the Open Championship to people for
striking one particular shot, he'd have let me win at least
one for my 2-iron play, one such shot of mine, he wrote, '. . .
would have brought light to the eyes of Samson'. He'd
wander up to me and splutter and mumble and stroke his
ginger moustache and say 'Good boy, well done,' and be
off. I never in my life spoke to Bernard Darwin, of *The
Times*, who during a long life was considered to be perhaps
the outstanding golf writer. I saw him around, but he was
an old, old man then, and I never was able to speak with
him. Henry Longhurst was rather a mystical figure in those
days. Of course, these fellows, the writers for the 'quality'
papers, were laws unto themselves, with masses of space to
write in. They were not really required to mingle with
the players, and no doubt didn't much care to, and in fact
were not even obliged to report every professional event.
They'd be at the Open Championship, the Match Play
Championship, the Ryder Cup match, and not much else.

If Longhurst was a mystical, rather distant figure in my
tournament days, throughout the seventies we drew closer

and closer together and in the end, as I have said, I was to think of him as my closest single friend. I hope he thought that of me. Television brought us together, televised golf, which Longhurst had virtually started many years earlier, when the first broadcast amounted to Longhurst, a cameraman and a sound man standing beside a green at Moor Park. Television for me started modestly in the early sixties when Ray Lakeland, a BBC producer from Manchester now retired, asked me if I would like to go up the tower and just tell the viewers how the course was playing. I said, 'Sure, fine.' Henry Longhurst and Bill Cox were the regular commentators at that time, with John Jacobs and Ben Wright on hand. Jacobs eventually became established in golf with ITV, while Ben Wright has made his name in the United States as a CBS commentator. I did two or three programmes without payment, then Lakeland said they'd better put me on the payroll. It was to be £15 a go. I had heard that the BBC was not exactly effusive in the matter of fees, but that seemed to suit me well enough. Longhurst at this time was rather distant – courteous, but not a man to come up and throw his arms round your shoulders. He would appear in old tweeds, cap, green flak jacket padded with down or goose feathers or whatever, which all good huntin', shootin' and fishin' chaps would wear. He would appear without notes, sometimes with a copy of the *Daily Mail* or the *Daily Telegraph* – no doubt he thought the *Guardian* altogether too radical – and he would look at the front page, scan through the critics, then start on the crossword.

Time, and work, brought us closer together. Bill Cox seemed to drift out of the commentary picture, I drifted in more and more. Bill eventually vanished from the scene and how that happened I simply do not know. There were people to say I had pushed him out, but that is certainly not my recollection. I just don't know what happened between him and the BBC. Bill, an outgoing roly-poly figure, was a good tournament player in his day and had played in a Ryder Cup team, and as a commentator on television I thought he was all right, tremendously enthusiastic, occasionally rather breathless, and, like most good teachers of the game, possibly inclined to talk a shade too much about the technicalities, the swing and so on. Thus Longhurst and I worked more and more closely together, and in fact found an increasing amount of work coming along from the US television networks.

I was to see the anguish and the bravery of the man when his son and his son-in-law were both killed in tragic accidents. His son-in-law died in the Australian bush. Apparently his car broke down, and he committed the cardinal error of leaving it, of not staying with it. He was a big, strong man, but the heat was so intense that he walked only five or six miles along the road before he collapsed and died – and then was only some five hundred yards from a sheep station and safety. Longhurst was quite distraught about this, because he worshipped his daughter Susan, a lovely girl, and he was proud of the fact that Susan and her husband were so close and so happy. Within the same twelve months his son Oliver, who was in the hotel management business, was killed in an air crash in Swaziland. I hope my presence and friendship were of some comfort to him. He was then in his sixties, and perhaps he was beginning to feel the stresses and strains of a life he had lived very fully. No one could have accused Longhurst of taking over-much care of his body. He was fond of a very regular sip. The Americans dubbed him Henry 'Don't mind if I do' Longhurst, or 'Henry Longthirst'. Possibly around the same time came the advent of the cancer which in the end was to devour him. But, of course, he struggled on.

When he died Henry left his wife, Claudine, and his daughter Susan. Claudine is a delightful lady, half-French I think, long-suffering maybe, but artistic, religious, a WVS enthusiast, a very good landscape painter and creator of the most beautiful Christmas cards from pressed flowers. Susan has never re-married – perhaps she is still in love with the memory of her husband.

Henry was godfather to Simon, our youngest, his present a silver tankard inscribed 'To S.P.G.A. from H.L.'. Longhurst, Cliff Michelmore, Bruce Forsyth, Colonel Tinker Jackson and Mrs Kate Alvin were the godparents. Longhurst came to stay with us in Leeds, the night before the christening. Henry was slightly perturbed by the whole thing, and on the morning of the day, he said, 'I'm not too sure I should be doing this job. Religious instruction is not my strong point, and I am not sure I can lead your son along the true paths of righteousness.' He was really quite concerned. He didn't like the business of going to church – felt a touch uncomfortable there.

I had become known as his 'minder', the travelling companion who made the arrangements and got things done. I had been joining him on trips to America, where we worked for ABC, and had covered the US Open for the BBC and so on. Longhurst had been in the extraordinary situation of working for both ABC and CBS. Such a luxury can no longer happen. If you are any good, one network wants you on an exclusive contract. Longhurst brought something new to US TV commentary – fresh terminology, phraseology, charm, the accent, and silence – and they loved him for it. They loved his voice, his phrasing, his enunciation, and what really amazed them was that Henry never seemed really prepared. But he always was, in his fashion.

They tell the story of Henry up the tower at the 16th green of the Augusta National course, at the Masters, a few seconds before the programme went on the air. The director was making his last-minute check around all the commentators, or announcers as the Americans call them, and he spoke to each in turn at their various positions around the course. He called Longhurst, 'Henry, are you there?' Silence. Again, 'Henry, are you there?' Silence. The seconds were ticking past, air time was approaching. 'Henry, Henry, for Chrissake are you there?' Silence. At last, at the very last moment, came the voice, 'Yes, I just had to go down to get my shoes.' There was a brief but total silence from everyone listening. Go down from the tower? For shoes? Then it was red light, on the air, the show under way. No one ever discovered why he had 'had to go down' for his shoes. Perhaps no one ever asked him.

The Americans, of course, had masses of statistics to hand, pen portraits of the players, dressing-room interviews done before tee-off, anecdotes, and what they called 'colour', and at the drop of a hat could rattle out that so-and-so was married, with three children, had won the Pensacola Open last year and to date had won $110,397 this year. Henry kept away from all that, left it to the others, made room for it all, so that the end product, when all the pieces of the voice jigsaw had dropped into place, was well balanced and varied and integrated. They were amazed that he was so easy and relaxed and professional.

This is not to say that he did not make mistakes. Towards the end, if he wasn't careful, he could make mistakes of omission, and I saw it as part of my job to keep a check on this. He might miss the fact that, at St Andrews, for example, the wind had turned right round so that the big hitters, instead of taking a 4-wood off the tee then a 9-iron, would be thrashing away with a driver, hard as they could, and hoping to get over the burn with, say, a 5-iron. Such things occasionally slipped past him. They slipped past him only because at St Andrews we would probably be staying at the Old Course Hotel, with the television commentary box on the roof, so that in fact we scarcely went out of the building. And I speak of a time when he was getting along in years, when his health was failing and he would virtually be going from his bedroom to go to work and not setting foot outside at all. In such circumstances, mistakes could easily be made. But he did have such a remarkable turn of phrase and sense of the history of the game that one could listen all day long. I learned a great deal from him, not only about television and commentary, but about the economy of words.

He was the one who encouraged me most with my writing, over the final ten or twelve years. I had a column in *Golf International*, a Mark McCormack magazine. Longhurst wasn't just being polite – he didn't have to be – but he encouraged me. I think he enjoyed my sense of the ridiculous. He wasn't concerned that my spelling was about 12 handicap. He did like crisp writing, and he taught me the value of being able to write a newsy, interesting, sometimes controversial piece in less than eight hundred words. He once told me that he had never written anything more than nine hundred words for the *Sunday Times*, in all his unbroken years there.

Henry lived in a pair of old windmills, Clayton Windmills, Hassocks, Sussex, on the South Downs a few miles north of Brighton. The windmills, can you guess, were called 'Jack' and 'Jill', and I believe they were protected buildings. In any event, Henry always seemed to be in a state of benevolent feud with one local authority or another over the buildings. He did add a modern wing to them at one point, and lived comfortably. Longhurst loved the windmills, enjoyed immensely sitting out there on his balcony on a lovely day, with views over the beautiful mature Sussex countryside. It was a very romantic setting. But the whole place must have been hell to live in – no mains water, a private water supply from a little pump. When it snowed, which will happen more often than the Brighton brochures might mention, he had to negotiate a drive some three hundred yards long, up from the public highway. I remember him telling me that he had once left his revered old soft-top Mustang car at the bottom of the hill one snowy night, and walked home up the drive. When he got back next day, some yobbos had slashed the canvas roof, and let the snow in. This sort of thing distressed us both, infuriated us, but Longhurst had experienced it all. One of his boasts was that throughout his life he had been able to meet all sorts, rich and poor, high and low, without ever feeling uncomfortable. That was perhaps his idea of being a democrat. In the bigger windmill, 'Jack', he had the whole of a large circular floor, which I believe had once been the grain store, as his office. Lots of books and papers there, a very old desk, with a big laundry basket beside it. It was a lived-in place, nothing chi-chi, clutter all around. In the laundry basket were all his past columns for the *Sunday Times*, all written in longhand, all on foolscap, going back months and years. I wonder what happened to them – probably taken away and burned.

Henry had rather a distinctive sense of humour, which was sometimes droll, sometimes dry, whimsical, even bizarre, but it was always manifest in stories, and in the telling of stories, rather than in jokes or one-line 'wisecracks'. The man was quite simply a marvellous story-teller. He was intensely patriotic in the sense that he took a very deep delight in Britain, in the society which we have here, in the fact that it is a rich and sophisticated society, with so many variations of mood, manners, speech and culture compressed into these little islands. He loved the regional flavours of our land, he loved our institutions, like British Rail, the Post Office, the Law, the way we govern ourselves, the heckling at elections, the existence of Hyde Park's Speakers' Corner, the fact that our institutions do have the merit of working, with their unspoken codes of morality and in spite of their shortcomings. He took great delight in the paradoxes which these things throw up and much of his humorous story-telling emerged from these paradoxes. He was convinced without the slightest doubt that the British had been good for the world, and I think that in some strange way he found this reflected in golf,

saying of his endless travels that no country in the world
had such a variety of golfing experience and pleasures
encompassed in such a convenient space as the British
Isles.

For all his vast experience as a commentator, Longhurst
always maintained a somewhat arm's-length relationship
with television. He knew nothing of the mechanics of
the thing, the engineering (indeed he had no reason to),
but although he never let it show, he was always as
nervous as the next man and had a very leery attitude to
making mistakes, mispronouncing names, and committing
Spoonerisms. The prospect of Hunt and Coles being
drawn together, playing together, and having to be
mentioned in his commentary, always struck a good deal of
fear into him! Although Longhurst was well aware of all
such perils in the game, nevertheless he enjoyed all the
classic muffs and hazards. As when Judith Chalmers,
finishing off a Fanny Cradock cookery programme in
which Fanny had been making doughnuts, said 'I hope you
enjoyed the programme, and may all your doughnuts turn
out like Fanny's.' Or when Alan Weeks, reporting a world
speedway championship from Cracow, said, 'And here
round the last bend comes Ove Fundin, fighting his
bucking machine.' 'Oh dear,' said Longhurst, 'takes a very
brave man to risk words like that in a crisis.'

Henry Longhurst's mother, clearly a remarkable lady,
lived to a great age, well into her nineties. Henry delighted
in telling the story of his mother and 'the moon'. It referred
to the first landing of American astronauts on the moon,
and Longhurst painted a lovely picture of the whole world
being agog as they went closer and closer, wondering if they
would make it, wondering if they would find the moon
covered in diamonds or green cheese, or would there be
little creatures running around, and these brave men
conquering the unknown just like Captain Kirk and the
starship Enterprise, and similar fantasies galore. And

eventually, with everyone glued to their television sets, they landed and Neil Armstrong stepped down and said the immortal words: 'One small step for man, one giant step for mankind.' Now Henry rushed into his mother's room, glass in hand, quite overcome, and shouted, 'Mother, they've landed, they've landed, they've done it.' And the old lady, in her nineties, looked at him coldly and said, 'They never ought to have gone up there, they had no business going up there!'

Such contrariness delighted Henry. Often his stories had little merit in them, but were enlivened simply in the telling. Once a bunch of us were sitting around when the Birthday Honours were announced, and there was the usual chatter: 'Oh so-and-so's got an MBE, did you see that whatsisname got a knighthood?' Longhurst was eating a chocolate digestive biscuit at the time, and he turned and said, when it was announced that someone in show business had been knighted, 'I don't know about him, but the chap who invented these biscuits certainly should have got a knighthood.'

When I started doing commentaries in America, he couldn't quite believe that they would want him to stay with me and join in, that there would be two 'Brits' on the same broadcast. In fact ABC had quite a few letters from viewers wanting to know why they had all these 'foreign' commentators. The expense of getting us over there was quite frightening. We had first-class air tickets, we were met everywhere – Chicago, New York, Los Angeles, Atlanta – by a young student, or a young man starting his career as a junior with ABC, and whisked off to our hotel. There would be the usual magnificent double room for each of us, and, say what you like, Longhurst got it right when he said that these American hotels were 'the most magnificent transit camps in the world'. They had huge beds, a television set with eighteen channels to choose from – though usually with inferior reception, but never mind, it

Superstars in moments of glory

Ben Hogan, Canada Cup,
Wentworth, 1956 (*Action Photos*)

Jack Nicklaus, St Andrews, 1978
(*Syndication International*)

Arnold Palmer, still winning in
1980 (*Peter Dazeley*)

Gary Player, Lytham Open, 1974
(*Syndication International*)

Above left
Mark McCormack, the guru of golf *(IMG)*

Above Refreshments with Henry Longhurst at Wentworth and *(left)* cartoonist Roy Ullyett's tribute *(Peter Alliss)*

The sun didn't always shine, even for Severiano Ballesteros, Jimmy Tarbuck, Lee Trevino and Bobby Charlton (*Ian Joy*)

Not the old Penfold man but Ronnie Corbett in disguise (*Ian Joy*)

Dick Martin of *Laugh-In* and the incomparable Bing Crosby (*Ian Joy*)

Perhaps my favourite
picture with father
Percy (*R. Saidman*)

With son Gary
(*Keith Hailey*)

was all there. Some of it was glittering rubbish, of course, which is a matter of opinion, but it was all there – instant hot water, baths and showers, multitudes of towels and tissues, everything sanitized, snappy room service, everything you needed. The coffee shop would be open at all hours, and if the 'Chef's Salad' wasn't all that great it didn't matter. To us the whole thing was always magical, and we would scamper around like small boys, trying everything, poking fingers everywhere; we couldn't quite believe that 'they' would be paying for everything. Our expenses often came to more than our fees. In the early days, we would be getting a couple of thousand dollars a trip, and our expenses were certainly at least the same, and it was quite staggering to think that it made sense for them to pay out that kind of money. But no doubt there was a place for it in their budgets, carefully calculated. It was no charity.

One of Longhurst's most famous and successful capers involved Concorde. It had not been flying in regular service for too long when Henry said, 'We simply must try to get on Concorde – but we can't charge them – Concorde is ten per cent more than the first-class fare.' So the plan became that we might go over on Concorde, come back tourist and equalize the fares, so that ABC would not suspect we had been overstepping the mark. This was for a trip to Washington, for a US PGA Championship. Henry unearthed an old chum working for British Airways, who said he would Telex and ask them to check what the reservations were like for coming back and whether there might be a chance of being up-graded to first class. We had given little thought to the return journey – we were going Concorde! This caper, I felt, underlined the lingering undergraduate streak in Henry.

In Concorde, we sat up in the front seats close by the machometer. There I was with the old boy, the great man who had always believed in trying everything at least once –

he'd been down in a diving suit in Shatt-al-Arab in the Gulf, flown over the Rockies in a helicopter, gone down the Cresta Run, shot a stag, flown all the way from London to Hong Kong before jet aircraft, on an inaugural flight, had been involved in the creation of the Killarney golf course with the rather preposterous Viscount Castlerosse, and there he was in the faster-than-the-speed-of-sound aeroplane. Like a couple of schoolboys we waited for Concorde to rush away, and rush away it did. Oh, what excitement! We had a couple of drinks before lunch, a very, very nice lunch – Dom Perignon champagne and a 1963 claret – and suddenly it was 'A liqueur, sir?' Well, why not, perhaps some Drambuie, which happens to be my favourite – it crucifies me, but I do love it so. Then it was 'Another liqueur, some more coffee, Mr Longhurst, Mr Alliss?' Then 'Yes, sir, we'll be landing in twelve minutes.' It was scarcely credible. We had watched the machometer going through the speed of sound, then twice the speed of sound, and we could not believe we had arrived. We went to the hotel, put our feet up for a couple of hours, went to the golf course, came back, feet up again, met at about seven-thirty. Henry had a couple of his nice Beefeater martinis – he did enjoy these – then dinner with his adored lamb chops; he really did worship American lamb chops with the crispy skin. Bed by nine-thirty, which with the time change was 2.30 a.m. in London, late enough, but for the first time in my life I woke next morning without suffering jet lag in the slightest.

The irony of all this was that the tournament was washed out. We had gone over for Saturday and Sunday only, we were to broadcast Sunday's play only, and the entire day was rained off. We both had other commitments and had to be back Monday. ABC gave us special dispensation to do that. So there it was. I was the only person to get 'on the air'. I managed to say something live, only around fifty words before it was stopped, and Henry said precisely nothing. We had gone over on Concorde, all expenses paid, and had done virtually no work, and now were on our way home. Henry found that vastly amusing. And when we got to Kennedy Airport in New York, the powers-that-be there had followed the washed-out golf on television, felt sorry for us, and since the plane leaving shortly was virtually empty, asked if we would mind moving up to first class. Would we mind! (I should say that while this was an international airline, it was not British Airways.) So home we came in style, and the giggling schoolboys took over. On top of Concorde and the return trip home in first class, Longhurst, when he had done his sums, reckoned we had made a profit of £37.40 on the trip. His delight and joy knew no bounds. He thought this hilariously funny.

So we continued to go to and fro across the Atlantic, more than once every year, for a variety of chores, covering the great championships for television. David Foster, the chief executive of Colgate-Palmolive, was especially generous to Longhurst and Alliss, and to very many other people around the world. This ought to be acknowledged. Foster is a remarkable man. He was born in England of American parents, when his father came over just after World War I to start the Colgate company in the UK. He went to school and university here, served with distinction and became a lieutenant-commander in the Fleet Air Arm in World War II, and in time became the overlord of Colgate. As men of vision go, in the business of professional sports promotion, Foster had no peer. He put Colgate into golf and tennis, skiing and other sports, and I think it is true to say that every professional event which Colgate sponsored, in the US, UK, Europe, Australia, Far East, wherever, was televised. The rationale was that women bought all the Colgate products, including the men's toiletries range, for husbands, brothers, sons, boyfriends, and almost all of his promotions were in women's sports. When he resigned in 1979, the new regime at Colgate effectively took them out of sports promotion, which was a great loss to professional sport everywhere.

Foster's hospitality was immense, but Longhurst, the wise man, always used to say that they could well afford it since the company was trading very successfully and the few dollars we cost them were lost in promotional and advertising budgets which ran into millions of dollars. At the same time, he would say that it was very easy for the likes of us, very privileged people, to be carried away by all that. The important thing was never to look upon it as a birthright, but to accept it graciously with the thought that it would not last forever, might never happen again, and when it was over, to have no regrets.

For me the transatlantic journeys go on, but I must say I have never become blasé about it. To this day it is still an enormous thrill for me to travel. I just cannot be doing with people who say, 'Oh God, what a bore, I have to go to America again.' For me it is still all an enormous adventure, another point I suppose I picked up from Henry Longhurst. He used to say that you should always go with your eyes open, look at the local architecture, the flora and fauna, listen to the people, try the food before you decide you don't like it, think, learn, observe, don't tell the people what they are doing wrong, look for the best of things, and enjoy them. Those hours we spent together, crossing the ocean and living in distant hotels, made lots of time for talk. We had long conversations about everything, and Henry, from the maturity of his sixties, was very conscious of the fact that he had not been a very nice person when young. Looking back on it all, he saw himself as having been very pompous and pedantic, rude and altogether rather less than attractive. His contemporaries, I suspect, might support that view. He regretted it all very much. He was in fact a very emotional man, and he often seemed quite taken aback when people wrote to him, admiring his work, saying how much pleasure his broadcasts had given them. He did not answer enough of the letters, I thought. If the reply required simply a thank you, he perhaps might not bother. Longhurst was well aware that life is not fair – and he knew very well that talent and opportunity and even privilege were not handed out evenly. He won a by-election at Acton in 1943, while he was a captain in the Army, and probably thought he was going to rush down to Westminster and change the face of the world. He enjoyed his time there, but was ousted, in good company, in 1945 when Churchill was deposed in favour of Attlee.

The last few years of his life were dreadful. He tolerated massive surgery for cancer, but the disease eventually became terminal. When he could no longer work or travel, we used to call him from pretty well all over the world. His American friends, particularly young Terry Jastrow, loved to do that. Terry had started off as Henry's 'gopher' – he would go for him to the airport, collect his luggage, drive him to the hotel, check him in, fetch drinks and generally take care of him. And within eight years, Terry had become a whiz-kid director – young, vibrant, able and attractive and one of the big success stories in US sports TV. I saw Henry a couple of weeks before he died in July 1978, then went off to work abroad. We called him, as usual, from Hawaii this time and were able to dial direct to the Sussex windmills. The old boy was sinking. I said, 'Henry? This is Peter Alliss, I'm calling from Hawaii.' There came the perfect Longhurst line, 'Good God, I hope you haven't reversed the charges!' The last conversation I had with him, on the telephone, certainly made me blub. It went, 'I'm very near the end now. I've never been a very religious man, but I know that you and I will meet again, many years from now, in another place. The one good thing about me going first is that at least it will afford me the opportunity of finding the sponsor's hospitality room.'

I was in America when he died and the news came through, and I had to broadcast the fact to the American public. There were lots of sniffles and snuffles then. Coming home from that trip, I saw Clive Jenkins, the trade union leader, loquacious as all Welshmen, in the first-class lounge and therefore presumed he was travelling first-class. Quite right too. Henry would have approved. He had little love for trade unions and certainly none for militant trade unionists, but he always believed that if you were a success, a star, as Clive Jenkins certainly is, then you should travel like one.

I inherited the Mustang car, and still have it. Sadly it is in a poor state of repair, and I don't know if I shall ever be able to resurrect it. In his better days, Henry used it to go down to Pyecombe, the pretty little golf club just over the Downs from his windmills, and where, at the time of his death, he was president. Completely in character was his instruction that £50 should be sent to the club to provide a round of drinks for all at the bar on the Sunday following his death, but that on no account was the club flag to be lowered, and that on no account should any club competition be postponed or cancelled.

He once did a writing job for someone, and stipulated that the payment should not be in cash, but should be a case of champagne, Bollinger, and Imperial pints at that. I asked him why Imperial pints. His answer seemed to sum up much of his philosophy of life.

He said, 'It affords you the opportunity of offering your wife a small glass.'

CHAPTER NINE

Television

A New Life

At Mauna Kea in Hawaii, in 1968, I did the last of my Shell *Wonderful World of Golf* films for television. Jimmy Demaret and Gene Sarazen were the commentators for the series. At the time I was hitting the ball quite magnificently, better than at any other period in my life, and putting, cross-handed, quite abominably. Demaret delivered himself of the deathless line that I had set back cross-handed putting by at least fifty years, and not much more than one year later, the whole thing virtually came to an end for Alliss the golfer. After the 1969 Ryder Cup match, in which the pattern of fine driving and pathetic, almost pathological, putting persisted, I declared that I no longer wanted to be selected for international play, and in fact took part in very few events of any kind in the seventies.

Now my fame and public persona, for what they may be worth, on both sides of the Atlantic, are as a television commentator, and it is quite extraordinary how people in their twenties or even early thirties have not the slightest idea of my early career. They come up to me and say, 'Did you ever play?' I find it quite difficult to say simply, 'Yes, I played.' I find it quite difficult not to ruffle the feathers and be self-effacing when what I really want to say is, 'Did I play, did I play? Of course I played, you bloody fool – don't you know I won more than twenty major tournaments, half a dozen national championships and played in eight Ryder Cup matches and ten World Cups?' Perhaps it is because they are accustomed to the fact that the famous sports commentators – Harry Carpenter, David Coleman, Brian Moore, Eddie Waring, Peter O'Sullevan – have been journalists and broadcasters first and have not competed at the highest level of their sports. At all events, television both here and in America has become immensely big for me, and has given me what few men can hope for – a second career, a second way of life, and I am hugely grateful for it.

With hindsight, I can now see the sixties as an important apprenticeship in it. The various Shell films I took part in gave me a direct experience of playing golf and golf shots specifically to the camera. They gave me some experience of talking directly to the camera, which can be a very spooky experience for the uninitiated – as you can see on almost any quiz or chat show – plus some idea of being interviewed, and conducting interviews. During the same period, Michael Seligman of Creative Film Makers asked me to be narrator for several of the annual films made of the Piccadilly World Match Play Championship at Wentworth, and other golf films, and there I learned a little of reading lines to the picture, of getting the timing right, of accenting one word or the other, of getting pronunciation and intonation right – the things which are the stock-in-trade of the good actor, the good broadcaster and which in time he does instinctively. And towards the end of the decade I was doing more and more direct commentary with Ray Lakeland of the BBC, and sitting avidly at the elbow of Henry Longhurst.

The people in the business will tell you that colour television is the most powerful single advertising medium yet devised by man, and certainly its influence on all our lives is immense. It is rather frightening when you consider that one is able to see war, for example, being fought live in our living rooms, as we did from Vietnam. All of that is a much wider issue, of course, but the remarkable thing about my experience with television is that I have never found my job overly difficult. I would not want to give the impression that it is all a piece of cake, but when it comes to casual chat, ad-libbing and talking off the cuff, I seem perfectly at ease. I have never worked from cue cards, and I imagine that would be quite difficult for me, too automatic, too confining. In fact, I am amazed at the number of programmes which apparently cannot be performed without written aids. Chat shows which are supposed to be totally informal and spontaneous, even those conducted by famous broadcasters, need cue cards, the words held up on cards or boards beside the camera. You've seen it all – the bland, smiling host walks in and says, 'Good evening, welcome to the show, tonight we have Joe Bloggs, a wonderful chap who has done . . .' All this is *written down* for him on cue cards, right through to the 'Goodnight'. I find all this very strange.

Yet without being a professional in the sense of having been in the game all my life, man and boy, without any formal training as such, there I was by the end of the seventies with programmes galore – ten *Pro-Celebrity Golf* shows, six of *Around with Alliss*, as well as the *Play Golf* series, six more involving mixed foursomes with two men, two women professionals, half a dozen major tournaments here, half a dozen in America, plus the *Golf Review of the Year*, plus odd sports programmes, plus, plus, plus. I seemed to be on the air every week of the year. Of course it is easy for people to assume that all this means two or three thousand pounds a pop. It doesn't. Only now is money coming my way. I hope it continues. Like everyone else, I get twitched up from time to time about when the next cheque is coming in to pay the bills and taxes and to take care of my people and maintain whatever lifestyle I have established for them.

People take television for granted now. It is part of the furniture, but more positively part of a way of life for all of us. And commentators are taken for granted, and patron-ized outrageously by people who simply do not comprehend how difficult commentary is. So many people seem to think that it is just a question of turning up, sitting down, watching a monitor, talking, then going home. Not so. Put these same people in front of a microphone or a television camera, and they would be paralysed. Not only that, but it is much easier to be a guest on the Michael Parkinson show than it is to be Michael Parkinson. And there are commentators and commentators, all with idiosyncracies and failings and shortcomings. I have been accused of prattling too much, and perhaps I do, but I rather take the view that golf commentary should be conversational in the way that ice-hockey commentary, for example, never could be. Other people have other attitudes. John Jacobs on ITV and Alex Hay on BBC are inclined to be concerned with the golf swing and its technicalities, more concerned with how players hit the ball than much else and that is perfectly understandable since both of them have spent their lives teaching the golf swing. Ben Wright, very successful for CBS in America and with ITV here, is an excellent companion and raconteur with a striking command of accents. Ben has obviously decided that a bit of erudition will do the Americans no harm, and a specimen snatch of Wright commentary might be, 'Here is the mighty Jack Nicklaus striding down the magnificently prepared fairway. He now draws his 3-iron from his bag and launches the ball like a speeding arrow from a bow, and it plummets down on the prepared surface, the greensward, leaving him a not-over-long putt for his birdie,' and on and on and on. Frank Chirkinian, his American producer – occasionally known as the 'Armenian camel-trader' – once said to him, 'Goddammit, you son-of-a-bitch Limey, I can't understand a word you say, but I tell you the day I do understand any of your effing language, you'll be fired.' That was meant as a compliment so perhaps Ben's technique is just right.

The commentator should have a clear idea of his

function. One of the great arts in television sports commentary, possibly the basic art, is in appreciating the power of the camera, and therefore of knowing when to stay quiet and say nothing. The voice can never compete with the camera. This is a visual medium. Those big electronic cameras are so powerful, so embracing, so penetrating and provide such fantastic pictures, that commentators had better not try to compete. The commentary must therefore complement them. The sensible commentator is one who will take the picture as the foundation and try to put a bit of his own baroque on top of it. As you will have guessed, I enjoy talk, I like conversation, so I am perfectly happy to watch cricket, for example, with the television picture on, the sound off, and be tuned in to the radio commentary. I like the chit-chat of radio, having listeners' letters read out, the reminiscing of the commentators. Because of the power of the picture in television, there ought to be less talk. But, I say again, the commentator should have a clear idea of his function and of his audience.

I believe it is my job to point out to the viewers the difficulty, or the ease of the shot, the magic, the genius, of the player. I try to explain the technicalities involved in the sport, in support of what the picture shows, and to interpret as best I can the problems the players face, what they are trying to achieve, and to some extent (though this is intrinsically impertinent) to interpret their mental attitudes and processes in their approach to the sport and its situations. I also feel I should have some background knowledge of what is going on in golf generally, what is happening behind the scenes at the tournament of the day. Yet I am not much for going into locker-rooms and being Charlie Charmer with the players. I prefer to pick up snippets of gossip and background from a variety of people, from caddies, PGA officials, and perhaps only a few of the players. This I think is important – one could easily become biased towards or against one player or the other. In general I arrive, go straight to the commentary position, socialize just a little during the odd break in transmission, but get away quickly when the work is done, not hang about when it is over. One should not have favourites.

The audience, the mere existence of the audience, can be a problem if you allow it to be. At a big American championship, the Masters or the US Open, the network people will tell you that the audience will be twenty-five to thirty million people. If you gave that a second thought, why, you'd never utter one word. Henry Longhurst rationalized this by taking the view that it was plainly not true, and that what you were really doing was talking essentially to two people, at home in their own sitting-room, having a cup of tea or a glass of beer. I try to extend that by imagining I am sitting in a grandstand on the course, or walking along the side of a fairway with a friend, talking about the play, and he is the one with the programme. The conversation might go:

'Hey, it's 11.45, who's due now?'

'Well, that should be Thomson and Locke.'

'Isn't that Locke in the white cap?'

'Yes, that's them, over there.'

'How are they doing?'

'Well, there's the scoreboard, let's go over and check.'

Conversational. Golf lends itself, as cricket does, and other sports do not, to that chat. I know, of course, from the letters I get that there are a tremendous number of people who follow golf on television who do not play the game and who do not really know the terminology of the game. And too many sports commentators as a whole, I think, assume too much knowledge on the part of the viewers and prattle on about birdies, eagles, sweepers and strikers, tight heads and flankers and peeling off, and every field position in cricket, every piece of a horse's harness. The occasional explanation of these terms is in order. It's great fun to be able to inform people, to let them learnalong – there is so much we don't learn in school, but learn in life from looking and listening.

Television commentators are terribly exposed to mockery and ridicule, and even imitation and impersonation. Perhaps that is the ultimate accolade. Dorian Williams was the man who used to say 'orf', and then he tried to say 'off', but didn't always succeed and I am not even sure that he need have bothered. Eddie Waring is criticized severely in the North of England because of his Rugby League commentaries, but he is accepted nationally as the voice of Rugby League. They say that Tommy Cooper is the most impersonated man in the British Isles, but Eddie Waring must run him a close second. I wonder about Eddie sometimes, not that I know him too well. He takes *himself* rather seriously when he should take *his game* seriously, and I think his Northern critics may have a point when they say he does little to raise the game above a rather basic level of appreciation. Eddie does say some funny things, I suspect many of them heavily rehearsed, but he has become a character, a much-impersonated comic character. Eddie is the least concerned about all this, and that may be his ultimate accolade. And since no one has started impersonating me, there may be a lesson for me in all this.

But I do like television. I do like the people in it. I think the BBC sports people, certainly the golf crew, are very fine people. Cameramen, riggers, drivers, engineers, production and direction people, they have all grown along with the game, so much so that many of them have become players. They take their clubs with them to events up and down the country, play whenever they can, even take practice swings in the television compound, where all those huge trailers are parked. The technical and engineering side of BBC broadcasts are of the highest standard, and they work small miracles within the restricted budgets which always seem to apply. The Americans by contrast have so much more equipment, such bigger budgets, that every aspect of their productions seems much more complicated, much more sophisticated – I am not sure which is the correct word – than the British. Yet I am also not sure that the end effect is any better, if indeed as good as ours.

One thing that constantly amuses and bewilders them is our 'studio'. Studio is a rather posh name for what is essentially a wooden shed perched on top of a scaffolding platform, usually behind a green at some suitable point on the course. It usually leaks. This is where the commentators, Harry Carpenter, the 'link' man who opens and closes the programme, our scorers, our caption and graphic people, all work in close proximity and as often as not in harmony. Rough wooden tables are knocked together bearing three or four television monitors which are often very dodgy, often facing the wrong way so that we have the sun shining in our eyes and we cannot quite see the pictures. Scorers in between the commentators keep the results up to date. People are talking constantly. Caption men scuttle about. They are the fellows who prepare and superimpose on the screens diagrams, headings, scores and so on, laid over the golf picture.

Harry Carpenter works in his own 'studio', which is no more than the end wall of the shed featuring a map of the course and a leader board or scoreboard of one kind or another. Rather like those busts of Mozart or Beethoven, Harry, from the nipples down, simply does not exist for the viewer. Yet in all this confusion, he is a master professional, cool, incisive, riddled with nerves like all the rest of us, yet totally in control. Carpenter is renowned in the trade for the perfection of his timing. The director will say, 'We have a forty-five-second introduction, Harry,' or 'We have fifteen seconds left on air, Harry,' and Carpenter time and again will find exactly the right number of words – all the facts correct – to finish right on the button. He is a master, and I burst with admiration for him. He, Frank Bough,

Dickie Davies, Tony Gubba, David Coleman – they do an enormously difficult job so well and make it look so simple; they are supreme professionals.

In the midst of all this apparent shambles and chaos, and it is only apparent, I can hear through my headset all the talk-back, all the director's instructions to everyone, cameramen, commentators, graphics people, all the words from everyone. The Americans can't quite believe the wooden hut thing and they are astonished that we still use this 'open-line' technique, with everyone hearing everyone else. Some years back they used the same system, but now in America I hear only the director talking to me, nothing else. That lightens the load somewhat, but on the other hand I do like to feel that I am in contact with my director, and with the BBC I have a 'lazy microphone', a separate mike which I can use by pressing a button, and speaking directly to him, perhaps to check a score or a fact. During a pause, he can answer me. In the US system I feel that my microphone is live all the time, and that I am somehow cut off, not master of my own destiny. The mike is not in fact live. A sound man controls it separately, and when the director says 'Go, Peter,' the sound man switches me live again, and I am off and running. In the US, they are under greater pressure, or apparent pressure. One reason is that hiring and firing is much easier over there. If you don't deliver the goods, you are fired. I sometimes think it is harder to get out of a job in our country than to get into one.

In contrast to our 'studio on stilts', a temporary affair, in America I have a studio of my own in the shape of a trailer, a huge mobile caravan parked quite near the clubhouse. I have an armchair, a desk, pads and pencils, sandwiches, soft drinks, hard drinks, wine, fruit, and I even have my own man scoring for me. There are two television sets, one showing the live transmission, the other for action replays, slow motions, leader board, and so on – all this basically for a two-and-a-half-hour programme on Saturday and two and a half hours on Sunday, and that would be a major programme, or 'telecast' as they call it.

This is luxury, of course, and in a way, Henry Longhurst and I pioneered this system. Previously, we would have been out on the course, positioned high on individual towers above a green, where we got wet when it rained, froze when it was cold, baked when it was hot, in company with a cameraman and scorers. The Americans thought this was necessary. This way the commentator would soak up the atmosphere of the event, and the ambience of the particular hole he was covering, would get more 'colour' into his work. We didn't quite think this was necessary to make it authentic, and we converted them. It started when Henry said one day, 'You know, we could do commentary on the US Open Golf Championship from my front room if we had a line, a microphone and a picture. We don't have to be out on the course – we don't even have to be there.' That made a lot of sense to me, and the Americans eventually went along with us. For ABC in America, Jim Mackay and Dave Marr still like to be outdoors, on a tower behind the 18th green, so that they can check wind, rain, weather and playing conditions. I take the view that you can tell it's raining when you see the umbrellas go up, and you know the wind is blowing when you see flags and trousers flapping, and trees nodding. You don't have to be Sherlock Holmes to check if the wind is against at the first hole. No matter, I now sit in splendour in my caravan, very civilized. And when it is all over and I step out, I am liable to be ten yards from the clubhouse. Under the previous system, I'd probably be at the 14th hole, furthest point out on the course!

The systems are different in odd particulars, and I like the challenge of the differing systems. US televised golf is simple in the sense that they cover only the third and fourth rounds of a tournament, on Saturday and Sunday. This is spreading slowly into British golf coverage, and more and more stroke-play events will be covered only on the two last days. The exceptions, I suppose, will be the Open Championship and the World Match Play Championship. The costs are virtually the same, but one does cut down on showing so many of the 'also-rans'. Of course sometimes the also-rans come through and become important and may even win the tournament, but usually after two rounds the tournament will have fallen into place, into a pattern in which we can concentrate more on the leading players.

The Americans are on the air for only a couple of hours each day, and so there is no real comparison between the systems in matters of scheduling and workloads. For their US Open, they now have a continuous four-and-a-half-hour telecast in which they seek to show every hole, every shot of the winner, or the leader. They attempt to tell the audience absolutely everything. Televised golf, televised sport in the US is an overpowering mass of statistics, scores, results, captions, sketches, graphics, piles of detail superimposed on the picture. They say that this is because so many people in America watch television in bars and clubs, where there is noise, conversation, music going on. They reckon that their viewers should be able to follow the action even when they can't quite hear the commentary. Since plenty of people have written to me saying, 'You talk too much, you prattle, do please shut up,' perhaps the Americans have got that right. Or do the British just naturally prefer more silence?

The Americans do like colour in their programmes, which really means gossip about the players – 'I was talking to so-and-so before he teed off and he said how he had stopped taking the injections/the kids had 'flu/his wife had run off' – that kind of thing. They are always very impressed by the quality of the BBC's coverage, by the skill of the cameramen and by the stamina of the announcers, and say so openly and graciously. But above all in the States, everyone is always mindful of the show, the dollar, the profit, and particularly the ratings. In a society geared to success, the ratings are all-important.

In television terms, golf in the US, as in the UK, is a minority sport. With the very odd exception, it does not compete with American football, baseball, basketball, just as golf in our country does not compare in public interest with football, racing and some other sports. The concern for ratings is well illustrated by what has happened at ABC, the company I work for in the US, and which may have a bearing on the future of televised golf in our country. In 1978–79, ABC made a profit of $200 million. They had had a major slice of the American PGA Tour, the regular round of tournaments which runs from January almost into October, week after week. ABC were paying some three million dollars for televising the majority of the events on the tour when Dean Beman, Commissioner (which means chief executive) of the Tour, upped the overall price to some eight or nine million dollars. ABC said no, thank you very much, and opted out. The other networks, NBC and CBS, took up the slack between them. However, ABC still had the US Open, the British Open and the US PGA Championship, none of which were negotiable by, or in the gift of, Beman.

From a ratings point of view, an entertainment point of view, the early-season events were important. They were few in number – the Bing Crosby tournament at Pebble Beach, the Los Angeles Open, the Bob Hope Classic in Palm Springs and the Hawaiian Open. All of these are played in January, at beautiful venues, usually in lovely sunny weather when most of the Northern and North-eastern states of America are snow-bound. And these are the states with the big populations, and therefore the big viewing audiences. American sports played in the winter are then in mid-season. After this early-season splurge of tournaments, which get huge attendances and good television ratings, and until mid-summer, there is really no more golf on television in America than there is in Britain. ABC were prepared to sacrifice this important winter sector because the trend in golf ratings has been going down for the past few seasons. The reasons? For one thing, if there was a run of one network doing several weeks in succession, they found that the commentators were running out of things to say about the same golfers week after week. For another thing, there was no more 'Big Three' in golf. Arnold Palmer, Jack Nicklaus and Gary Player for one reason or another were not around as they had been in the sixties and into the seventies. There was a new crop of tournament players, most of them from the colleges, almost all of them looking alike and playing alike, and ABC seemed entirely prepared to accept the loss of the routine golf event, while retaining the plums of the big championships. The Masters, which is televised by CBS, is the only one they do not have.

ABC had the reputation of being the Sports Channel, the 'Network of the Olympics'. They bowed out of that too, letting the Moscow Olympics go to NBC in 1980, and, as it happened, they were lucky – American athletes did not take part, and the Olympics must therefore have lost a huge slice of its potential American audience. ABC has a *Wide World of Sports* programme at weekends, which is a steal from the BBC's *Grandstand*, and although they dropped out of the PGA Tour, they killed the opposition with this. They placed their golf coverage, as indeed the BBC does, into this programme, and they simply made up for it by extending the other sports. And sometimes they would put on a big movie which really hit the golf figures and the PGA Tour. So it all gets back to the ratings, the dreaded ratings.

Pressure is enormous in America, where I find that people get to work earlier, they work harder, they take shorter lunch breaks. Of course, the dollar is almighty. It's no disgrace to earn money, no disgrace to drive around in a superior car, no disgrace to 'serve'. America is becoming one of the last bastions of service and politeness in the world. Waitresses say, 'Hi, good morning, good to see you, have a nice day, y'all come back and see us, y'hear.' All right, maybe a lot of it is insincere, said with rather a glazed eye, but it might bring them a tip and tips are not automatic in the US. People still want to earn tips. You stop for petrol and a mob will swarm over the car and check the oil, the tyres, the water, battery, clean the windscreen, almost without having to be asked. Everyone wants to get on and do things. Having said that, everyone is always mindful of the fact that they might get the sack, so it does keep people on their toes. They complain that the unions have taken over almost everything in the country; they are beginners when it comes to the ludicrous things that abound in Britain.

They use masses of equipment, masses of people. That's their style, and the advertisers will pay in the end. All of it makes me think of the Americans at war, and the cynics who say that they never fire a shot unless they have their own personalized jeeps, the Coca-Cola machine, the four-course lunch, candy and gum, with the waiting helicopter and a Purple Heart for getting up before seven in the morning. But you'd better face it, they do it their way, and that is their way. No point in going over there and telling them it is wrong to drive on the right side of the road. They have a huge country, masses of equipment, masses of people, masses of wealth and power – enormous costs, enormous profits, and they have done it all with their own sweat and energy and ingenuity. By contrast, the BBC seem always to be scratching for money and means. Of course, if everyone paid the licence fee, it would probably cost no more than a fiver and there would be plenty of funds available. But people cheat, and don't pay and that's how it is here. There the whole caper is different, the pressures are different, even if they may be equal. During an Open Championship here, we can be live on the air for six or seven hours, so we are perhaps slower, more relaxed, more discursive. In America the show is geared to being punchy, factual, hard-hitting, newsy, because 'we don't have time'. Above all else, Americans love a winner, love the sight of victory. They do not go much for pretty pictures for their own sake, those lovely opening or closing shots of striking landscapes which the BBC do so well. If the event is at Pebble Beach, that would be an exception. There they are likely to have a camera in an airship, showing pictures ranging round Carmel Bay and the Monterey Peninsula and the 17 Mile Drive, with whales in the ocean and breakers crashing on the California shore, but basically they would never dwell on rhododendrons at Wentworth, a lovely garden, a robin on a bush, or the sad dunes and estuaries of St Andrews or Muirfield or Turnberry.

The top people in American television, such as Chuck Howard, Jim Mackay, Bob Goodrich and Jim Jennett are very well paid, with salaries running into six figures. They are all bright, attractive, talented people. And on the executive side, I think the medium attracts talent and great characters. Take Cliff Morgan, BBC Head of Sport, one-time outstanding rugby player for Wales, and an enormously amusing man. I once said to him, 'Why don't you do more broadcasting, you have a marvellous tone and timbre to your voice, I used to love those radio programmes you did, on music. How did you get interested in music?' This was clearly a mistake. All the old Celtic flamboyance came out, and he said, 'Well, boyo, I can remember going on my father's shoulders when I was a little boy, up the mountain from our village, and as he carried me on his back I could almost feel the lumps of anthracite still embedded in the skin from forty years of working in the mine. We climbed higher, ever higher, and the air was getting purer and purer, and suddenly I could hear the massed voices of the Treorchy Male Voice Choir' – or whatever it was. No doubt some of it was true, but the rest was pure mumbo-jumbo. Lumps of anthracite embedded in the shoulders indeed. But it was all passion, all Wales, all Cardiff Arms Park and the British Lions, emerging from a simple question.

Young men like Morgan seem to be in command in television, and I like that. Alastair Milne, Ian Trethowan and the others, are all in their forties or early fifties. When I was in my twenties, everyone in control of everything seemed to be sixty-five, or even seventy. Or perhaps I'm getting older.

Television is my thing now. I am so proud to be part of it. The future of television is unlimited. There will be a tremendous movement in video cassettes and discs during the rest of this century. Over the past few years, when these things cost around £700, I wonder who on earth would pay such money. But increasingly I hear people say, 'We'll be out to dinner, doesn't matter, we've set the machine to get *Dallas*.' No doubt the porno and blue-movie merchants will be rubbing their hands, but we will be feeding ourselves much more information through television screens and video tapes. Education will be transformed, I believe. Golf tuition and sporting highlights will have their place. One problem at the moment is that the existing systems are not standardized and there are conflicting companies. But I am sure costs will come down and the whole thing will be enormous. I certainly plan to be part of it.

Pro-Celebrity Golf

I confess, without being ingratiating, that the thrill of going to a truly great hotel, walking through the portals, is still very much with me. I have been lucky in this respect in my life. I have been to many of them, around the world. But there is a very particular thrill for me in walking through the doors of Gleneagles Hotel, in Perthshire. Gleneagles Hotel is the only five-star hotel in Scotland, one of not all that many in the UK, and for me now, as it was in 1953 when I went there for the very first time, it is a place of surpassing beauty and wonder. We used to go there in the fifties for the Gleneagles-Saxone Foursomes, which came along in the autumn, the closing event of the golf season which then was almost entirely domestic, and it made a marvellous 'end-of-term' jollyup for everyone involved. I seem to remember that it was 37s 6d *table d'hôte* all in, and five shillings extra for a private bathroom. Rather different now. The 1980 rate, I believe, was around £75 for a double room, bed and breakfast, service and VAT. After that you could think of lunch and dinner and green fees and so on. Yet there are many people who will say it is the least expensive five-star hotel in Europe. With television, I suppose I go, and have done for some years, three, four or five times a year, and probably spend two and a half weeks there in all. This is a very privileged position to be in, and I am never unmindful of that.

Television, of course, has made this possible, and specifically the BBC Pro-Celebrity series which we have been filming for some years. This is essentially one professional and one amateur celebrity from show business or public life, matched against another pro and another celebrity in a team competition in which the pros remain throughout the series, and amateur celebrities change more or less each match. I had no idea, say ten years ago, that televised golf would grow so much, would boom, in fact, in the way that it has done. In my early days with the medium, my life seemed settled at Moor Allerton and was perhaps closing in around giving some lessons, playing a bit, running the shop and the club. I was forty, and that was that. Or so it seemed. When the Pro-Celebrity series started, my salary with the BBC was quite ordinary. The first of the annual series was held at Turnberry Hotel, on the Ayrshire coast, and looking back, that year presented perhaps the most star-studded cast we have ever had.

There was Telly Savalas, then beginning the enormous reputation he made with *Kojak*; Fred McMurray, a household name in the film business; Johnny Mathis, one of the great modern balladeers; Bobby Charlton, Henry Cooper, Ronnie Corbett and Johnny Rutherford who, I now realize, is one of America's greatest racing drivers, certainly on a par with Stirling Moss and Jackie Stewart. Turnberry Hotel is almost as magnificent as Gleneagles – some people call it Gleneagles-by-the-sea – but its appeal is different. There is the splendid, classic links of the Ailsa Course, the stunning position of the hotel on a rise looking across the Ailsa and Arran courses to dazzling seascapes of the Firth of Clyde and its islands, and the mountains of Arran. It is all a very dramatic scene, but when we filmed there, the weather was quite appalling, with rain and wind and storms, the whole thing quite ghastly. Yet no doubt because of the personalities, the Kojaks and Mathises, the series took off in spectacular fashion in terms of viewing figures. Suddenly BBC people were rushing around saying, 'Do you realize we had x millions?' In fact, the Bobby Charlton match from Turnberry had around $3\frac{1}{2}$–4 million viewers, which was phenomenal for a filmed golf show. Shortly afterwards, the series, which is filmed in August and transmitted on the air early the following year, moved to Gleneagles, which is a shade more opulent, and slightly more central for access, and has remained there ever since. The 1981 series may go to Turnberry again, just for a change of scene.

Almost every celebrity known to play golf has been on one series or another. Notable exceptions would be Bob Hope and James Garner, who is said to have been almost up to professional standard when he was a younger man. Always one commitment or another prevents him from coming. It has been a great delight to meet these people. We are inclined to hold the 'stars of the silver screen' in some kind of awe, but it is not until you actually shake hands and stand beside them and have a good look that you realize that many of them are really rather insecure, rather ordinary, not at all intellectual or physical giants. Alas, many of them are riddled by their own devils, just as much as a small shopkeeper in Islington or a wealthy landowner in Cornwall might be.

Burt Lancaster, for example, was always one of my heroes, still is for that matter. I remember him so well in the circus film *Trapeze*, with Gina Lollobrigida, doing all his own stunts. And in *Vera Cruz* in the scene where he snapped Cesar Romero's long cigarette holder. And in *Gunfight at the OK Corral* and countless Westerns and adventure films. I always admired his physical presence, that striking walk with the short steps, an arrogant, animalistic, rhythmical walk. He was very courteous, but difficult. I was given a page of notes on him, listing his hobbies, pastimes, interests, history. One note said that some years earlier he had become so obsessed with golf that he had neglected work and had hardly done anything else for about three years. His overheads continued, of course, there was little money coming in, so he quit golf and went back to work. I thought this was an interesting point to develop, and tried to lead him into that, that golf was one of his great loves. He said, 'No.' I said well you used to play a lot – 'No.' It was very much a Gary Cooper conversation, and he was quite unresponsive. I rather gave up on him.

Some of the celebrities, I'm afraid, took liberties with the sponsors' hospitality, signing for everything. Mars bars and packets of tees in the pro shop, and were not averse to going through the *à la carte* and even to getting into the Dom Perignon. The event was sponsored by the BBC, by Sports Marketing and Management, a promotional company, and in more recent years by Marley Tiles. The BBC do the actual production, and retain all UK television rights. SMM contract, transport and accommodate all the talent, and retain all television rights worldwide outside the UK. SMM take the view that since the amateurs do not get paid, you cannot ask people to come from Hollywood or Spain or Australia or Tooting Bec, then tell them they have a fixed menu and are allowed only one drink. It has to be all or nothing. And people, I fear, do abuse it.

SMM do an exceptional job in the Pro-Celebrity. They have to deal with the television company, the BBC. They have to deal with the venue, Gleneagles Hotel these past few years, which means British Transport Hotels Ltd. They have to deal with the sponsoring company, currently Marley. And each year they have to find two professionals who are available, suitable and interested in doing the work, plus a succession of celebrities who can play golf to some kind of standard and who also are available and interested, and each year they must ring the changes and find new faces. The only word for it all – they do it so very well – is legerdemain.

Incidentally, so many people have asked me why Waterford Crystal and Marley are in on the event. As sponsors Marley Tiles put up the Marley Trophy and the prize money, with Jack Aisher, the boss of the company and a great personal fan of Gleneagles – he goes there privately at other times with his family – attending each year and supporting the series in person. The Waterford people provide the lovely crystal ware which you see being given to the players at the end of each programme. They are involved simply because, in the person of Colm O'Connell, they were the first company – as far as I know the only company – to come along and offer their goods, free, without the slightest stipulation about being mentioned in any way on the shows. Simple as that.

Another of my latter-day heroes was Dennis Morgan. I spent a lot of time at the cinema when I was in my early teens! Morgan was a musical comedy chap with, I suppose, a light baritone voice. He was invariably the good guy who always got one of the girls – handsome, with thick waving hair, he was the Nelson Eddy type. But he turned out for us in rather bad shape. He too obviously liked tasting the grape, and although he had a good-looking swing, he himself looked quite dreadful, with bloodshot eyes positioned somewhere behind his ears. At that very first hole, the 8th, he squirted one right off the toe into the ferns. By the time Morgan had gone three holes, he looked in deep trouble. A flask was sent out from the clubhouse, and he rallied enough to make a game of it and finish the show. All part of the service.

How could one ever forget a week with the late Bing Crosby? At that time he was not too strong, frail, ageing. He was an entirely pleasant man, steeped of course in show business – he had quite the most astonishing wig I have ever seen which fitted sweet as a nut – but not one to talk much about it all. He was a good conversationalist, enjoyed his life, loved the game of golf, loved the people he found in golf, loved going to Scotland. He enjoyed his Scotch and soda at the end of the day, and did every single thing smoothly and quietly. One thing he said which I cannot forget was that every single day of his life he tried to learn something – a new word, a new phrase, a new thought, a new fact. Just something more about life. Pity more of us don't do just that.

I sometimes wondered why the celebrities did it all, since they got nothing out of it, apart from a few days at Gleneagles. Yet so many of them came back time and again, desperately keen to do well, to play well, to win. The classic example was probably Sean Connery. He works terribly hard and is probably hugely wealthy. He did tell me that he had had lots of bad business ventures, bad schemes, lots of rip-offs and lots of the money dissipated. But he slaves on, doing maybe three or four films some years, and yet has really no material possessions at all. His wardrobe comprises a few pairs of shoes, a couple of jackets, half a dozen slacks and some sports shirts and that's it. His wife Micheline is the artist and collector of the family, and they live in a very beautiful house opposite Puerto Banus, near Marbella on the Costa del Sol. But he personally doesn't have any possessions and does not seem to want them. He is very proud, however, of a Scottish charitable trust he has set up with Sir Ian Stewart, the Scottish industrialist.

Connery has an enormously fierce competitive spirit. He has always taken the game tremendously seriously, and works very hard at it, but his golf really has not improved as much as it should have done, considering how long he has been playing and how much he puts into it. For a big man who in many ways is so graceful physically, with that panther walk, somehow on the golf course it all becomes a little wooden. On the other hand, a fellow like Bobby Charlton, despite his fierce hooker's grip, is all balance and smooth rhythm, and gives the ball a fair old crack. Jimmy Tarbuck, one of the best celebrity players we have had with the exception perhaps of Ted Dexter, always desperately wanted to win, and almost always played well, but simply could not win for a long spell. It was 1980, after quite a few years, before he did. On the other hand, Eric Sykes, who by any judgment is not one of the best golfers we have had, won the overall Stableford prize in 1979, which delighted everyone for Sykes is one of the most loyal supporters of charity golf. Bruce Forsyth was always very keen and serious about the event, with his twinkling little steps. Henry Cooper, who moved so smoothly and elegantly as a boxer, really rather lumbered around on the course, and like Connery looks wooden, but when he has it going well is a very tough competitor indeed.

One odd thing about the series over the years, and it involved a Henry Cooper match, is that only once have we had to re-do a hole. It was the first hole, and all four players played it so diabolically badly, on top of which we had a camera fault, that we did it all over again. Apart from that, there have never been any re-takes. Every shot you see on the finished television programme is what happened as it happened – there was never any 'Oh let me try another shot at that.'

James Hunt, world champion racing driver, confirmed something which I had suspected, namely that racing drivers go into everything, try, try, try, one hundred per cent all the time. Jackie Stewart had certainly shown us that, a few years earlier at Gleneagles. He had not played the game for many, many years, and I daresay when he did he was not terribly good, but he just forced the ball off the tee, forced it up the fairway, forced it into the hole. Hunt, perhaps a 16-handicap player, was exactly the same. He drove with an iron, and appeared in the most disgraceful clothes: plimsolls, tattered jeans and a grubby T-shirt, and we had many, many letters about it. People wrote saying how dare I be a party to allowing Hunt, with all his wealth, to appear at Gleneagles dressed in this way, and didn't I know that if they or anyone else turned up at Gleneagles to play golf like that they would be turned away? It was an interesting point and I was not entirely sure how I should answer it.

We have had Jack Lemmon, a charming man and one of the world's greatest comic actors; Robert Stack of *The Untouchables*, and Robert Sterling who declared that he had given Garbo her last screen kiss – how about that for your tombstone. Then there was Gerald Harper, Colin Cowdrey, Dick Martin of *Laugh-In*, Christopher Lee; Howard Keel of *Oklahoma*, a delightful man; Charlie Drake, Greg Morris of *Mission Impossible*, again a charming man, but one who didn't play too well; Dickie Henderson, Val Doonican, Richie Benaud, Peter Falk, Ted Dexter, Lew Hoad who practised solidly for a week then couldn't hit a shot for the cameras, and Adam Faith. I became firm friends with Faith. I liked his cheeky humour, and he too was a tremendous trier. There was Ray Reardon and Jimmy Hill and Jeremy Kemp and a host of them. And there were the marvellous impromptu nights in the ballroom, with Kenny Lynch and Bruce Forsyth in knock-up cabarets, Dennis Morgan and Johnny Mathis singing. Henry Longhurst was there to the end, but in the last few years was fading. The stars enjoyed meeting him, which he in turn enjoyed, and he always pretended he didn't know who half of them were. But, as ever, Longhurst knew a great deal more than anyone ever gave him credit for.

The professionals who took part in the various series – Tony Jacklin, Tom Weiskopf, Peter Oosterhuis, Johnny Miller – were basically a dull lot, even if they were all in their own ways different. Of course, in the early days it was an entirely new experience for some of them to be exposed to this kind of television programme, and some didn't quite catch on to what was required. Weiskopf, perhaps oddly enough, would have won on points, not only because of his majestic swing and the way he played and his presence – he must be six feet four inches tall – but he was articulate and willing to try. People say Tom is his own worst enemy which is probably true in that he is very self-critical and has a short temper and gets very annoyed when he plays badly. He has been dubbed in America 'The Towering Inferno'. Johnny Miller was always quite pleasant, but I suppose it is difficult to be a Mormon – no cigarettes, no tobacco, no booze, no tea, no coffee. He was there with a wife and a couple of children, but we didn't see very much of him; it was up to the suite, room service, food, television and bed, I suppose. Oosterhuis was pleasant and easy and quite prepared to be led along. I am just so sorry that he is not a slightly better player, because he would have been a wonderful champion and ambassador. He is a gutsy player.

When Tony Jacklin was on the show, he was beginning to go into the doldrums. We had very many letters when the programmes were shown saying, 'Can't you stop Jacklin moaning, in that mid-Atlantic accent?' I must say that I was not aware of it during filming, but it was quite apparent when the programmes were shown some months later. When he left a putt short, or didn't quite hit the ball as he wanted to, he said, 'Aah, did I hurt you ball, did I hurt you? Aaah Gad, Scottie, what the hell am I doin'?' (Scottie was his caddie then.) Since the other professional in that series was Johnny Miller, then in a slight decline, it did not make for sparkling television. Happily, Tony has worked his way through that period, and things are beginning to emerge for him, not least in television. He is easing his way into the commentary business, at which I think he will be very, very good.

Lee Trevino, however, brought a whole new dimension to Pro-Celebrity golf. He was brash, outgoing, an incessant talker, so much so that some of the other performers were a little scared of him. Lee in public is a complete extrovert, full of wisecracks, one-liners rather than stories. Sometimes he repeats himself, but I have noticed that each year he brings over some new material. He plays quite superbly, and he overshadows some of the other great ones. They can't keep up with his quips, and so are inclined to play poorly. Ballesteros did tremendously well when he partnered him, considering that his English then was rather halting. But Ballesteros has a fine sense of humour. Ben Crenshaw, too, was a perfect foil for Trevino, with his boyish good looks, his Texas accent and a certain dryness in his style. And in 1980, we had a superb series of matches with Lee Trevino and Fuzzy Zoeller. Zoeller is a man who thinks that life is not such a serious business, and he matched Trevino quip for quip.

Trevino is a strange man in so many ways. At Gleneagles, he is always on time, always available, always impeccably turned out, always has an hour's practice behind him, no matter how early we may start. Yet he keeps socializing to an absolute minimum. He is perfectly friendly to everyone, but at the end of the day he may only have one glass of beer in our hospitality suite, then he vanishes, has dinner in his room, watches television, and gets to bed early. And I believe that at home with his family, the happy-go-lucky public image is replaced by the attitudes of a disciplinarian who gets close to being a Puritan if necessary. He explains it by equating the life of a professional golfer to show business and says that when he goes down to the course in the morning and the cameras start turning, he is on stage. Then he will stand on his head if the producer wants that. He reckons he is being paid to entertain people. But when the camera stops turning at five o'clock in the evening, he is off stage, and doesn't want to run the rigours of a public dining-room, with all the hassle of autographs and people talking about the weather and how his back is and so on.

So, for me, the Pro-Celebrity series have been a wonderland: of meeting so many people, of being involved with success and of going back again and again to Gleneagles Hotel, which I love. I realize that I have been going to the place for more than a quarter of a century, and so many of the welcoming faces are still there. The hall porters, Big John McGillivry and Billy Lynch, the night porter Bob Thomson and Ian Robertson in the garage, who puts such a sheen on the cars; Tony, the Italian *maître d'* who only recently retired but comes in on busy nights; Ian Marchbank, the professional who fusses and fidgets during filming, keeping the crowds off his precious greens, and Derek Brown in the professional's shop; Jimmy Bannatyne, the general manager who has been there for more than a decade and has seen everything.

And here I should acknowledge the exceptional BBC team which has made the series such a success. In the early days, production was handled by Alan Mouncer and Slim Wilkinson, engineering by Ted Bragg. Now David

Kenning and Richard Tilling take care of production and direction, Sam Branter is our electronics wizard and Alistair Scott our talented editor. Annette Faydenko is Kenning's secretary, Frances Freeman is Tilling's, girls wise in the ways of television and its temperamental men. All these people are expert people, the absolute core of the entire operation.

Gleneagles is a very beautiful place with lovely gardens, lovely golf courses, lovely vistas and excellent service. What I do not like is the property development which Bovis are putting up. It seems to me to be incongruous, not Scottish, not Gleneagles. Pity, because Perthshire is one of my very favourite regions in all the world.

I think I am privileged to have been part of the series, especially since I still somehow think I am not really a professional at it, rather a gifted amateur. And I am also lucky in not being self-conscious, at least now, in front of a camera. Someone once said I was just an instant reporter, show him a picture and he'll find some words. I certainly would not say I could walk on to the stage of the Palladium, and I am certainly not one for rehearsing too much. Just a small and lucky talent, that's it.

Around With Alliss

Playing a few holes of golf, on a beautiful course, on a pleasant day, with a famous personality whose conversation might range widely and entertainingly over this and that – what could be more enjoyable? This, with perhaps a bit of tuition from me thrown in if the need arose, was the concept of a rather unusual television series made by the BBC in 1979. The notion, as I mention elsewhere, came from Bob Abrahams, BBC sports producer, who thought it might make an interesting combination of the chat show and a popular sport with pretty 'visuals'. It made an unusual series in the sense that it was successful beyond any of our hopes, it was cheap by television standards and a year later the BBC felt able to invest in a second series.

Hunt the celebrity was a game we had to play. I suppose the ideal half-dozen people for such a purpose would have been Bing Crosby, Bob Hope, Frank Sinatra, Arthur Scargill, Kevin Keegan and Margaret or Denis Thatcher, but the major problem was, and is, getting people of this calibre to the place you want them on the day you want them. Very difficult. They are all very busy people. And whoever was to appear on the show had to be able to make a reasonable pass at the ball; he could not be an absolute beginner, a non-golfer. That would have been altogether too boring for the audience. After searching around, the BBC came up with Mark McCormack, Michael Parkinson, Dan Maskell, Leslie Thomas, Douglas Bader and Hugh Scanlon.

Although Ian Wooldridge was busy at the time putting together a big documentary on Mark McCormack for ITV, no one had done very much with Mark McCormack on television, and I thought it was a pity to throw the chance away. McCormack had been a first-class player in his day, as we have seen. Michael Parkinson was something of a coup. He had spent a good deal of time declaring that golf was rubbish, a waste of a good walk and so on, and in fact had been president of the Anti-Golf Society. However, someone had tempted him on to a golf course, he had hit a few decent shots, and had been hooked – a late convert, always the most dangerous kind.

Dan Maskell was entirely in character, exactly as you would imagine from his Wimbledon voice and appearance on the screen – a lovely, gentle man. Leslie Thomas, the journalist-turned-author, was fascinating if a little nervous at the whole project. Then there was Group Captain Douglas Bader, Battle of Britain ace and subsequently boss of the Shell aircraft fleet, a hard man, very right wing, a flog 'em, hang 'em man, pipe clenched, smoke belching, stumping around on the tin legs which had meant almost constant pain for more than forty years – a very exceptional man.

But for me, the most intriguing of all was Hugh Scanlon, the Communist Lord. Hugh, erstwhile boss of the engineers' union, had been a member of the Communist Party in his younger days, but what was most intriguing to me was that none of the people like him, the radical, socialist, change-the-world-at-a-stroke people, seemed to be very radical, backs-to-the-wall types in their later, golden years. Hugh was not trying to prove anything, demand anything, dominate anyone. Listening to him was rather like listening to Mannie Shinwell. Out of government, out of power, out of public life, these chaps seem to talk nothing but sound sense. If you took George Brown, Harold MacMillan, Scanlon and Shinwell and told them to get on with it, they would probably run the whole show perfectly well, even if some of them had been rabid extremists in their early days. I believe Shinwell, for example, held the view that we should get all our priorities settled and concentrate the entire resources of the country in a massive assault, each year, on one major problem – one year education, the next year roads, then health, housing, railways in turn – and get each one put right. Someone would have to have massive powers, and it may be very idealistic, but it is a very attractive notion.

Of course, out of power, it seemed they could say things they would never have said when in power. Hugh Scanlon was still very much for the workers, but he did say plainly that there had to be discipline, that workers had to earn their wages, and they had to produce the nation's wealth. Then retired and living in the Broadstairs area, Hugh was a keen and passably good golfer. He was an amusing man, with a sharp sense of humour.

We filmed him down at the Manor House Hotel at Moretonhampstead, on the edge of Dartmoor, in April 1979. In the evening, we had had a pretty good dinner, and no one had stinted on the smoked salmon, the tournedos, taken with more than a few glasses of claret, and when we moved into the Manor House's 'Cathedral Lounge' for coffee and the rest of it, there was a log fire burning in the huge fireplace. Scanlon noticed the fire going down, but not the young waiter who, just at that moment, was bringing in the coffee, and he said, 'Throw another couple of peasants on that fire!' Then he did see the young man, and said quickly, 'You shouldn't have been listening to that, lad – never mind, if you ever get fired, call me and I'll fight your case for you at the Industrial Tribunal.' Then with a little laugh, and slightly under his breath, he said, 'And, of course, you'll lose!' I felt it was somehow a serious joke. I don't know if he tried to use humour deliberately, to keep the common touch, but he was certainly much more fun than most of the politicians I have met, yet at the same time it was clear that he had a very strong sense of responsibility. Of course, once a man has declared himself in public life, then moved in another direction – from Karl Marx to the House of Lords is quite a step – he really is an Aunt Sally to be shot at. But it may be that the House of Lords, for Hugh Scanlon, represented no more than evolution and maturity.

This series of six programmes was brought in for less than £50,000. When you consider that we traipsed more than a dozen people to the Manor House in Devon, to Hollinwell on the Notts-Yorkshire border and to Parkstone in Dorset, with all the required equipment and with transportation, hotels, food, salaries, etc., to be paid, it was cheap at the price, so much so that the BBC were persuaded to do it again, with other people in other places, in 1980. Our first venture then was to the lovely Rosemount course at Blairgowrie, where we had Bill Maclaren, the BBC rugby commentator, and Jim Watt, the world boxing champion, in their differing ways two braw Scots laddies. Maclaren really is the glorious amateur, his commentaries revealing quite clearly his deep love for his own game. A Hawick man, he has virtually never left his home town. He was a very promising rugby player in his early days, but his career was stopped by tuberculosis, and he has stayed with schoolteaching, stayed with the local education authority, never left his lovely, beloved Borders, never gone on tour, been content, if you want to say so, to be a big fish in a small pond – and it is certainly not for me to start telling him he is wrong. Jim Watt had just taken up golf, rather surprisingly for a Scot. He turned out to be a super guy, with a very clear picture of his life, what he was doing in the fight game, what he wanted to get out of it – a very rational man, I decided.

We moved to Royal Porthcawl, where my father's career really started some sixty years earlier, and filmed Max Faulkner and Max Boyce, the Welsh entertainer who seems to have made a career of rugby football. Interesting how Boyce and Billy Connolly and Jasper Carrot have had great success with what I might call regional humour, if that does not offend Connolly. Max Faulkner was rather nervous, but bright and lively as ever. We finished the series at Woburn, with Victor Matthews and Andrew Barlow. Matthews, the tycoon of Trafalgar House, Cunard and Express Newspapers, must have known at the time that he was about to become Lord Matthews, but never once mentioned it. He was very interesting on the subject of unions, and his creed obviously was that 'management must be allowed to manage'.

Andrew Barlow was the youngest heart transplant patient, and working with him was for me a rather harrowing experience. I had just been watching Dr Jonathan Miller's series on television on how the body works, and, of course, the heart is a very emotive lump of meat. Here was this young man who had been told not to drink, not to smoke, and was doing both. He had been prescribed pills which contained cortisone, and was beginning to become plump. I kept thinking, couldn't help it, how long might he live, because suddenly one realized that one was looking at, and talking with, a man who was absolutely delighted simply to be alive, and yet with a future that was totally unknown. It was a very strange, salutary experience. He was just one of the twelve people we had worked with on the series, part of a great patchwork, but the other elements, even the success of the programme, seemed quite trivial compared with young Barlow and his problems.

Play Golf

Some time in 1977 Gordon Menzies, producer of BBC Scotland educational programmes, called me and said, 'I've got some money left in a budget. Would you be interested in doing a golf instruction series?' The answer was yes, and again it was remarkable how we got through the work. At the Downfield course, near Dundee, we taped two programmes a day, ten in a working week, despite the fact that the television people said that for one reason or another this simply could not be done. And, I should say, despite the fact that the weather was basically quite foul. We had four guinea-pig amateurs, two men, a girl and a boy, and the boy, Duncan, who was a beginner, got the golf bug quite badly, and has gone on to become a very nice little player indeed. We had a variety of professional guests – Jean Donald, a very old friend from Slazenger days and a cracking lady; John Panton, one of my very favourite people; Greg Norman, the young Australian giant who was to have such a fine year in 1980, culminating in his win in the World Match Play Championship; Tommy Horton,

Maurice Bembridge, John Stark from nearby Crieff, Bob Jamieson from Turnberry Hotel and Ian Marchbank from Gleneagles Hotel.

We were just beginning the last programme, a day and a half ahead of schedule, when Bruce Allen of BBC Scotland came over to me and said, 'I must shake you by the hand.' 'Why?' says I. He said, 'This thing has been one of the most professional operations I have ever been associated with.' I thought there was some joke coming, and said rather guardedly, 'What do you mean?' He went on to say that none of the BBC people had thought it could be done so quickly and that it was basically down to me and to my ability to turn up ready and on time, then remember the introduction, get the thing done and keep the conversation flowing, with always something new to say, to be cued-in and cued-out, thank the people for watching, remembering to link into next week's programme and who will be on it and the whole bit. 'It has been marvellous,' he said, 'we could have been here for another four or five days. As it is we have done it, and we are under budget and I am very pleased to have been here and to have worked with you.'

I felt like Superman. I thought this was the most enormous compliment, probably the nicest thing I had ever had in television work. If you get compliments from the experts, the professionals, that is as much as you can hope for, as far as you can go, since in my case I still felt in a way that I was, and still am, an amateur at the television game. Henry Longhurst used to say that we were the last of the amateurs, because we felt in a way that the best of the amateurs would be wholly without meanness of spirit, would be totally dedicated, and yet would have a thoroughly professional approach to the work. I suppose that is why, even if they annoy me with their aloofness occasionally, I am glad that the Royal and Ancient Golf Club of St Andrews, and the United States Golf

Association, the governing bodies of the game in the world, are as they are, and are as grand as they are. That is as it should be with governing bodies of anything.

Compliments from the public, on the contrary, are something else. I do not entirely trust the public compliment. In conversation, people will say, 'Isn't so-and-so awful? Isn't the BBC/ITV awful?' But if they happen to meet so-and-so, this changes to a rather gushing, 'Oh we do enjoy your programme so – it really is wonderful – so much better than the other side.' Then they meet the other side and say exactly the same, which means exactly the opposite. The fact is that both television networks put out first-class work, as good as anything in the world. All this is a form of nerves, of fear, of trying to impress people, of getting close to the stars, the old 'jersey-tuggers' again. I suppose it comes from some kind of longing for self-expression.

This sort of behaviour perhaps reaches its peak with the people who run on to the field, chasing after the players at the finish of football, rugby, cricket matches to jump on their backs and pummel them and almost wrestle with them. And not all of these people are youngsters. They are dangerous, unnecessary and a pain in the arse. They never seem to consider that these players have been functioning at maximum intensity, making a total physical effort, for an hour and a half – all day long in the case of cricket – and they are suffering all kinds of reaction at the finish. Some are totally let down and depressed. Some are totally raised up, elated. They are in a highly charged emotional state and the last thing they want is this mob. That's why you'll see the odd batsman sweeping the bat around himself as he leaves the field, fending them off.

The public are necessary, but in their proper place, and increasingly that proper place is behind barriers. The public make life difficult for the sportsman, and nowhere more so than in the business of autographs. They'll come at

you en masse, shoving sheaves of paper under your nose –
no pens of course – and say:

'Sign that.'

'It's for my nephew, write "To Fred".'

'Sign that.'

'Who are you?'

'Are you Ballesteros?'

'Who is it?'

'Sign, sign.'

An overstatement, madame? Of course it is – once more
we are talking of a very small minority of people. Not all the
public behave in this way. I get hundreds of letters each
year from all kinds of people, many of them quite old
people, who may never have played golf, and it is quite clear
that they are all genuine supporters of golf on television.
And the great majority of people who come to watch and
make up the gallery at *Pro-Celebrity Golf* and televised golf
matches, where there are not admission charges, behave
perfectly well. Lee Trevino has a great line for the people at
such events who don't quite behave as well as they should,
who hustle him while we are actually working and filming.
He says in effect, 'Now don't be too demanding, I'll see you
when we have finished. Don't forget, you got in here for
nothing, you are not providing my bread, someone else is
doing that this week, you haven't paid, so stay cool, don't
be greedy and demanding, I'll do it all at the end of the day.'

Perhaps that is how we got through *Play Golf* in double-
quick time – no public, no autographs!

CHAPTER TEN

Build Me a Golf Course

Around 1967, I had a letter from this fellow in Belfast, called Tom McAuley, which said in effect, 'I am the most highly qualified construction engineer in the world, and you are very famous in golf. We should design golf courses together.' David Thomas, my lifelong friend and I had discussed golf-course design often enough, and between us we had seen, indeed played on, enough courses around the world to have lively opinions on the subject, although I am not sure we had given any serious thought before this time to actually getting into the business. We were both still playing tournament golf reasonably well, but after talking to McAuley, we decided to give it a try.

We got a couple of reconstruction jobs in the Manchester area, at Didsbury and Northenden, realigning a few holes, building a couple of new holes, that sort of thing. This taught us a lot, and also gave us our first experience as businessmen of the golf-club committee – and not, I fear, our last. We were to discover that we had still much to learn about these gentlemen. Funny thing about golfers and golf-club committees – they really are convinced that they know what a good golf course should look like, and why it should look the way it does, and they think they know a great deal about grass. The truth is (a) they do not play the game all that well and (b) they are drawn from the club membership, which means the general public and therefore they have no technical qualifications whatsoever about greenkeeping. In this respect, too, we were to learn that possibly the worst man to have on any greens committee is a farmer. The whole thrust of his psyche is to grow things, whereas the golf greenkeeper does not want to grow anything, except grass, and that under very tight control.

However, all that was to come. Tom Scott of *Golf Illustrated* introduced Bernard von Limburger, a very fine, experienced European architect who had built most of his courses in Germany, Austria, Spain and Switzerland. He was an old chum of my father's from Berlin days. His remaining ambition – he may have seen it as a swansong since he was then seventy – was to build a course in the UK.

The first major job we had was at Clandeboye in Northern Ireland. It was to re-vamp nine of the twenty-seven existing holes, then add nine new ones so that the club would have thirty-six holes. From Limburger we learned a lot about the whole business, and the basic steps. Next was a splendid scheme in Iran, on the Caspian Sea, for the Bank of Omran, which really meant, I suspect, for Princess Ashraf and her brother, the Shah. McAuley and Limburger spent a couple of years on the project; it was never completed.

By 1973, we had separated from Tom. Money was the main problem, how to divide the spoils. Tom thought that if he was doing most of the work, he should get most of the profit. We felt that if we were bringing in the business, we should get an equal share. Next came Nigel Whitfield, from Parkstone, a chum and a surveyor, who lasted about nine months and left for very much the same reason. Perhaps we were bad employers, or partners, in the sense that as tournament golfers we had always been accustomed to paying our own expenses travelling up and down the country, working Saturdays and Sundays, never able to claim anything from 'the company', not knowing anything about overtime or double time or daily rates. We simply worked until the job was done, and perhaps we expected to see everyone else work as we did, and leave the money in the business until it prospered. We went through a variety of surveyors, and David Thomas, overseeing the bulk of the work on the ground, had obviously little experience of quantities at that time. Payments, completion dates, contractual difficulties, the wrong seed mix, bad weather, bad maintenance – we were quickly exposed to the perils of building golf courses! We survived, greatly helped by Bernard von Limburger – but he was based in Germany, and becoming less spry.

Two big jobs came in, at Hessle Golf Club near Hull, and at King's Lynn in Norfolk, and interesting case studies they made. At this time we were using a construction company called, believe it or not, Bale and Hay Ltd, and had a loose arrangement with them to pass work to each other. The Hessle club had a very pretty, mature nine-hole course on a pleasant site. It was right on the line of the huge new Humber Bridge, however, and the club was invited to move and given immense compensation. As with Moor Allerton, the members wanted the compensation, but did not want to move very far. Accustomed to driving seven minutes to the golf club, why should they now have to drive thirty-seven minutes, they asked themselves. Since no one can conjure up a perfect site exactly where it is wanted, there were problems. Some of the potential sites we looked at were little more than mangel-wurzel fields.

We had lots of problems at Hessle, not least with stones and stone-picking. Stone-picking is one of the banes of golf-course construction. Even if the client knows you will be working on stony ground, only when the ground is opened does the committee realize what is involved. So you have a clause in the contract to clear stones. You start with a standard machine which will pick up stones of at least one inch in diameter. Inevitably some stones are missed. The client, the greens committee, says, 'That job is nowhere near done.' So you come back and do it again. Then it rains for a few days, and more stones come up, and you do it again, and all of this means time, which means money. Eventually you find yourself in a situation in which the club seems to be accusing you of having planted the stones there in the first place. This is where problems of writing contracts and the retention of money by the client can become a nightmare. Clients will withhold £20,000 when only a few hundred pounds' worth of work is at issue. There is a continuous battle to satisfy the customer, and salve your own conscience and pride in your work.

British Industrial Sands were the landlords of the King's Lynn club, which had a lease with only fifteen years to run. There was a good deal of high grade sand under their pretty course and BIS wanted to get it out. They told the club they would find them another site, build the course and clubhouse, do everything for them if they would move to another site. We found a cracker at Castle Rising, only a few miles from the town. It had lovely woodlands with good undulation in the ground, a pine-birch-heather type of terrain. It was perhaps not the easiest place to grow grass – rather boggy in parts, a very sandy, acid soil, with a good deal of moss and lichen around.

Eric Dodds, a solicitor in King's Lynn, was the captain and driving force when it all started. BIS were excellent landlords, but Dodds had tremendous battles with his own people. Some of them had the weird idea that they had BIS over a barrel, and could screw the last penny out of them. They did not seem to realize that BIS could simply have sat on their lease for fifteen years, and when it ran out the club would have been invited to leave with precisely nothing – nothing that is except the problem of finding alternative land, buying it, and building a golf course and clubhouse with their own money! Sane men, when they become members of golf-club committees, act very strangely at times. We were rather pig-in-the-middle in all this, although the BIS people we dealt with were absolutely first class.

The club wanted more and more for less and less. During construction the watering system – for which we were not responsible – went awry, a very dry summer came along, the grass would not grow, everyone was bitching and moaning instead of pulling together and a lot of time was wasted. They wanted to chop down trees here and there. We could do that in thirty seconds as against the seventy years the trees had been there. They seemed to think that we could grow grass in a desert overnight, and plant trees that would grow thirty feet in an afternoon. All very educational.

On top of all that, Bale and Hay went broke, the classic situation of a construction company that had diversified into too many areas, then found that they could not get the work to sustain the staff and the expensive machinery. From them, we inherited Patrick Dawson, Boris Hayklan and Bill Squires. Dawson was an enthusiast and enormous driving force, and still is. Squires was a dour, dogged Yorkshireman. But then Alliss and Thomas can be pretty dogmatic at times, and I suppose that is how we all got along.

In any event, David and I had been coming round to the belief that being golf-course designers was somehow not quite enough. We thought we should be responsible for design *and* construction. The system that seemed to prevail was for the golf architect – Frank Pennink, Charles Lawrie, Fred Hawtrey, Henry Cotton et al – to produce a design and a set of drawings for a fee, give the client a list of bona-fide constructors, and let the client put the work out to tender; and usually the lowest tender would be accepted. The architect would make four or five supervisory visits during construction, but would not be able to alter anything substantially if the work was done. Alterations after the event would cost the contractor, and therefore the client, additional money.

We thought it more sensible to do everything. We would put our own project manager on the site. We would hire labour and machinery. We would buy the materials. We would sell a complete package, marry the work closely to the design, and the whole thing would be better and cheaper for the client. Ordinary contractors, we found, took tremendous shortcuts. Since mistakes are always costly to repair and since the major profit in the whole business comes from the construction element, it seemed the rational way to go.

Our first overseas venture was at Almaina Park at Alicante on the Costa Blanca in Spain, and a cautionary tale that turned out to be. It was the brainchild of two extraordinary Jewish cousins from North London. They had had assorted careers in their time, but when we came across them in the early seventies, they were in the property business in the Alicante area. This was just before OPEC and the three-day week of Edward Heath's government convulsed all our lives, and at that time one could still buy an apartment, even a small house, in Spain for a few thousand pounds. The two cousins had built a development of houses on a dramatic hillside site behind the city of Alicante, had plans for tower blocks of apartments on the beach and had found a site near the city for a total development which was to have two golf courses, a clubhouse with tennis, swimming, riding and all the rest, a hotel and hundreds of units of property, villas and apartments.

At the time, it looked an absolute winner. Alicante is a pleasant, cosmopolitan city of getting on for 200,000 people, a regional capital with an international airport, good public services, hotels and restaurants, lovely beaches nearby, and it was the gateway to Benidorm and a booming holiday coast which attracted hundreds of thousands of visitors each year. And it had a marvellous winter climate, the greatest of all attractions for the British and other Northern Europeans.

The project was launched with a grand Press conference in the River Room of the Savoy Hotel. Gabe Guteman, a lively American sales director, was appointed, founder memberships and subscriptions were sold, and we buckled down to our part of the job. Bill Squires went out as project manager in residence. David Thomas made many visits and spent lots of time there, we worked hard on the course and got it built and it was a fine course of which we were very proud. Then came some ominous rumblings from the hillside development. All sorts of unhappy rumours were being put about. Suddenly the whole project at Almaina Park, only five miles from the city, less than ten from the airport, was sold to Eurovillas. We were to continue with the work. We were still being paid, and our contract included half a dozen villa plots and possibly an involvement in the management of the completed development. We had decided to build eight-bedroomed villas for ourselves and become millionaires, and everything looked rosy. Then we heard that the water bills had not been paid, and that Eurovillas were in financial trouble. The whole thing ground to a halt, and we are still out some £35,000 on the whole project. We were learning that bad debts were a fact of life in the golf-construction business.

Almaina Park is still there, of course, the irrigation pipes and the drains still under the ground, but the whole place is in receivership. It is very sad – for a few hundred thousand pounds, the place could be resurrected, and someone would be sitting on a fortune. Next came Almeria, further down the coast, and we thought this would be a chance to recoup our Alicante losses.

It was a similar development, this time with a Slater, Walker company involved. We were to design the course, staff and manage the course and clubhouse and generally run the whole golf operation and retain all the golf profits. The developers would charge us a rental and get their compensation from the sale of properties. At this time, in fact, we had a fanciful plan to build courses and developments all over Europe, calling each of them 'The Champions' Club', so impressed had we been by the

Champions' Club in Houston, put together by Jimmy Demaret and Jack Burke. We would sell memberships, have our own homes on each course, become as rich as Kashoggi and it would all be totally grand.

But would you believe it? Slater Walker went under. Before they did, they had sold the Almeria development on to a Spanish company, which in turn sold most of it on to a Spanish bank, so we had rather lost touch with our original client. Now we were in the hands of people not much interested in golf, but only in property development. We were too, but the one basic point we tried to impress on them was that the golf course was the core of the whole thing, and the success of the entire project surely depended on the quality and beauty of the course, and its completion. Suddenly they wanted to take over everything. They stopped paying us. We stopped working. We left. Again it was all very sad, and it meant that with Alicante, Spain had now cost us some £60,000. Our first overseas ventures had not been sensationally satisfactory.

However haltingly, the world kept turning at home, in the UK, and there was work from Wigan for the borough council, possibilities at Peterborough, Hill Valley and Blairgowrie. Wigan, or rather Leigh, was for nine holes, and David Thomas by this time had decided that his golf would not improve too much and decided to go full-time into our design and construction business, and since then has played a critical part in it. Peterborough we now see as one of our mistakes. The Development Corporation there wanted us to design, build, staff and manage a new course for them. We didn't take the risk. We should have. The course has been a real money-spinner, tremendously successful.

Hill Valley near Whitchurch was the brainchild of two very likely lads, Albert Minshall and Leslie Welsh. We built the course round the site they had chosen for their hotel, on a difficult piece of ground, and got a good, if not too casy, course out of it, but it was Blairgowrie that we thought simply had to be a real plum. Everyone in golf knew the famous Rosemount course up in Perthshire. It is a gem in Scottish golf. The project was to build a second eighteen holes, not in two loops of nine but in such a way that the entire thirty-six would provide various permutations of play. Many of the local people were against any idea of a second course. Extraordinary general meetings were held, people met in local village halls, and there was a good deal of Scottish 'girning' about the whole scheme, since they had some idea that the existing course, their pride and joy, was to be changed, which was totally wrong. The mood of the final meeting seemed against the project. David Thomas made his final presentation. Pat Dawson made his final presentation. I said a few words. Going back south in the car, the others were very melancholy, very down in the dumps, saying, 'They won't do it, they'll never agree to it, we've had it' and the like. I said impulsively, 'I'll just bet you both a fiver that we do get it.' We got it. I never have collected those fivers, although they have made up for it in many other ways.

Blairgowrie was a very interesting site. Three-quarters of it went through thick heather, pine and gorse. The adjoining landlord had a huge estate and along his boundary fence you might have thought that five feet one way or the other would have made no difference, but there were niggly arguments about boundary lines. There was a problem with stones. The property there is high, with lots of snow, ice and frosts in the winter, and the course can be closed for eight, ten weeks. But it is a magnificent setting and it will settle down and mature very well. The broom is growing, and already the original two open fields are nicely covered. Each hole plays along its own avenue, the holes are tight and narrow and in time it could become a real classic.

The site is critical to the golf architect. The first thing any golf architect worth his salt will say to his client is,

'Show me your site.' Until he has done that, until he has seen the piece of land in question, there is virtually nothing else to discuss with the client. I am sure that most golf architects would agree that, as far as the UK is concerned, there are two prime sites to work on. One is through seaside sand dunes, where our classic links courses are laid out, and the other is through heather and pine country, again with a sandy sub-soil and with a reasonable amount of movement in it – that marvellous heather, pine, gorse, bracken golfing ground that has given us, for example, Sunningdale, The Berkshire, Woodhall Spa, Gleneagles, Parkstone, Ferndown, Broadstone. I am not a great fan of downland golf, up and down and across valleys, over mainly open and exposed land.

In the midst of all this came an approach from the Jersey Tourist Board. They were concerned at the amount of golfing holiday business going to the Costa del Sol and the other Spanish and Portuguese coasts. They accepted that the weather was better there, but Jersey was very much nearer to the UK market and things were beginning to be more expensive in Spain. La Moye in Jersey is a very full, very busy club with a course that had been re-jigged and was now a better test. Royal Jersey is on public land, with a right of way across it to the beach, and it is plagued by picnickers and rather open to the elements. Land in Jersey is hard to find, and expensive. We discovered a piece on the north-west tip of the island, about 150 acres, rather rugged and rough, with stunning views, a clifftop walk and even some old German fortifications. It had the potential of a fine, heathland course along the cliff tops, but when the wind blew, you couldn't stand up. In spite of a lot of hard work by us, the Tourist Board decided against the project. Run on tight, commercial lines, I believe it could have succeeded.

Despite our experience in Spain, we soon discovered that the jobs were still about. It was clear that in this business, there was to be no even pattern of work; you had to be philosophical and take the work where you found it, home or abroad. Once more, in the mid-1970s, it appeared that we were about to conquer the world with projects lined up in Borneo, Nigeria, the Ivory Coast and, back in Europe, in France.

In Borneo, our client was the government, and the government's representative, their resident engineer, was an enthusiastic 15-handicap golfer who had very fixed ideas on how a golf course should look, and how the specification should be applied. We were building to an American specification, very clearly set out, but the thing became almost a nightmare, what with rains, washouts, re-seeding, the very humid climate and interference by our resident engineer – a perfect illustration of how a little knowledge can be a dangerous thing.

Next came West Africa. A local architect had been commissioned by the East Central State Government of Nigeria to build a motel and rest and recreation centre at Ogutu, up-country. He contacted us, suggested we could build him a golf course, and the very first thing we discovered is that Nigeria, beyond any reasonable doubt, has some very strange customs when it comes to money.

As a result the job became a nightmare, and there were times when we wondered if we would survive, much less finish it. We still have around £20,000 locked up in the country which we are not allowed to take out. We thought of all kinds of schemes to get our hands on it, including buying an aircraft to fly it out, then selling the plane, but we failed. However, we did have one success there. We took a rather revolutionary attitude to grass. Greens in Nigeria had always been 'browns', simply oil poured on sand and rolled flat and firm. We noticed that we were more or less on the same latitude as Singapore, where they grow grass perfectly successfully in roughly the same climate; so why not in Nigeria? We took advice from Tifton College in

Georgia, USA, famous for its work in agronomy. A professor there assured us that grass would grow in that part of West Africa and we imported, secretly in two suitcases, the stolons. These are in fact plants, rather than seeds, which are planted and grow very quickly, spreading out sideways. What you then do is thin them out and replant, and you have a green within weeks. Later we repeated the process in the Ivory Coast. The greens aren't like Surrey or St Andrews, the grass is much rougher, and the greens don't quite look like billiards tables, but they are grass greens, with a putting surface.

In the Ivory Coast, we started the Presidential course at Yammasoukra in September 1977, and at Abidjan, the capital, there were nine holes public, eighteen holes private, on adjoining locations. In contrast to Nigeria, the Ivory Coast was paradise. It is a well-organized country – indeed in terms of the black African continent, it is a model state. President Félix Houphouet-Boigny is a first-class man. Yet work in these countries is so difficult, the weather so dramatic. We had one washout there, in which rain removed four fairways and greens, simply washed them down a hillside taking all our precious grass, seed and topsoil with it. We felt like Walter Huston and Humphrey Bogart in that final scene from *The Treasure of the Sierra Madre* – all the gold dust blowing away in the wind.

We tied in with a Paris-based company, Golf Européen, which had been doing some work in Europe but a lot of the time not being paid, or being paid very little very late. There was some distrust in the early days of the association, until they saw that we were getting the work done, and that the money came in. There was a new course at La Baule, starting at the end of 1975, a reconstruction at Mougins for the Cannes Country Club, and a new course to be done at Lacanau, near Bordeaux. But in the midst of all this, came crisis.

David Thomas had a neighbour in Cheshire who was

always interested in what David was doing. He was Michael Renton, chairman and managing director of Chancery Trust Ltd, a secondary merchant bank which he had formed. He had done some very astute things in business and gained a reputation for himself. David told him that most things were fine, but the one area that bothered us was finance and financial control, and that neither he nor I was particularly qualified to run a company with big sums of money involved. Renton suggested that Chancery could provide a service for us, and we agreed that it would buy twenty-two per cent of our company. At that time there were four partners: David, Pat Dawson, myself and Boris Hayklan (the Hay of Bale and Hay). Boris by then had rather lost interest and got into other things, and he now owns a big hotel in Cheltenham. Chancery bought his shares. Unfortunately, through a lack of real understanding the company became overstretched. Chancery eventually put in Richard Harding as part-time financial director, we paid them a management fee for his services, and he turned the thing around. Of course, we had work in hand, and some money was coming in, and fortunately we got two very big jobs which helped Harding put things straight. By the end of 1979, we had bought back the shares from Chancery and were independent again.

Chancery Trust subsequently merged with Arbuthnots, who were very big in the city of London, and Michael Renton became chief executive of the new company, and moved to London. So there was another stanza in the saga of Alliss and Thomas, makers of golf courses.

Next came Lucien Barrière and his company who own a chain of casinos and hotels in France, including the casino and L'Hermitage Hotel in the lovely resort town of La Baule, on the Atlantic coast at the southern end of Brittany. The hotel, managed by Gérard Mauger with his wife Andrée, is very attractive. The company had a small golf course with a pretty château-type clubhouse, but they ran into a water problem. They were given planning permission to develop the land, and found another site about five miles from the town. Finding such land in France is very difficult. Farmers have colossal power and political clout. There are not great runs of land. Farms are likely to be small and rather patchwork, scattered about in bits and pieces and handed down through the generations (this is a part of the problem for agriculture in the EEC).

Two and a half years after we had broken the ground at the new La Baule course, the French Open Championship was played on it, and we could take a proper pride in that. Of course, climate and grass down there are excellent – plenty of rain and sunshine. But La Baule, like so many other places, was not without its problems – from the committee. They had said, 'We want a new course, we don't want it too difficult because our best player is 5-handicap; we want two loops of nine; we don't want it too long because most of our membership is old, but we would like to be able to play the French championships from the back tees.' To get all that into eighteen holes is a rather tall order, but we got through it quite well. We did not install the irrigation system. A friend of a friend of a member was commanded by them to do that – he may well have been the local plumber – and botched the job. The Toro equipment was fine, but there were changes made in the fairway lines, wrong couplings went in, valves were wrong, pumps were wrong and the long hot summer of 1976 did not help.

They also decided that a local man would dig out the huge lake, about five acres in extent, which we wanted to provide the irrigation supply. That turned out too deep at one end, too shallow at the other, so the water capacity was insufficient. No one seemed to spot these things – everyone just sat around and did nothing and said it was someone else's responsibility. We gave the course its first cut, as required contractually, and left. When we went back on an inspection visit, the grass was three feet high! We almost lost it all, and had to scramble in a reaper to cut it at a cost of thousands of pounds. We made mistakes here. Our engineer did not pipe in a few springs properly, and this caused great problems which took years to correct; even now it's not perfect.

At Mougins, the brief we shared with Golf Européen was to extend the course and make it bigger and better. The extra land they provided was on a slope, and stony – difficult indeed. They did not want to spend too much money (!), and when we had done our best they complained, and talked of withholding money. At Bordeaux, the specification for the Lacanau course was for 6,600–6,700 metres. They changed that. Minutes were taken, signed, then lost, abandoned, forgotten, ignored. 'You said it was to be 7,000 metres,' they'd say, 'and the lake was to be 10,000 square metres and we measure it as only 7,500 square metres.' We'd say, 'We've made it smaller because it didn't look quite right, but we've made it deeper to hold the same volume of water.' In some cases this is just to get out of payment of the full contract price. Perhaps it is just bloody-mindedness. Perhaps it is all political. There is an eventual battle, an eventual settlement and everyone but us accepts that honour is satisfied. However, we were finally satisfied with Lacanau – it will become one of France's really fine courses.

Perhaps there is just something in the French mind that we do not understand. We would talk across the table and discuss plans and prices. They would say, 'Oh, that's too much.' We would say, all right, we can cut down the size of greens, of water hazards and water features and the drainage. Drainage is usually the most expensive item. So we'd say we'd cut the drainage bill from £40,000 to £20,000, and put in fewer drains, and if after a year or two there were wet patches, we would add drains then. But when the time came, they would have forgotten – and would demand to know why they did not have a complete drainage system, as the contract said originally, and a dry golf course. So there is further conflict.

Maybe they just don't like us British all that much. Maybe they have never forgotten that we have fought with them for about a thousand years. Maybe they cannot forget that with the Americans we bailed them out twice this century. But, politics aside, in golf course architecture you have to accept that drains do break, that you cannot tell finally how water will run until the course is built, that trees and bushes and grass take time to grow, that a golf course is a living thing, in short: 'If you want to see my course at its very best, come back in twenty-five years' time.'

From all this we had learned one thing – patience. Golf courses need time. When a golf course has been designed and constructed, and the grass germinates, that is merely the moment of birth, and the next five years are vital, as is the quality of the greenkeeping after construction is finished. In probably only one course have we not had post-construction greenkeeping problems, and that was at Blairgowrie, where the greenkeeping staff accepted our greens and tees in sequence, and took them over formally and went on to do a good job with the new course.

Sometimes you have the impression that life, at home as well as overseas, has to be one long compromise. This was brought home to me by the disappointment we had at Turnberry Hotel. We were asked in 1975 to quote for alterations to the Ailsa Course, in preparation for the 1977 Open Championship which was to be played there for the first time. We thought this would be an outstanding opportunity for our company, Golf Construction Ltd, to make its mark in prestige terms, and David Thomas, Pat Dawson and I went up there, looked very carefully at the entire property, spent a lot of time on it, and made a three-part presentation. We proposed a major scheme which involved altering about forty bunkers, but the plan they eventually approved was a much lesser one.

Meanwhile there was a huge wrangle between the Royal and Ancient Golf Club, staging the championship, and British Transport Hotels Ltd, owners of the property, as to who should pay for what, and what precisely needed doing. I should have thought that BTH, who have always struggled to make Turnberry Hotel really profitable, should just have taken the situation by the scruff of the neck and said, 'We'll do it – we'll find the money somehow.' As it was, the whole thing turned out to be the usual compromise, and we put in six bunkers, a new tee, realigned the 18th tee to eliminate an area of crowd congestion around the 5th green, 6th tee and 17th green areas. All in all I suppose it went fairly well, but it was a case for me of what might have been.

In all the discussions, Jim Arthur, consultant agronomist to the Royal and Ancient, was present, as was Tom Telford, then the BTH grounds and golf courses superintendent. They seemed very anti-Golf Construction.

It was made very clear to us that we were not to use any material that was on the property. Everything had to be brought in. Now there are plenty of places at Turnberry where we could have excavated material. The huge practice ground could have provided turf for tees and tee surrounds. In the end, after much nagging, they gave us a piece of the rough, yes *rough*, which we used for a new 8th tee, and which we cut and fed and eventually made a perfectly good tee.

It seemed to be one continuous battle. Some of the new bunkers were cut so badly that it almost looked deliberate and they had to be re-done. Only about one-third of the work we recommended was done. The Open of 1977 became one of the classic championships of history, because of the par-busting duel between Watson and Nicklaus, but under well-nigh perfect weather conditions only three players finished under par. I certainly hope that changes will be made for any future Open there, although the costs will have escalated by three or four times. Turnberry is such a majestic setting that it was a tragedy our changes were not all done to make it the very best seaside course in the country. Hard by the water, with holes 4, 8, 9, 10 and 11 hanging over the sea, it could be made just about the most dramatic course in the world.

Perhaps communication, or lack of it, was part of the Turnberry problem, with all the parties. And certainly communications problems, in the sense that people do not listen to what you say, or do not want to hear what you say, may have been part of the next story that unfolds, at the Belfry, Sutton Coldfield.

We were first approached by Alan Hunter, the estates manager for Greenall Witney, the brewers who owned the Belfry Hotel, to build an eighteen-hole course on the land around their hotel. We suggested that they should get the PGA involved so that they might get a major tournament played there. We designed eighteen holes, and Alan went off. Next thing we knew was that Greenall had appointed PA Consultants to find a partner for them in the project, and James Cook of PA produced Ellerman, the shipping and travel group. Now the concept was to be thirty-six holes, the PGA was involved and was to have its national office on the site, and the biggest drama of all was that the Belfry was to be the site of a Ryder Cup match, as soon as it was ready. We were asked to produce 'the championship course and one other course'. We did various routes and designs. They had to buy additional land for this and finished with some 325 acres. Much of it was agricultural land, under potatoes, owned by farmers who had contracts with Smith's Crisps and Golden Wonder, so there was a good deal of compensation paid to them.

We saw the Belfry as something different, something special, a very big deal indeed. And we both had a very strong feeling about the whole thing because of the PGA presence, and the brief that it was to be a Ryder Cup venue of the future. We produced a package at a price of £380,000 which we thought adequate but not extortionate. We would not make a vast fortune out of it, but, as I say, we had this strong feeling of personal involvement, personal responsibility.

The package, the design, was difficult. It was basically indifferent land, with nothing very dramatic about the site, which was a flat, open valley. We saw the need to build up greens, make mounds to hide one thing from another, anticipate lots of planting so that, come the year dot, the fairways would be separated and the place would look more like Wentworth. We absolutely had to get it right, and David used to go to bed thinking, 'God what happens when Jack and Lee and Tom and these guys come to play it? What will they think of it?' He'd lie awake, I know, thinking of ways in which to make it more difficult, super-special, super-sophisticated.

So the money started to fly out of the window. There were two lakes, a big one at the top of the property, and a smaller one lower down which could be kept in balance by a reverse pump. But we needed so much fill that the lakes kept getting bigger and bigger. There was a main public road running along one side of the site, and the best screening for that was a mound. This might well have been an extra on the contract – we didn't press it. But we had heavy machinery running all over the place for three months. We had six big Volvo BM dumpers, six-wheelers, paddling around. I shudder to think of it now – £300 per day, each. We had two D8s and a D9 for quite a while and they were £35 per hour, working for about five weeks! We certainly didn't take much money home from the Belfry job, I can tell you. But we opened the Derby course on schedule on 1 May 1977, and by agreement held back the Brabazon course, the championship course, for an extra four or six weeks to get the extra growth it needed.

There were the inevitable weather problems during

construction, a hot dry summer in 1976, a virtual drought the following summer, then at the end of 1977 a deluge of rain. We had germination by that time, but we lost lots of the finer grasses which were simply washed out. The stronger grass, the rye, remained in places. Now rye grass grows vertically, not sideways, so it looks green, but it had no volume to it, no fat, no cushion, and so the ball went right to the bottom. We put in all the most sophisticated and expensive Toro grasscutting and maintenance machinery, but I'm afraid the greenkeeping was just too much for the people we left there. They did not seem to realize that with all the heavy machinery on the site for such a long time there would be lots of compaction around the place, and that during the first six months they should have been busy letting the fairways breathe – aerating, hollow-tining, breaking up the surface, feeding it, top-dressing it, re-seeding where necessary. They seemed afraid to get to grips with it. So, for the first two years of its finished existence, *we* got all the blame.

Including our one year of post-construction supervision, we finished in 1978, but we felt we had a moral responsibility to the place and we went back, and back. There were continuing problems with water, and irrigation. There were problems with greens. The Penncross seed, on the sand and peat greens which we had built, needs regular work, virtually every month, to keep out thatch and compaction. The greens need hollow-tining, slitting, scarifying and fertilizing regularly, which is no more than routine greenkeeping practice in the United States, but not as yet in this country. On these greens, the ball should pitch and stop. For a while at the Belfry, every shot was going through the green. The Ryder Cup match of 1981 had been scheduled there for September. With several more growing seasons from 1978 through to that date, I believe it could have been played there. But at the English Classic in summer 1979, Brian Barnes and several other players made a public damnation of the course, and the PGA decided to move, making a commitment to Walton Heath for 1981. There had been problems with stone, and some contractors were not one hundred per cent on the ball with the result that some parts were left untidy. But three hundred acres or so, with streams running through, need a *lot* of maintenance. I would say now that there were not enough men on the course in the early stages, also that some of those present did not perhaps take enough pride in their work.

The recurring problem of 'germination' is so critical to our work, so much the subject of squabbles and wrangles with the client, that it has almost become funny – but not quite. We have spent an enormous amount of time trying to see that contracts are written so specifically that there never can be any misunderstanding between us and the client, but I am not sure that even after a dozen years we have got it right. Perhaps no one quite gets this right. Germination, I suppose, can be taken to mean that grass is growing, and the moment of germination is usually taken as the time when the architect and constructor can hand the course into the care of the club's greenkeeping staff. But when is that? What do we mean by 'grass growing'? Do we mean a beautiful carpet of green? Do we mean the first sprigs of grass coming through? And if we mean that, how many sprigs per square inch? If you stand fifty yards away and look at a green and it has a fair overall cover, is that the moment of truth? It is difficult, very difficult to define contractually. Clients do not always accept our interpretation. After germination, we undertake to do the first two grass cuts, and give a one-year guarantee to come back and overseed any areas which have been washed out, which are thin, or whatever. As I said, perhaps our one outstanding success in this area was at Blairgowrie, where the existing experienced greenkeeping staff passed and accepted each tee, green and fairway as we went along. Greenkeepers are critical – they are the men who have to bring the course to prime condition in the five years *after* we have built the thing, and handed it over.

For us, making golf courses has been a marvel. Our experience in so many different countries has been infuriating, frustrating, stimulating, fulfilling. On reflection, it may have been the most important slice of our lives because the thought that must sustain every architect, every builder, is that his work may well last one hundred years. Golf courses are good monuments to leave behind.

So much depends on the land, the money, the water, and above all, the client. What does he want? What is the purpose of his course? Is it to be a so-called championship course, a resort course, a pleasant suburban setting for the local golf club? Priorities are essential for the designer. Our ideal client would say, 'I have a very fixed and clear idea of what I want. I want a resort-type course, say, which is playable by the majority of golfers. I have a nice piece of land, somewhere between 125 and 155 acres, with a little bit of undulation, with water running through it which we can use, and I have sufficient money to do the whole thing.' We have not come across too many of these animals, but if we did, we would then want a very frank discussion of just how big, how grand, how exciting he wants to see his project on completion.

Robert Trent Jones, famous for his philosophy of moving mountains of earth and excavating enormous lakes and water hazards, has summarized his own attitude as 'to make a course on which it is difficult for professionals to make birdies, easy for the average player to make bogeys'. I think that says it rather well. We try to make the same set of hazards apply to all the players, from different tees. The professional tee is tucked back out of sight into the woods. The average golfer has no right to be there. He plays off a middle tee, with his club medal tee say ten yards further back, and the ladies' tee would be set forward, all playing into the range of the same hazards.

When we started we made greens which were rather simple, only because we did not have enough experience. Now we try to look at the broader concept and use existing mounds and contours in the overall design so that the natural mounding runs itself into the green and the whole thing, not just the putting surface, is landscaped. This is a Trent Jones technique, in which he landscapes the whole unit, then cuts bunkers and putting surfaces out afterwards. We also now try to set the greens rather across the line of the shot, which lets us place bunkers in many positions to give more interesting, varied and more difficult pin positions.

The ideal would be a course which gives the most pleasure to the most people. From the back tees it would be a positive challenge to the highest class of player. And from the ladies' tees it should be a relatively equal challenge, offering the same problems of hazards as face the very best player. Having said that, it is not too often easy to get all the factors right. You have to think of getting the balance right – two short holes on each nine, one or two par fives on each nine, with the rest balanced between short, medium and long par fours. You have to consider in which directions the holes should best run, and the direction of the prevailing wind. Should the holes run with, against or across the wind? Where does the sun rise and set? You don't want the first hole to play into sunrise, the last into sunset. And ideally no short holes should run in exactly the same direction. And how shall we relate the standard scratch score to par? So many factors, and all of them governed by the shape of the site – square, diamond-shaped, a long skinny rectangle, or almost anything you can conceive.

There are so many set ideas, taboos, in golf-course architecture, and I think most of them are nonsense. You would be crucified if you built the Old Course at St Andrews today, with all those hidden bunkers, enormous greens and fairways crossing each other, as at Alwoodley in

Leeds. Royal Lytham begins with a short hole, Lindrick ends with a short hole. Neither should be allowed. Yet these are great golf courses which have survived for years, you just can't be dogmatic about it. What about Cypress Point at Monterey in California? There are two holes there which are both only around 300 yards long, but they are two of the greatest holes I have ever seen in my life. Funny little holes, hidden away by sandhills so that you have to drive with a 4-wood or 4-iron, then chip from the top of a hill, or if you want to blast away with a driver, then you might never see your ball again. Then there is the 16th across the water at Cypress Point, or that dinky little 7th hole at Pebble Beach, just 108 yards, downhill towards the water. These are dream holes, marvellous holes that you would want to put into any course you ever made. I do like a balance of holes, but I think long iron play is rather going out of the game – I like to see a few par fours of more than 400 yards which demand 2- and 3-iron seconds.

In all of this experience, we had nothing but help from the Americans. One of the most fascinating features of American life is how open their society really is, how much information they make freely available to you. Perhaps they are just surprised that we should want to know how they do it, and intrigued that we should be interested in how they build, what kind of sands, seeds and mixtures they use. Their climatic changes are very different, much more extreme, with parts of the country suffering hurricanes, burning hot summers, freezing winters, wet in the North-west, arid through the South-west, and most of the Northern and North-eastern states under snow for two or three months each year. This has made them work harder, study more, become more sophisticated and scientific in the growing and development of grasses. And they spend fifty times more money than we do to get it right. At their average semi-private club, a club where you can play by paying a green fee as opposed to a private club which is exclusively for members and guests, they will think nothing of spending £25,000 on fertilizers, insecticides, seeds and the like. No machinery, no wages, just material – an enormous amount of money by British standards.

It has to be said that there is much of a sameness about US Open courses. Every venue I have seen I would call a parkland course with the exception of those in the Monterey Peninsula area – Cypress Point, Monterey, Spyglass Hill, Pebble Beach – I would be happy to play Cypress Point for the rest of my life. Most American courses are tree-lined, with heavy grass rough, but no heather, gorse or undergrowth as we know it. Yet they are always splendidly maintained, in excellent condition with perfect organization, huge clubhouses. But then American golfers are prepared to pay, to pay for service and quality, and shout loud and long if they do not get it. Not many clubs in the UK have subscriptions of more than £200 at the moment. That is less than $500. And that is for one of our very best clubs. For the Americans, $500 is a joke. Their facilities, budgeting, greens staff are all immense, and the courses are all immaculately groomed.

Yet the people in Britain will say, 'Ah, but it's not seaside golf, it's not links golf, it's not open and exposed, it should be rugged and rough.' That is the 'outdoor boarding-school' syndrome – run through a field of nettles in the snow at 5 a.m., come back to a cold shower and a lump of porridge with salt on it, prefects give you a good flogging, do you good, and sleep with boxing gloves on. Don't believe all that crap –all that does is make you a colonel in the KGB.

But now there may be a marvellous finale to the story of our experiences in building courses. Down at Liphook in Hampshire there is a fellow by the name of Ken Wood, with a lovely piece of property called Old Thorns Farm. He always wanted to have his own golf course. His property is quite near Forest Mere, which he once part-owned. His own residence, an eight-bedroomed manor house, is to be the nucleus of our clubhouse. There will be twenty-eight suites, with planning permission for a further thirty. There is a swimming pool, and saunas, beauty and massage parlour facilities for business seminars are also planned, and the whole thing, I am obliged to say, is a dream, a dream which we, Golf Construction, hope to make come true. There are lovely views, with water, and the landscape is like the Old Course at Sunningdale, like Swinley Forest, Woking, Parkstone or Ferndown. To my knowledge, it is the first time everything has fallen into place. The financing is there. The ground is right. It is being done by professionals in every aspect. We have a great opportunity to avoid all the mistakes that all the golf architects have made, or have had to make, in the past. It should be just about ready in late 1981, and we will get it right – for Ken Wood, and for Golf Construction Ltd.

CHAPTER ELEVEN

The Way Ahead

Once upon a time, a man named Ernest Button lived in a big house by the 17th green of Parkstone golf course. Button was the head of PA Management Consultants, a company of 'headhunters' in London. One of the functions of PA was and still is to find high-powered executives for high-powered jobs and Button's clients were the companies seeking these people. So in business terms, Button operated at a high altitude, and the whole thrust of his life was research, analysis, interview, the psychology of people and all the rest of that. One of his personal thrusts, perhaps obsessions, was organization and efficiency. I was professional at Parkstone in the early sixties and had long conversations – it should be said arguments – with him on how all this could be applied to professional tournament golf and golfers.

Ernest was quite persuaded that if a competent golfer practised a ten-foot putt often enough, he would eventually be able to hole every single one. He insisted that if such a man practised hard enough, long enough, intelligently enough, he must become a champion. He totally rejected the existence of any 'X-factor', any human error or frailty, the degree of dampness on a putting green, the nap of the grass (which required further acts of judgment) or the state of a man's digestive tract at any given moment. We had heated discussions on the subject, but he was very pedantic, would not be moved. He resolved to bring together a team of young players and train them and condition them for tournament play and in a word to sponsor them, and to my knowledge this was the first sponsorship of a tournament team in golf.

Private individuals for many years have gone out of their way to help players financially, and not every sponsor has been greedy, not every player has had misfortunes with sponsors and managers such as Orville Moody, David Graham, Lee Trevino and others have had. And many golf clubs, in particular Jewish clubs such as Coombe Hill, Moor Allerton, Dunham Forest, Dyrham Park, Potters Bar and others, have been very helpful to young players. But Button did it very scientifically, as you might expect from such a man. He brought together a team of young men who were to be trained very seriously in golf, in physical fitness, whose diets were to be regulated, who were to live and work and travel in a properly scheduled fashion, all subsidized by Ernest Button, administered by Max Faulkner. The project did well. It did not produce an Open Champion. It broke up as the fellows grew older and decided to go their own ways, but all of his team – Brian Barnes, Tommy Horton, Mike Ingham, Sandy Wilson, Ian Clarke – have gone on and in their different ways made something of their lives, for which they should be grateful to Ernest Button.

All this is by way of a preamble, and we now skip forward twenty years to 1979 and the Dunhill golf team. Some background to this concept is now required. The Dunhill company produces many high quality products – handbags, toiletries, leather goods, cigarette lighters, and is now very substantially into the leisure clothing business, with an elegant and expensive range. It also markets cigarettes, cigars and tobacco products. Dunhill is part-owned by Rothmans International, the world-wide company which, using one brand name or the other, has been very extensively involved in sports promotion in the UK. There was a Piccadilly golf tournament as far back as 1962, played at Hillside in Lancashire, and won by Peter Thomson, and from 1964 to 1976 Piccadilly sponsored the World Match Play Championship at Wentworth, after the British Open the most important, most exciting, most watched event in the country.

For commercial reasons, Rothmans withdrew from all sports sponsorship in 1976, but by 1979 were ready to come back, at a different level, with a different philosophy, and they should have been welcomed. I really cannot imagine what professional golf would do, what professional sport would do if cigarette companies pulled out of sponsorship entirely. It would leave an enormous void. The late seventies were a difficult time for sponsorship, and for cigarette company sponsorship in particular, probably because smoking is always a difficult, emotive subject – for governments, for health authorities, for do-gooders, for authoritarians, even for the people who smoke.

Dunhill decided to start at a youthful level. They promoted an amateur event in which any club member in the country could participate. And they decided to form the Dunhill golf team of young professionals. The concept was to select four promising young players who would each be given a wardrobe of Dunhill clothing. They were to be provided with cars. They had an annual retaining fee on a three-year contract, reviewed each year, and they were to keep all of their tournament winnings. A manager, Jim Lynch from the Stoke Poges club, would look after them and I – and here I declare my interest – was to be director of the entire project.

It was a wonderful opportunity for four lucky lads, but there were major problems in finding them. The selection process would be difficult. In January 1979, for example it would have been easy to sit down and list on a piece of paper such names as Howard Clark, Sandy Lyle, Michael King as very promising players who might have welcomed such sponsorship. In January 1981, we might have had to think of young Brian Marchbank, or of Peter McEvoy, or Ronan Rafferty, outstanding amateurs who might have decided to play professional. But Dunhill took the view that they should not be seeking players with existing reputations, but should rather look for unseasoned lads who had a chance to succeed and stood to benefit most from this kind of assistance.

Other factors applied in the selection process, and any selection process I find fascinating. If you are selecting the England football team of the moment and Kevin Keegan is fit and in form, then you don't spend much time discussing his position – you simply write down Keegan. But if he is not available and there are two or three alternatives who are almost equal in ability, which one do you choose, and why? So many factors had to be considered with the Dunhill boys.

First, was it essential that they all had the 'players' card', that passport from the European Tournament Players Division of the PGA which would permit them to play in all events controlled by the ETPD? Had they all finished in the top sixty players in the 1979 season, which would exempt them from pre-qualifying for the tournaments in the 1980 season? If they were not, could we reasonably expect them to pass through these pre-qualifying requirements and gain entry to the tournaments proper? Next, if they did that, would they be good enough to 'make the cut', after thirty-six holes of the tournament proper, and so play all seventy-two holes of the tournament? That would be a major target for them, since all players who complete the seventy-two holes proper of 'this' week's tournament automatically qualify for direct entry into 'next' week's tournament. Those are the rules of the game the lads would have to face. We chose Donald Armour, Garry Cullen, Dennis Durnian and Willy McColl, and of the four only Cullen had finished in the top sixty in 1979. The others would have to go through the mill, take their chances with all the pre-qualifying systems and so, apart from any anguish involved, build up their experience and, we hoped, their confidence.

Certainly they would have to wear the clothes well, drive cars sensibly, refrain from insulting anyone and behave in a tolerably civilized manner. Dunhill took the position that the boys were *not* going to be sacked if they scored eighty or eighty-one. But since the public image of the company and of the team was all important, they definitely *would* be sacked if they didn't appear to be trying, if they did not work hard enough, if they misbehaved or became a nuisance. All told, it was an interesting re-entry into the game by a very important company. It was not unreasonable to imagine that if it had succeeded, the future investment of Dunhill in professional golf might be considerably extended. But that was a point that seemed wholly lost to certain members of the ETPD.

At the annual general meeting for 1980 of the ETPD, held in the press centre at the John Haig Tournament Players Championship, at Moortown Golf Club, Leeds, in September, those present passed a resolution that no company could sponsor more than one player, commencing April 1981. This meeting was attended by some forty players, from a total membership of more than two hundred.

This decision seemed to me to epitomize all that is and has always been wrong with the tournament game, going back to my own time and before. The players and their organization simply do not seem to have the faintest knowledge of the facts of business and commercial life. They do not seem to have the slightest idea of how to treat sponsors and sponsoring companies. What the players decided at Leeds meant in effect that a company, if it had a mind to, could spend £500,000 on one player – but could not spread that £500,000 across ten players. It is another aspect of what I call the Rolls-Royce syndrome, the mentality that afflicts so much of life in our country, which says if I can't have it you can't have it. You know the kind of thing – instead of saying, 'Look at that magnificent Rolls-Royce – by God, I'm going to work my tail off until I have one,' people say, 'Why should *he* have a Rolls-Royce when I don't?'

It was a piddling decision, because it meant that the only people who would suffer would be the young fellows, the little men, not the Lyles, the Faldos and the Ballesteroses. I was delighted to learn that Dunhill had their lawyers looking at the decision with the thought of challenging it, in law. It remains an illustration of the fact that the players still somehow believe – as they did in my day – that the game and the sponsors owe them a living and that they, the players, are somehow doing the sponsors a favour by turning up and playing in their pro-am and in their tournament. As often as not, they play these pro-ams, with three or four sponsor's guests, people important to the sponsor's business, and treat them with boorishness or indifference. In October 1980, I read that Freda Weetman was planning to sell all Harry's *objets d'art*, trophies, souvenirs, memorabilia or whatever from his career, with the idea of helping youngsters in the game. But if Dunhill are hit on the head, you would find yourself wondering why she bothers with such a noble plan.

The players still do not seem to realize that they are in show business, that they are in competition with an increasing number of sports and leisure activities for the public's pennies, and for exposure in the media. They do not seem to take note of the fact that with the exception of the Open, the World Match Play and, significantly in 1980, the Bob Hope Classic, golf attendances were going down. And surely they should observe that the big crowds at the Bob Hope Classic went to see the show business personalities, and not the golfers. They do not accept that they are in a minority sport that will never really challenge the big ones in our country, which are football and racing. There is a limit to where golf can go in Europe, with only some thirty weeks in the year that can be used for tournaments. Almost all these weeks are being used, so that the quality and not the quantity of events has to be increased, and the players are simply not doing enough in this respect. Moreover in recent seasons they seem to be taking events to courses of very high quality and consequently are perhaps neglecting areas starved of golf. They really would do well to spend some money on a proper market research programme to investigate the potential and the needs of the game, and act on the results.

Golf has to live with a whole new world in which there is a market for the best, but in which people are not much interested in anything else. And although it is a subject quite obviously close to my heart, the professional game must have a rational policy about television – and there is just a danger that already there may be too much golf on television.

I have called this chapter 'The Way Ahead'. I wanted to try to take a look into the future, at best a perilous business, though if I am lucky and reach the allotted span, I will be taking a peek into the next century. That is twenty more years, and I daresay they will be eventful years, and when you reach the age of fifty, you know that they will whisk past very quickly. It would be fanciful to suppose that in the year 2001 we shall be shuttling to the planets, lunch will be one small tablet, every telephone will have its own television receiver and our cars will be running on one small eternal energy pack, silent and smokeless. But I suspect the world does not turn quite that quickly.

One of the most interesting developments in the game in the past few years has been the emergence of women's professional tournament golf, and the creation of the Women's Professional Golfers' Association, associated, I am happy to say, with the PGA proper. In the United States, with its greater resources, its greater population, the ladies' tour has been going along with increasing success for some thirty years or more. Here they are just into their third year, and with some forty or fifty players regularly involved, it will take a few more years to build up. Its existence owes a great deal to Vivienne Saunders, whose enthusiasm and determination have helped make the whole thing possible.

I accepted the presidency of the WPGA because I believe in its future, and because I believe I can help them. I made it clear that I would not want to be a president who merely presented prizes, but suggested that I try to help with publicity, advice, with getting sponsors and discussing venues. We are very lucky to have as our executive director Barry Edwards, and his wife Carol who handles press relations. Edwards is greatly experienced in marketing, which is exactly what the new organization needs. They have done an outstanding job, and in 1980, only their second full year, they were in profit.

The leading money-winner in 1980 was the Scottish lass, Muriel Thomson, with £8008 in official prize money, the fifth girl on the list won £5172, the tenth £2871. So at the moment no one is getting very fat. But sponsors are coming along. At the moment, the top prize money, for the British Open, is around £15,000, and I am sure the money will increase year by year. The promotion of these WPGA events is attractive to various companies. The Carlsberg company has made a substantial investment in the women's tour, which you may think odd. Is lager considered a women's product? Perhaps not, but the Carlsberg people note that some forty per cent of their sales are now coming from supermarkets, and women do the supermarket shopping. Hitachi, too, are into women's golf, tying it in with dealer promotions and dealer entertainment. The point is that club golfers can identify with women's golf more closely than they can with the game of young giants like Lyle and Faldo and Norman, who hit the ball miles. Club players, with their very best shot, will hit the ball about the same distance as the girls do. And all the girls are well aware that sponsors and sponsors' guests are critical to their future, so they work very hard at their public relations and the whole image of women's pro golf. No club throwing, no squabbling about rules, no bad behaviour of any kind here.

Under the direction of Edwards, it will all come good. It will demand progressively more media coverage. It may be some years before the girls force their way into television, and they may need to produce a superstar to do it, but give it time, give it time. It has a chance of becoming more international. In Australia at the end of 1980, I talked with some of the Australian girls who had tried the US tour. They had found it very tough going, financially as much as anything else. The women's golf tour in the States is just as expensive as the men's and I suggested to them that they might think of playing a few seasons in the UK to get some experience, learn to play, learn their trade before tackling the US on a permanent basis. I believe our British tour will be stimulated by players from Australia, New Zealand and South Africa, as the men's tour has been over the years.

I cannot foresee major changes in the playing of the game. Look back twenty years and there is very little difference. Graphite and aluminium shafts have come and gone, without lingering long. We may get round to synthetic surfaces for greens and tees – some interesting work is being done in that area. Amateur championships and amateur tournament golf, which with the exception of the Walker Cup match has lost its audience, will not, I fear, get it back. But more and more leisure time, shorter working weeks and longer holidays will mean that more and more people will want to play the game, and with the pressure on land, and the cost of land, there will be many problems. More and more courses will be needed, and I hope that more and more local government authorities will come to provide them, and to see that they can build and operate golf courses profitably. And existing clubs will have to make better use of the plant – somehow make the clubhouses into social centres every night of the week, and fill their courses every hour of the day.

And here we might consider the most neglected people in the whole spectrum of the game, the greenkeepers. As president of the British Golf Greenkeepers' Association, this is close to my heart. Walter Heeles from Knaresborough wrote and asked me to be their president. I accepted on the grounds that it would be impossible for me to go to all their dinners and events – each section has an annual dinner – but I would try to help in every way I could, mainly by publicizing their work. Golf club attitudes to greenkeepers just do not seem to change. I see so many greenkeepers' sheds looking exactly like the one I knew as a boy, forty years ago. If there is any running water, it will be ice-cold. There is hardly ever any hot water, no proper loo, no place to cook hot food, no place to wash – often greenkeepers take their food in rooms which contain chemicals and peat and golf course materials. Few clubs provide uniforms and waterproof clothing for people who are liable to be out at all hours of the day in all weathers. Of course, there are a *few* good clubs who do.

Our ideas in these respects are light years behind the Americans, and I say that not believing that it is necessary to copy everything the Americans do. They do spend a lot of money on greenkeeping, though, and money is the root of this evil in our country, with club committees and management responsible for the lack of it. Lots of greenkeepers themselves, of course, still live in the dark ages – they won't change, won't move, won't adapt, won't even try. And I often wonder why women are not employed on golf courses. With the sophisticated machinery available now, there is much less physical labour involved than before, and I would have thought women could do most jobs in maintaining courses these days. Greenkeepers, like so many others in the game, can do with much more support.

Young professionals coming into the game, or youngsters planning to come into the professional game, must be helped more. So many youngsters are beaten before they get started. I heard of one young man who won his player's card at the winter school, and qualified for the tournaments, then played his first seven tournaments without winning one penny of prize-money. Now how does that fellow pay his bills? The ETPD must find some way to help people like him. We cannot hope to duplicate the American college scholarship system, where their universities offer scholarships to promising young players which allow them to study half the time and play golf the other half. And to spur them on there is competitive golf between the colleges which puts a fine edge on their performances and gives them intensive competitive experience, so that when they do go into the professional tournaments they have some idea of what to expect. Perhaps we should have a new category of 'pre-professionals', so that promising amateurs who wanted to play professionally might have, say, six months' help before they started. We have plenty of residential colleges and universities which are closed for many weeks in the year and which could be used as bases for such courses. I'm sure there are enough companies around, like Dunhill, for example, which could make it financially feasible.

I do see some warning signs for the future. In the United States, they are playing for a total of $12 million, in the UK for some $3 million and in Japan for probably rather more than that. In America, they seem to think that 'CBS will pay, ABC will pay, NBC will pay.' I am not so sure. I see these young American professionals coming out of the locker rooms, boys who have done nothing very much, and saying, 'Where's my car, where's my courtesy car, where the hell is that damned woman who's supposed to be driving me?' That 'damned woman' might well be the wife of the boss of the Chase Manhattan Bank, doing her bit without payment or thanks, to help the tournament along. So much is taken for granted. We assume all over the world that the television companies will go on forever, that sponsors will go on forever.

There was a world conference of all the PGAs in Australia in 1980, when they discussed yet again a world circuit. That is becoming a hoary old chestnut first talked about more than twenty years ago. In fact, I believe there is just too much golf being played around the world at the moment, and in that sense a world circuit exists even if it is not centrally co-ordinated. The players have events in Canada and the US; East and West and South Africa; Australia, New Zealand and Japan and the Far East; the UK and Europe, and, increasingly, South America. And all these events offer very attractive money. Costs are becoming enormous, costs to sponsors, costs to spectators. I am not sure just how much growth is left in the tournament game and already there are some indicators that one or two tournaments in America may drop out. One could see a US tour running from February to the end of August, with the Americans free to play anywhere else in the world between times, but you can be sure if anyone is going to control a world circuit – and it will need an overriding governing body – it will be the Americans.

I am also occasionally amused at the statistics of success and failure in professional golf. Surely, anyone considering it as a career who was then told that only some twenty-five players, that is ten per cent of the members of the organization, made a profit in 1980 from official winnings, and also that of some 300 young fellows who go to Portugal to qualify for their ETPD cards, only one or two *break par* over four rounds – any sensible man told that would simply never start the business, would go off and dig ditches, or be a property dealer or a prime minister. But there is never any shortage of débutants – the game is ultimately about glory as much as money.

Parting Shot

You have read my version of all that has happened to me in my first fifty years. All I now want for the rest of my life is to try to bring up my children sensibly, look after my people, and in whatever I am doing, do it to the limit of my ability. There is much still to be done, many places still to go, many people still to meet. And my credo is still best contained in that Harry Secombe song that sustained me many years ago:

> They say I've reached the time of life,
> That's slightly past the prime of life,
> And yet, and yet, towards the sun I'm turning.

> They tell me I should save myself,
> It's time that I behave myself,
> And yet, and yet, there's bridges still for burning.

> Let the young and foolish pick the blossom on the vine,
> There's years to waste, before they'll taste
> The flavour of the wine.

> The rosebuds I've been gathering, the children I've been
>   fathering,
> May fade and die, take wings and fly and leave, to my
>   regret,
> And yet, and yet, it seems to me the best is yet to be.

Sometimes I think I have been blessed in life – so many people have helped me along the way. This is a list of the 'few' and I doff all my caps to all of them: Anthony Reid, Marshall and Carol Bellow, David and Karen Wickins, Ronnie Sumrie; Dick Penfold, Humphrey and Michael McMasters, Buzzer Hadingham, Leslie and Freda Shoesmith, Ian Peacock, Ian Mitchell, Jimmy Ross, Tom Gambol, John Reid, Frank Jobson, all Slazenger at one time; Muriel Jordan, Fred and Hilda Wormold; John and Lynn Greenwood; Sam and Stella Goldman; the Fingrets – Stanley and Shirley, Peter and Anne; Aubrey and Pam Phillipson; Lord Belwin; Charles and 'Fofo' Dunsdon; Roy and Beryl Beckett, John and Flo Mason, Jimmy Cooper, Gordon Dean, Jimmy Tarbuck, Bruce Forsyth, David Gow, Geoffrey Ford, Roy Cooper; Maureen Greig, Cliff and Jean Michelmore; Glyn and Helen Thomas, Ann and Jeff Rutherford, Jock and Elsie Anderson; John Plank, Harry Dickens, Michael Seligman, Phil Pilley, Ken Young; Alan Payne, Johan Sigurdson, Stuart and Wendy Barber, Freddie Wallis, Malcolm Chisholm, Victor Sandleson; Colin McInerney, Lionel Fynn, Ian Prentice, Archie Preston, Malcolm Green; George Makey, Justin Rickards; Peter Gammon, Ray Connium – and the old boys, in the beginning, who encouraged me when I was a lad at Ferndown.

My fondest regards to all of them and to my acquaintances everywhere.

INDEX

ABC TV, 71, 145, 155, 160, 161, 162, 176, 178, 179, 238
Aaron, Tom, 86, 124
Aber, Doddy, 66
Abrahams, Bob, 146, 193
Abrahams, Sir Charles, 50
Acheson, Dean, 42
Adams, Jimmy, 43
Aisher, Jack, 186
Ali, Muhammad, 9, 103, 144
All England Lawn Tennis Club, 144
Allen, Bruce, 199
Alliss, Alec, 18, 25, 28, 41, 42, 45, 46, 47, 58
Alliss, Carol, 45, 59
Alliss, Gary, 43, 45, 59, 152
Alliss, George, 20
Alliss (Grey), Jackey, 56, 57, 58, 59, 62, 64, 65, 72, 73, 74, 75, 76
Alliss, Mrs Percy, 18, 20, 55, 59
Alliss (McGuiness), Joan, 41, 43, 44, 55, 56, 58, 59, 62, 64
Alliss, Percy, 17, 19, 21, 25, 35, 41, 58, 90, 130
Alliss, Sara, 73, 76
Alliss, Simon, 71, 76, 155
Alliss, Victoria, 73–6
Almaina Park GC, Alicante, 70, 207, 208, 209
Altrincham GC, 12
Alvin, Kate, 155
Alwoodley GC, 63, 224
Aoki, Isao, 52
Armour, Donald, 231
Armstrong, Neil, 160
Around With Alliss, 71, 146, 169, 193–8
Arrowe Park GC, 28

Arthur, Jim, 218
Assistants' Match Play Championship, 35
Attlee, Clement, 165
Augusta National GC, 53, 117, 155
Australian Open Championship, 110, 120, 121

BBC TV, 71, 72, 83, 144, 145, 146, 153, 155, 168, 170, 173, 175, 177, 179, 181, 183, 184, 185, 186, 192, 193, 194, 196, 198, 199, 200
Bader, Douglas, 12, 194
Baiocchi, Hugh, 101
Ballesteros, Severiano, 10, 11, 92, 103, 114, 115, 118, 132, 138, 191, 201, 233
Baltusrol GC, 114
Bannatyne, Jimmy, 192
Bannerman, Harry, 140
Barber, Miller, 86
Barlow, Andrew, 197, 198
Barnes, Brian, 11, 85, 93, 135, 136, 137, 138, 221, 229
Barnes, Tom, 137
Barrière, Lucien, 214
Beaconsfield GC, 22
Beard, Frank, 85
Beatles, The, 47, 48, 147
Beckett, Beryl, 59
Beckett, Roy, 59, 130
Beeching, Dr, 48
Belfry, The, 135, 219, 220, 221
Bellow, Carol, 64
Bellow, Irwin, 60, 62, 64
Bellow, Marshall, 64
Beman, Deane, 145, 178
Bembridge, Maurice, 53, 95, 138, 199

Harry Cole

POLICEMAN'S PROGRESS

Being one of four policemen coping with the drunken, sex-mad, middle-aged, pear-shaped Clara, or sitting out a night with the neighbourhood ghost, or calming wayward Rosie, the local prostitute, who'd had her 'Bristols' bitten, must have been a lot more fun than digging out the late and seventy-year-old Elsie Morton, rotting in bed after not being seen for some weeks, dealing with violence, or bearing the news of fatal accidents to bereaved families.

PC Harry Cole, now nearly thirty years on the Southwark force, has done it all and there's consequently many a tale to tell. He produces his account of life on the beat with a combination of good humour and honesty that makes *Policeman's Progress* a rich mixture of riotous and serious reading. Harry Cole's loyalty to the force, but also his obvious sympathy for all reasonable human eccentricities, make one feel that he would be a good man to have around when there's trouble.

Fontana Paperbacks: Non-fiction

Fontana is a leading paperback publisher of non-fiction, both popular and academic. Below are some recent titles.